Analysing Organizational Behaviour

Analysing Organizational Behaviour

Edited by
Mike Smith

MACMILLAN

First published 1991 by
THE MACMILLAN PRESS LTD
Houndmills, Basingstoke, Hampshire RG21 2XS
and London
Companies and representatives
throughout the world

ISBN 0–333–51703–2 hardcover
ISBN 0–333–51704–0 paperback

A catalogue record for this book is available
from the British Library.

Printed in China

Reprinted 1992, 1993

Contents

List of Figures

Acknowledgement

Grateful acknowledgement is made to my daughter, Julie, for her work in producing the index to this book.

Note to the reader. In the interests of clarity, the masculine form has been used throughout the book.

MIKE SMITH

Preface

This book is a direct descendant of *Introducing Organizational Behaviour* which was published in 1981. We were delighted and surprised that *Introducing Organizational Behaviour* soon established itself in the market and became one of the leading introductory texts on organizational behaviour. However, time takes its toll and slowly it became outdated. Consequently we were asked by Macmillan to produce a new introductory book.

We have tried to maintain the same objectives – to produce a clear and concise account of the main developments in the field. In the main, this has meant that we have focused on the major trends and eschewed some of the more peripheral developments. In the main, we have only given key references rather than bombarding the reader with all possible references. The book was completely revised and renamed *Analysing Organizational Behaviour*. While keeping to a very similar framework, its scope was widened to include the topics of selection and training. In retrospect, their omission from *Introducing Organizational Behaviour* was unforgivable. Selection was probably the greatest growth area of the 1980s and training looks as though it will be the growth area of the 1990s. The authorship has also been widened to include teachers and researchers from outside the Manchester School of Management at UMIST. It is always sad to loosen ties with friends and colleagues but there is the advantage of including friends from other departments and benefiting from their wider range of expertise.

MIKE SMITH

Manchester School of Management

xii

Multiple Choice Question Bank

Multiple choice tests are becoming a feature of assessment in many introductory courses in organizational behaviour because they offer the advantages of objectivity and ease of marking. However, the savings in marking time are usually offset by the chore of preparing lengthy question papers.

To remove this problem, a set of over several hundred multiple choice questions from the domain covered in this book are available to lecturers in educational institutions. The multiple choice questions consist of questions whose answers are contained in this book and also questions which students could reasonably be expected to find in wider reading.

The booklet of questions also provides some guidance on formatting the answer sheet plus a floppy disc (5.25″) containing a program for marking the answers. The answers can be obtained from a file produced by an opscan reader or the file can be input by a data process operator keying in the answers.

The output of the program consists of two parts: an individual report for each student and statistics for the teacher.

The report for the student gives a standardized score for the whole test (parameters defined by the teacher) plus general indications of success in each subject area included.

The statistics available for the tutors includes a listing for each student of their overall scores and subscores. It also includes a listing of the proportion of students passing each question and an index of how well each question discriminates between students with high or low marks.

The booklet and program are only available to full-time teachers in recognized institutions. Orders must be official orders or on official headed letter paper. It must clearly state the name and position of the person ordering the booklet. To meet the cost of producing the booklet and providing the disc a charge equal to two-thirds the current price (in sterling) of this book is made. Cheques should accompany the order and should be made out to 'UMIST'. Orders should include an A4 self-addressed envelope.

Orders should be sent to

> Dr Mike Smith
> Manchester School of Management
> UMIST
> Manchester
> M60 1QD

1

A Framework for Analysing Organizations

MIKE SMITH
School of Management, UMIST

Organizations are very complex. Too complex to analyse in one go. To make the task manageable, some sort of scheme is needed. Fortunately, a scheme is available. It is a simplification because it does not show all the links and the interactions: but it is logical and covers most of the subject. The scheme is usually termed 'The Organizational Psychology Paradigm' and it is shown in Figure 1.1.

According to this paradigm, the analysis of any organization starts with analysing the jobs or roles within an organization. Indeed, in some ways, an organization is nothing more than a collection of roles. Job analysis is so important that many people have called it the cornerstone of industrial and organization psychology. Without understanding the role that people are required to fill and the jobs that they have to do, how can we even begin to understand how an organization works? It is therefore logical to start a book on analysing organizations by looking at analysing jobs and specifying the people needed to perform these jobs.

Once we have a clear idea of a job and the type of person who would be competent in the job we can start to work towards matching the person and the job. There are three main ways that the match between the person and the job can be brought about. We can select someone who already has the right characteristics. Or we can hire someone without all the characteristics but try to given them the competencies they need by some kind of training. Selection and training can be

1

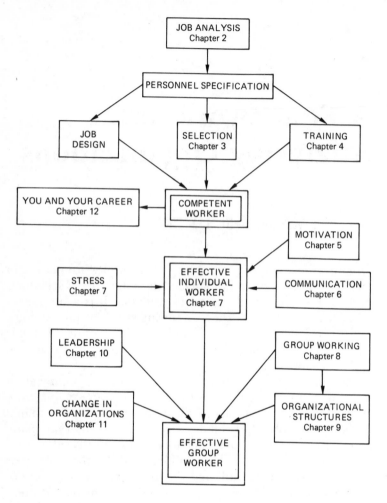

Figure 1.1   *The organizational psychology paradigm*

thought of as ways of fitting the man (or woman) to the job. This is usually known by the acronym of FMJ.

All other things being equal, it is usually more effective to select the right person rather than attempt to train them. Training is usually much more expensive than selection. Furthermore, training is usually much more chancy than selection since it involves an attempt over a short period of time to alter characteristics which are either innate or which have been built up over a lifetime. In most situations, it is necessary to select the best possible candidates and then give training to deal with any shortcomings they may have. Selection and training are covered in Chapters 3 and 4.

An alternative to both selection and training is job design. If a job can be organized in a way that 90 per cent of the population can do the job then neither selection nor training are needed. In theory, job design is much better than either selection or training. The costs are one-off costs and the results are almost assured over a long period of time. Human uncertainty is eliminated.

Job design is very similar to ergonomics. Ergonomics is not covered in this book because it is a fairly specialized field. It can be thought of as three domains: equipment design – making sure that the new lathe can be operated by people other than a dwarf 1m. high and with a 3m. armspan; workplace design – making sure that people are not asked to work in conditions that resemble a blacked-out sauna; and work patterns – making sure that people are not expected to work 50-hour shifts without any rest pauses. A better description of ergonomics is given by Landy (1985) and McCormick and Tiffin (1974). Job design is usually thought of as fitting the job to the man (or woman) (FMJ).

Selection, training and proper job design should result in a competent worker – that is, someone who is able to do the job. However, this does not mean that the worker *will* do the job. A person may be able to do a job but he or she may be unwilling to do so. Consequently, the topics of motivation and job satisfaction are also important. Even if a person is competent and keen they could still be ineffective because no-one has informed them of the goals and how these goals are to be achieved. Good communication is needed. There are also factors which prevent a worker from achieving their maximum potential. Such factors must be minimized to the greatest possible extent. *Stress* is probably the most important of these negative factors.

If everyone worked on their own in one-person outfits, the analysis of organizational behaviour could stop here. But the fact is that most people work in organizations containing many other people. The nature of these organizations has a great impact on the effectiveness of the people. In some organizations, highly intelligent, well-trained, motivated, well-informed and non-stressed individuals produce great results. In other organizations similar people are rendered only marginally effective. It is clear that an analysis of organizational behaviour must also take these factors into account.

Probably the best place to start analysing the organizational factors is to consider work groups. *Groups* can exist in many different types. They need to attract new members. They need to prevent too many members leaving otherwise they cease to exist. For groups to be effective, members must act in a fairly predictable way. How do groups ensure all these things? Very often, several groups combine to produce a larger organization. The way that they combine and the *organizational structures* can have a profound influence on the effectiveness of both the group and the individual.

According to some schools of thought, organizations need leaders – otherwise the organizations would stumble aimlessly about their environment. A leader is needed to give them a sense of direction and unity. However, research has shown that this view, although popular, is too simple. The whole concept of leadership needs to be analysed at a much deeper level.

The picture of organizational behaviour that has emerged so far will do up to a point and it would be an acceptable analysis in a static world. One wit said that two things in life are certain – death and taxes. He should have added a third – change. An efficient organization will do well, probably very well, for a time: but the environment around it will change, and competitors will improve. Despite the fact that organizations need to change they often encounter great inertia. So perhaps the final element in analysing organizational behaviour is to analyse the way that *organizational change* can be brought about.

Cross-Cultural Research

No single framework can be expected to cover all areas of organizations. The framework on which this book is based is no exception. One omission in particular, cross-cultural aspects, needs a brief mention.

Looking to the future, the international aspects of organizational behaviour are likely to increase in importance. Huge, international trading blocks, North America, the Pacific Basin and the European Community, are emerging. The vast majority of studies quoted in this book are set in the USA, UK or Europe. To what extent are findings in one country applicable to another? At one time, great cultural variations were expected but much recent work has shown a high consistency from one country to another. One of the earliest international studies was Cantril's (1966) survey of the pattern of human concerns which covered 10 very varied countries. On the things that really matter the pattern of human concerns was very uniform – they were the avoidance of war, the avoidance of hunger and the maintenance of good health.

As we shall see in Chapter 2, analyses of managerial work in the UK and in the USA reveal very similar patterns. At one time it was suspected that various selection methods were biased against certain ethnic groups but careful analysis has shown that the level of any bias is small and that our initial suspicion was founded upon faulty data. The samples were small and we know that results based on small samples are very erratic. Some researchers were foolish enough to mistake this sampling error for genuine findings and tried to interpret their meaning. More recently, it has been suspected that the differences have arisen because researchers have mistaken the method of expression for the underlying facts. For example, many Western researchers have analysed leadership style in terms of two things; the extent to which the leader gets things done and the extent to which the leader considers the feelings of subordinates. The question arises, 'Do the same considerations apply to leaders in countries such as Japan or Hong Kong?' On first impressions the answer may be no. A considerate leader in the West respects the individuality of subordinates. Observations in Japan would probably show that managers act in this way much less frequently. However, Misumi (1985) points out that such a conclusion would be misleading. Japanese managers *are* just as considerate as Western managers but the consideration takes a different form – perhaps by being more careful to respect your age and position in the group. Future cross-cultural studies need to take subleties of this kind into account.

References for Chapter 1

Cantril, H. (1966) *The Pattern of Human Concerns*, Rutgers University Press, New Brunswick.

Landy, F. J. (1985) *Psychology of Work Behaviour*, Dorsey Press, Homewood, Illinois.

McCormick, E. J. and Tiffin, J. (1974) *Industrial Psychology*, Allen and Unwin, London.

Misumi, J. (1985) *The Behavioural Science of Leadership: An Interdisciplinary Japanese Research Program.* University of Michigan Press, Ann Arbor.

2

Analysing Jobs: The Manager and the Job

MIKE SMITH and LYNN DAVIDSON
School of Management, UMIST

A little green Martian visiting any organization in Australia, the USA or the UK would notice that the people in the organizations do not behave randomly. Neither do they all behave similarly. Except in the very smallest organization, perhaps a partnership, people tend to specialize in certain activities. Specialization happens because, up to a point, it brings enormous benefits. People can become more skilled at a narrow range of tasks than being an incompetent 'Jack of all trades'. It also helps others to deal with the organization. The Broken Hill Steel Company employs thousands of people – you can imagine the chaos in chasing up an application form if its progress had been allotted at random to one of the staff!

Specialization tends to take place around groups of related activities that have certain skills or functions in common. The classic functions were:

1. Production
2. Sales
3. Finance
4. Personnel

However, over the years, as organizations became more complex other functions differentiated out to include:

1. Research and Development (R&D)
2. Distribution
3. Data Processing

4. Administration
5. Buildings and Maintenance
6. Purchasing
7. Marketing
8. Legal
9. Technical

Of course, not all of these functions are present in all organizations. Marks and Spencers does not have a production function, universities do not have a distribution function and the two-man outfit next door is unlikely to have a marketing function. In very large organizations the functions are likely to have differentiated even further into finer specialisms. For example, the IBM personnel function is likely to be divided into recruitment, training and industrial relations.

Specialization has disadvantages. The biggest is a tendency to lead to rigidity. Once activities are grouped in a certain way, they tend to stay grouped in that way from inertia or because vested interests develop in maintaining the structure. Ultimately, the organization can become outdated. Fortunately, in most organizations only the key elements of the job are defined and individuals have some ability to mould the job to their personal tastes. Some of these individual changes will be beneficial and modern. In a healthy organization, these beneficial changes will be copied by others while the unhelpful changes are ignored. Consequently, there should be slow but inexorable progress towards a better clustering of activities. This process can only happen if jobs are not initially over-defined.

Whatever way the specialism evolved, it will be staffed by people behaving in fairly similar ways. Almost all people in the finance function add up lists of money and almost all in the distribution function schedule the delivery and collection of things. The recurrent groups of work-related activities are called jobs. One of the most basic steps in analysing any organization is to analyse how the activities are grouped together and how jobs are made up. Job analysis is often called the cornerstone of industrial and organizational psychology. It forms the basis of selection and training.

Uses of Job Analysis

The uses of job analysis are not confined to these two major applications. Blum and Naylor (1968) report 20 different organizational uses including:

better communication
job grading and classification
salary administration
transfers and promotion
career guidance
accident investigations
job design

A good job description can be a major factor in establishing a good relationship between a boss and his or her subordinate. A clear statement of what is and what is not expected from a worker does much to remove animosities that arise from misunderstandings. Good job descriptions do much to remove feelings of resentment and unfairness. Grouping jobs also helps to establish logical patterns for employee transfers and promotions. The similarities in the activities in different jobs can be highlighted and individuals can be guided to the jobs which suit them best. In many situations, job analyses can identify working practices and situations likely to result in accidents.

Methods of Analysing Jobs

Because job analysis is so important many methods of analysing jobs have been developed. The main advantages and disadvantages of most of these methods are outlined in Figure 2.1. Probably the most frequently used method is the questionnaire. Typically, the job analyst reads all the available documents and talks to job holders and their superiors. This gives quite a good list of the tasks that are involved. But because it is based on a small sample – only a handful of

1. **Questionnaire Method**
   - *Advantages*   Good for producing quantitative information and can produce objective and generalizable results; cheap
   - *Disadvantages*   Substantial sample needed; Substantial foreknowledge needed to be able to construct questionnaire; respondents must be able and willing to give accurate replies

2. **Checklist Method**
   Similar to questionnaire method but since responses are either YES or NO the results may be 'cruder' or require larger sample. They tend to require fewer subjective judgements.

3. **Individual Interviews**
   - *Advantages*   Very flexible; can provide indepth information; easy to organize and prepare
   - *Disadvantages*   Time consuming; expensive; difficult to analyse

4. **Observation Interviews**
   Similar to individual interview method but provides additional information, for example, visual or auditory information. The higher level of contextual cues make it more difficult for the analyst to be misled. The method may expose both the analyst and the worker to increased safety hazards.

5. **Group Interviews**
   Similar to the individual interview but they are less time consuming for analyst and some claim that richer information is obtained since interviewees stimulate each other's thoughts. They are more difficult to organize and there is the danger that a group is over-influenced by one individual.

6. **Technical Conference Methods**
   - *Advantages*   Quick, cheap and can be used for jobs that do not yet exist. Can avoid restrictive practices
   - *Disadvantages*   The 'experts' may not be true experts and an unrealistic analysis may result

7. **Diary Method**
   - *Advantages*   Cheap, flexible and requires little advance preparation. Useful for non-manual tasks where observation is of limited value. Can also be used in jobs involving a wide variety of tasks
   - *Disadvantages*   Needs co-operation from respondents; tendency to keep incomplete logs – frequent but minor items often omitted

8. **Work Participation Method**
   - *Advantages*   Can produce very realistic analyses
   - *Disadvantages*   Expensive, time consuming and can only be used for jobs requiring short training and no safety hazards

9. **Critical Incident Method**
   - *Advantages*   Focuses on the aspects of a job that are crucial to success
   - *Disadvantages*   Often produces incomplete data difficult to analyse

Figure 2.1   *Checklist Two: advantages and disadvantages of 10 methods of job analysis*

interviews – it does not give a good idea of how frequent or important each task is. The next stage is to construct a questionnaire and administer it to a larger sample. Typically, each task is accompanied by three scales asking how frequent, how difficult and how critical each task is. The scales are usually five-point scales. For example, job holders would be asked if a task is very difficult, difficult, neither difficult nor easy, easy or very easy.

Custom-designed questionnaires of this kind can be very accurate. Unfortunately, they are costly and time consuming to produce. Fortunately, there are standard questionnaires which can be used. Whilst the results are not quite as good, they are often better value for money.

The most established questionnaire for analysing jobs is the PAQ (Position Analysis Questionnaire). The PAQ was devised by McCormick, Jeanneret and Mecham (1969) after intensive research. A computer used a statistical technique called factor analysis to scan the data and find recurrent trends or dimensions. The six main trends were:

1. *Information input*: how information is obtained: visual, auditory, written, estimation, etc.
2. *Mental processes*: reasoning, decision-making, planning, analysing, compiling, etc.
3. *Work output*: physical activities and tools used, use of precision tools, controls, setting up, adjusting, physical exertion, co-ordination, etc.
4. *Relationship with other workers*: communication, supervision, type of contact, etc.
5. *Job context*: outdoor environment, physical hazards, personal and social aspects, etc.
6. *Other job characteristics*: such as apparel worn, work schedule, responsibility, job structure, etc.

Each of the dimensions is subdivided and the PAQ asks for information on a total of 186 job aspects. One of the great strengths of the PAQ is that the responses to many items are guided by benchmarks. Benchmarks are specific examples of typical responses in a category. For example, physical exertion may be graded on a 1–5 scale as follows:

1. *Very little*: occasionally lifts a piece of paper, flicks a switch, uses a telephone or keyboard;
2. *Some*: walks, stands frequently lifting up to 5Kg or occasionally lifting or pushing up to 10Kg;
3. *Moderate*: frequently exerting a force of up to 10Kg or occasionally lifting or pushing up to 25Kg, (e.g. auto mechanic or bus driver);
4. *Considerable*: frequently exerting force of 25Kg and occasionally exerting force of 50Kg, (e.g. labourer, porter, bulldozer operator);
5. *Very High*: frequently exerting force greater than 25Kg or occasionally exerting force of 50Kg, (e.g. hod carrier or miner).

The inclusion of these benchmarks (sometimes called anchors) has a great advantage. It takes a lot of the subjectivity out of the replies.

In a typical job analysis using the PAQ, the questionnaire is given to 12 people, usually the job holders' superiors, who know the job well. They complete the forms independently and the average of their replies is used. Sometimes the forms are completed by the job holders.

The PAQ has another great advantage. It is possible to combine the results from the job analysis to produce a profile of the characteristics which workers need. This combination uses a series of weights which have been obtained from research and the results might reveal, for example that a job needs someone who has good long term memory and good hand-eye co-ordination but does not need good colour vision or quick reaction times. In the next chapter it will be shown that statements of this kind are vital in selecting the right person for the job.

The disadvantage of the PAQ is that it is not sufficiently detailed for some jobs – especially management and technical jobs. In response to this Mitchell and McCormick produced *The Professional and Managerial Position Questionnaire*. A questionnaire which is good for analysing technical jobs is the *Occupation Analysis Inventory*, which was developed by Cunningham *et al.* (1983). The PAQ has been described in some detail because it is probably one of the best and most researched examples of standard questionnaires for analysing jobs. However, it is not the only questionnaire of this kind. Two others are worthy of special note. The *Job Components Inventory* was developed in Sheffield by Banks *et al*. It contains almost 400 items and it is particularly good in analysing clerical and technical jobs that involve mathematical skills.

One of the most exciting innovations in the last few years has been the development of the *Work Profiling System* by the Saville Holdsworth Organization (1988). The system involves three overlapping questionnaires suitable for managerial and professional workers, service and administrative workers, and manual and technical workers. There is an ingenious system which ensures that people are not swamped with 800 or so questions. Initially, they sort a set of cards to focus on the four or five areas most relevant to their job. They then only complete the questionnaires which deal with the subset of information which the cardsort has identified as useful. The questionnaire is computer marked and a very full report is generated giving a detailed analysis of the job. Furthermore, the system goes several steps even further. Using the system of weights the WPS translates the results of the job analysis into the human skills and characteristics needed to do the job. As a final sophistication the WPS then suggests tests to measure these abilities or questions which should be asked at an interview.

Flannagan's (1949) critical incident technique is frequently adopted in analysing jobs. Its essence is very simple. People are simply asked to list, not all the aspects of a job, but only those aspects which make the critical difference between successful job performance and unsuccessful job performance. The advantage of this approach is that only the important things appear in the job in the job description and they are not hidden in a forest of mundane, routine and easy activities. A detailed consideration of analyzing jobs and the dimensions of human performance is given by Fleishman and Quaintance (1984).

The Accuracy of Job Analyses

Whichever method of job analysis is used, sooner or later someone will ask the question, 'how accurate is job analysis?'

Clearly, this will depend on the expertise and experience of the analyst. A better way to frame the question would be, 'how accurate *can* job analysis be?' This question may, in turn, be broken down into two other questions: how reliable is job analysis and how valid is it? The question of reliability is the easier question to answer. As a slight simplification, reliability means, 'does it give consistent results?' One way of checking this is for two people to analyse the job and then compare the two analyses. If this procedure is repeated several times a statistical index of the level of agreement between the analyses can be calculated. This statistical index is usually the correlation coefficient. Perfect agreement is 1.0 and only chance agreement is 0.0. Generally, studies of this kind give high correlations of about 9. This tells us that two people generate fairly similar results. But job analysis might be unreliable, not because the analysts disagree with each other but because the results are unstable from one example of a job to another example. This can be checked by gathering information on several examples of the same job. Given a well-thought-out system used by properly trained analysts, very consistent results are obtained. Generally the correlations are in the .8 to .95 range.

The question of validity is much harder to gauge. As a slight over-simplification validity can be taken to mean, 'does the analysis measure what it is supposed to measure?' The way to handle this question is to compare the results of a job analysis with a perfect job analysis. The problem is, of course, that perfect job analyses do not exist – if they did there would be no point in bothering with the imperfect job analyses. An alternative approach would be to compare the predictions made from job analyses with reasonable deductions. For example, it could be expected that job analyses of senior management jobs reveal more long term strategic thinking than junior management jobs. As another example, if a job analysis reveals that a job involves a great deal of spatial reasoning, then it would be expected that people who are good at spatial reasoning should do better at that job than those who are not good at spatial reasoning. Unfortunately such arguments are never watertight. Some senior managers have difficulty in thinking and rely upon their subordinates. In order to measure ability we need to rely on tests. A poor result could arise because the job analysis is fine but the test used is poor. Taking all this into consideration it seems that job analyses are fairly valid and yield correlations in the range .6–.8.

It may seem that the issues of reliability and validity of job analyses are trivial and have little practical point. Nothing could be further from the truth. Job analysis forms the basis of many systems in industrial psychology. If the job analysis is not reliable and valid it is likely to be biased. Consequently any subsequent selection system or training methods run the danger of being unfair to women or some minority group. Indeed, in the USA firms have been heavily fined and ordered to abandon selection systems because they could not prove that their job analyses were reliable and valid.

Job Families

Despite its importance, job analysis is tedious and expensive. Some of the chore can be removed by using standard job descriptions such as *The Dictionary of Occupational Titles* (DOT) in the USA or the *Classification of Occupations and Dictionary of Occupational Titles* (CODOT) in the UK. Often, however, these sources are not appropriate. Effort would be saved by grouping similar jobs. When a vacancy arose it would be unnecessary to perform a separate analysis since the analysis for the family could be used. Arranging jobs into families would have other benefits too. We would be able to see the relationships between different jobs and this would help us to understand why jobs are organised in the way they are. They would also be helpful in giving careers advice. If someone was unhappy in their present job we could suggest a change to another job in the same family because we would know that it would involve a similar blend of skills and activities. Probably the best article on clustering jobs into families is by Pearlman (1980). He points out that the development of job families would lead to better selection. Instead of selection being employed on relatively few people in a single job they could be applied to larger numbers in a family of jobs. Because much larger numbers are involved it would make economic sense to provide more resources so that a really good system was produced.

Analyses of the Managerial Job

In any organization the job of a manager is a vital one. Furthermore, it is virtually certain that the vast majority of readers of this book are either managers or will one day occupy managerial positions. Consequently, it is worthwhile to focus upon the research obtained from analysing managerial work.

Definitions of a Manager

One of the most basic issues is to define, 'what is a manager?'. No single definition is universally accepted but one of the best is, 'someone who gets work done by other people'. The advantage of this definition is that it emphasizes that managers do not actually do things, rather it is their job to get other people to do things. This does not mean that managers are idle. Indeed, sometimes it is a lot harder to get others to do things than doing the task oneself! The definition also makes the distinction with operatives and specialists. An operative is the person who actually does things – either making things or providing a service. Specialists provide either the manager or the operative with information or advice. A training specialist gives advice and information about developing the skills and competencies of employees. A financial specialist gives advice on the recording and investment of money. These distinctions do not necessarily imply status or financial rewards. Some operatives earn more than their managers, especially when the operative's skills are in short supply. Some specialists have a higher reputation and status than the managers they advise. Another definition of a manager is someone who is responsible for ensuring that the organization's output is of greater value than the resources it takes in. This definition has the advantage of emphasizing the manager's reponsibility for organizing an efficient transformation process. In the classic

Marxian analysis, a manager is given three types of resources to input to his organization: people, money and land. The manager is responsible for combining these resources so that extra value is created. This value may not be expressed in money terms: the hospital manager's job is to ensure that the money he or she is given by the community delivers a standard of health care which is of higher value than the money received. The efficiency with which the manager achieves the transformation is often expressed as two important ratios. The most usual is the *percentage return on capital*: a manager who consumes 1 million dollars to produce goods to the value of 1.1 million is, all other things being equal, a better manager than one who consumes 2 million dollars to produce 2.1 million output. The other main index of managerial efficiency is the *value added per employee*: a manager who organizes staff so that when the surplus divided by the number of staff is 1,000 ecus (European Currency Units) is a better manager than one with an added value of 800 ecus per member of staff.

Levels of Management

Traditionally, managers are divided into three levels. *Junior managers* are those that directly supervise operatives. Generally, their job is to control the flow of work within limited and clearly defined areas. Often their job is to ensure that production plans or call rates are achieved to established standards. Their timespan of discretion is short in the sense that any mistakes they make will show up very quickly.

Middle managers supervise junior managers and usually call upon the advice of specialists. Their main job is integration and motivation. They need to integrate the work among the junior managers and to integrate the work of their department with the work of others. Their work is less structured. If they make a mistake it may be months before the chickens come home to roost.

Senior managers are usually heads of functions such as the personnel function or data processing. They usually report to the directors or the chief executive of the organization. The main job of a senior manager is to develop strategy, locate and exploit opportunities, give a sense of direction and establish an ethos. Their job is less structured and more ambiguous. The timespan of discretion is long. If they make a mistake it may be years before the chickens come home to roost. For example if the head of the data processing function mis-estimates the growth in demand and orders a computer system that is too small it will be years before the system is blocked. By that time he will have been promoted and will be heaping odium on his successor for not being able to cope!

Inevitably this short description of the different levels of management is a simplification. In practice, things are less clear. However, the description identifies a major point. Managerial work changes with seniority. Senior managers do not simply do more of the same kind of the tasks done by junior managers. These qualitative changes are important. The fact that someone is good at one level of management does not mean they will be good at the next level up. Often it seems unfair when a very efficient manager is passed over for promotion and someone producing worse results is promoted in his stead. What is usually happening is that someone has decided that while the individual has the right blend of characteristics for junior management, they do not have the right combination for senior levels.

Expert Analyses of Managerial Jobs

During the early part of this century, the dominant method of analysing management jobs was expert analysis. Two of the most famous were Henri Fayol, General Manager of a large French mining company and Luther Gulick. Their work established a number of important management principles such as the unity of command (everyone should have one, and only one, boss) and reasonable spans of control (one person can rarely effectively co-ordinate the work of more than six to 12 others). Their efforts can be summarized in the letters POSDCRB. In their analysis, management consisted of seven major activities:

1. Planning (setting goals and scheduling the stages to the goals);

2. Organizing (devising systems and divisions of labour);
3. Staffing (recruiting, training, motivating etc);
4. Deciding (seeking out and recognizing opportunities and allocating resources according to these decisions);
5. Controlling (checking that events are going to plan and taking corrective action if they are not);
6. Reporting (communicating upwards, downwards and sideways);
7. Budgeting (keeping track of the major resources of money and time).

The works of Fayol and Gulick were enormously influential and even today management is often viewed within this framework. Unfortunately, the framework is very stylized and very few organizations conform completely to this pattern.

Work Activity School

The work activity school, including researchers such as Kotter, Stewart and Mintzberg, studied what managers actually did. Kotter (1972) administered questionnaires to and observed 15 high-level general managers in the USA. He found that some of the most distinctive aspects of managerial work were the ways in which the general managers set the agendas for their organizations. The prioritizing of the issues that are important is crucial to effective management. As we shall see later, one of the characteristics of managerial work is a torrent of short term activities which appear to arrive in no particular order. The existence of agendas gives a sense of direction and allows the manager to assess very quickly whether he should or should not give much attention to a particular event.

Rosemary Stewart (1967) asked 160 British managers to keep a diary for a four-week period. Her analysis provided a great deal of information about how managers spent their time (see Figure 2.2). In more recent work, Rosemary Stewart (1982) has focused upon the degree to which managers are free to choose what they do. Generally, a manager's job is ill-defined and managers have a considerable choice about *what* they do (that is, they are usually free to set their own

	Stewart	Mintzberg
Formal meetings	7	
Committees	7	69%
Informal discussions	43	
Social activities	4	
Paperwork	36	22
Telephone	6	6
Tours	6	3

Figure 2.2 *How managers spend their time*

agendas) and *how* they do it. Over a period of time, managers will seek to change their job in fairly standard ways. Managers spend a lot of time reacting to others. But they will try to change this towards becoming the source of activities and changing the structure so that the balance of initiatives favours them. Managers will also strive to bring desirable activities under their own control and to off-load routine and time consuming ones.

Henry Mintzberg (1973) observed five managers over a period of one week each. He also analysed the way managers spend their time and arrived at results that were broadly consistent with Stewart. Mintzberg went further. He tried to distil the essence of managerial work. According to Mintzberg, there are three crucial aspects of managerial work:

1. brevity, variety and fragmentation;
2. emphasis on the spoken media;
3. emphasis on a network of contracts.

Mintzberg's research revealed that managers spend only a short period of time on any one thing before they break off and attend to something else. On average, the brief periods are about nine minutes. In junior managers the brief episodes are even shorter. In senior managers and certain functions such as accounting, the episodes are longer – perhaps as long as 20 or even 40 minutes. The episodes are very varied in content. The first may be a production problem. The second may be a financial problem. The third may be a personnel problem. The variety of a manager's job contrasts with the work of a medical practitioner. Their work episodes are also very brief – perhaps spending about 10 minutes with each patient. But each episode will deal with the same thing – health. Fragmentation can be viewed as a consequence of brevity and variety. Managers rarely tackle an issue at one go. In the first brief episode they set events in train. They are interrupted, deal with several other issues and return to the first event in, perhaps, the afternoon when others have gathered extra details and have prepared several options. The fragmentation, variety and brevity of managerial work has led some writers to conclude that the circumstances of managerial work are schizoid. Indeed, the torrent of activities inevitably produces another well-established aspect of managerial work – conflict and pressure. One of the standard myths about managerial work is that they are careful and deliberate planners and strategists. The work of Mintzberg and others repeatedly shows that managerial work is primarily reactive. As early as 1951 Carlson wrote:

> Before we made this study, I always thought of the chief executive as the conductor of an orchestra standing aloof on a platform. Now I am in some respects inclined to see him as the puppet in a puppet show with hundreds of people pulling the strings and forcing him to react in one way or another.

Managers hate written work. They much prefer to speak to the people concerned, either by a visit or by telephone. It would seem that managers distrust the written media for two main reasons. First, they know that by the time something is typed, signed and distributed it has probably been overtaken by events. Also, they appreciate that people are much more careful and guarded when they write things down. Hence writers tend to filter out the nuances which are hard to prove but which give vital clues to the true situation.

Managers work hard at developing a network of contacts. Much of a manager's work depends upon having up-to-date and relevant information. The need for specific pieces of information is hard to predict. It is therefore essential that managers know who has the information they require and that the person will be willing to give the information. By building a network of contacts managers aim to meet both requirements.

Another way of viewing managers is in terms of the roles they perform. Recently, Belbin (1981) has identified eight roles and has linked them to certain personality traits.

The role of *Chairman* involves clarifying the goals of the group and setting the group's agenda. A chairman will help to establish roles, responsibilities and work boundaries within a group. He will also sum up the feelings and achievements of the group and articulate group verdicts. Generally, a chairman will be a very trusting person who is able to accept other's strengths and weaknesses. He will also tend to be assertive but conscientious.

The *Shaper* is someone who takes an active part in setting boundaries and seeks to find a pattern in the group discussion. He pushes the group forward towards agreements on policy and taking decisions. Often, the Shaper is an outgoing person, who is somewhat apprehensive, tense and suspicious.

The *Plant* advances proposals, makes criticisms that lead to counter-suggestions and offers new insight on lines of action already agreed. In many ways he is the person in the group who sows the seed of an idea and then encourages it to flourish and grow. 'Plants' tend to be intelligent, perhaps introverted and tender-minded.

A *Monitor–Evaluator* is the analyst of the group. He will interpret complex written material and assess the contributions of others. He will be a sober person who is shrewd and calculating.

The *Company Worker* is the person who transforms talk and ideas into practical steps. He considers what is feasible and trims suggestions to make them fit established systems. The company worker is tough-minded, conscientious, practical and trusting.

A *Teamworker* focuses on the interpersonal behaviour of a management group by supporting others and building upon the ideas and suggestions of others. They attempt to draw the reticent into discussion and they generally promote a team spirit by first trying to avert disagreements or smoothing things over if a disagreement occurs. Teamworkers tend to be outgoing, group-oriented, trusting and accommodating.

The *Resource Investigator* is the person who forages in the external environment for new ideas and developments. On their own intitiative they contact other individuals or groups and negotiate on behalf of their own group. Resource investigators tend to be relaxed extroverts who are imaginative and experimental.

The *Completer* is the final management role identified by Belbin. The completer emphasizes the need to complete a task to schedule. They promote a sense of urgency and galvanize others into action – sometimes by spotting oversights and errors. A completer is usually characterized by two traits: conscientiousness and a fairly high level of anxiety.

Belbin's team roles are important for two reasons. First, they link management activities with personality. Using a fairly standard personality test it is possible to guide or select individuals to specific jobs. Second, they emphasize the fact that a management team needs a variety of styles if it is going to work – for example a management team where everyone is either a 'shaper' or a 'plant' would be disastrous. It suggests that perhaps our unit of analysis should not be an individual manager but rather a management team.

Implications for Management Training

As Chapters 3 and 4 show, the analyses of management jobs have clear implications for the selection and training of managers. However there are great discrepancies between experts' analyses of management jobs and the results analysing what managers actually do. According to experts, managers should be thinkers, planners and organizers. Yet in practice most managers are reacting to events without much deliberate control. What exactly should management education be doing? In the past, management schools have taken the intellectual approach and have tried to develop the reasoning power of students. Subjects have been studied in ponderous depth and detail. Seasoned managers have then complained that what is taught in management schools is largely irrelevant to the real job of management. Perhaps what the schools should be teaching is the art of superficiality and how to maximize the information that can be gained and

the decisions that can be made in nine minutes. Perhaps! But
that could be viewed as merely accepting things as they are
without trying to improve them. However, a really enquiring
mind would then ask what evidence there is that the experts'
view is really the best?

Women in Management

Throughout this chapter we have consistently referred to a
manager as he. This is not an oversight nor was it done to
goad and infuriate Germaine Greer. It is simply a reflection of
the fact that the vast majority of managers are men. It is,
however, necessary to end this chapter by looking at this
phenomenon and indicating how the situation may be changing.

It is a paradox that although we talk about the start of the
leisure society, more people are at work now than at any other
time in history. A part of the increase in the number of
workers is due to the growth of the population, but in
industrialized countries at least, the major cause has been an
increase in the proportion of women who are working. In
Britain the proportion of women in the workforce has steadily
increased and by 1989, women made up 44 per cent of the
labour force and this figure is expected to rise to about 50 per
cent within the next decade.

However, women's advances into what have traditionally
been men's jobs (blue- and white-collar jobs) are still very
small. Women are still markedly under-represented among
managers and administrators. In the EEC countries and
Scandinavia, the figure ranges between 11 and 17 per cent
with the UK leading with 22 per cent of all administrators and
managers being women (Davidson, 1989). In the USA, with
the strongest legislation affecting the employment of women,
the ranks of female managers tripled during the 1970s. In
1980 almost a third (30.5 per cent) of all managers in the USA
were women. Today, this figure has risen to over 38 per cent
(Powell, 1988).

Nevertheless, women are still likely to be employed in traditional female areas such as catering and retailing. A British

Managers	No. of women	% who are women
Managers in wholesale and retail distribution	218,000	30.2%
Managers of hotels, clubs, etc and in entertainment and sport	119,000	40.7%
Office managers	55,000	25.6%
Production, works and maintenance managers, works foremen	29,000	7.5%
Farmers, horticulturalists, farm managers	25,000	10.8%
Others	85,000	
TOTAL managerial	531,000	22.7%

Figure 2.3 *Representation of women in occupational groups*
Source: EO Research Unit, 1985.

Institute of Management survey (Alban-Metcalf and Nicholson, 1985; Nicholson and West, 1988) showed that women were found less in the manufacturing sector and more in the service sector. Women were also more likely to be found in certain managerial functions such as training, office administration and personnel (Davidson and Cooper, 1987). In both the USA and UK, the percentage of senior female executives is very small – about 1 or 2 per cent.

The question arises, 'why does such widespread under-representation occur?' There seems to be no real evidence to suggest that women are inherently less suitable for management positions. Indeed, numerous cross-cultural studies comparing males and females in terms of managerial efficiency and performance conclude that there are far more similarities than differences.

Any differences tend to be found not in the way each sex manages but from factors associated with the low proportion of female managers, differences in attitudes and the different life circumstances of female managers. Recent British large scale surveys allow comparison of the profiles of women and men managers. Firstly, the female manager is less likely to be married and is more likely to be divorced or separated and less likely to have children (or have fewer of them). The pattern of work in the home often results in marriage and family supporting men managers but hindering women. In addition, women managers are far more likely to be a part of a dual career partnership.

Women managers tend to hold higher educational qualifications and occupy more specialist positions at every level of management. In their career patterns, women are more radical in their job changes and move faster between jobs after changing employer as they climb the managerial ladder. In terms of attitude, women are more self-directed, motivated and are less concerned about fringe benefits, pay and status. Alban-Metcalf and Nicholson found that women managers viewed themselves as more sociable, intellectual and ambitious than the men.

Women managers currently occupy the status of a minority group in a milieu dominated by policies made by men. It is therefore not surprising that research indicates that they are subjected to a greater number of pressures – especially the strains of coping with prejudice and sex stereotyping, overt and indirect discrimination from fellow employees, employers and the organizational structure. Furthermore, there are pressures caused by the lack of role models, coping with the feelings of isolation and the burdens of coping with the role of the 'token woman'. All of these pressures are in addition to those of maintaining a family and home. This does not mean that women cannot cope with managerial jobs, only that they are often faced with extra pressures not experienced by male managers. Many organizations need to take this into account and to adjust their organization and policy accordingly.

References for Chapter 2

Alban-Metcalf, B. and Nicholson, N. (1984) *The Career Development of British Managers*, British Institute of Management, London.

Banks, M. H., Jackson, R. R., Stafford, E. M. and Warr, P. B. (1982) *The Job Components Inventory Mark II*, Manpower Services Commission, Sheffield, England.

Belbin, R. M. (1981) *Management Teams: why they succeed or fail*, Heinemann, London.

Blum, M. L. and Naylor, J. C. (1968) *Industrial Psychology*, Harper and Row, London.

Carlson, S. (1951) *Executive Behaviour: a study of the work loads and working methods of managing directors*, Strombergs, Stockholm.

Cunningham, J. W., Boese, R. R., Need, R. W. and Pass, J. J. (1983) Systematically derived work dimensions', *Journal of Applied Psychology*, 68, 232–52.

Davidson, M. J. (1985) *Reach For the Top: a Women's Guide to Success in Business and Management*, Piatkus, London.

Davidson, M. J. and Cooper, C. L. (1987) 'Occupational stress in female managers: a comparative study', *Journal of Management Studies*, 21, 2, 185–205.

Fleishman, E. A. and Quaintance, M. K. (1984) *Taxonomies of Human Performance*, Academic Press, London.

Flannagan, J. C. (1949) 'Critical requirements: a new approach to employee evaluation', *Personnel Psychology*, 2, 419–25

Kotter, J. (1982) *The General Manager*, Free Press, New York.

McCormick, E. J., Jeanneret, P. R. and Mecham, R. C. (1969) *Position Analysis Questionnaire (PAQ)*, Occupational Research Center, Purdue University, Purdue, USA.

Mintzberg, H. (1983) *The Nature of Managerial Work*, Harper and Row, New York.

Nicholson, W. and West, M. A. (1988) *Managerial Job Change: Men and Women in Transition*, Cambridge University Press, Cambridge.

Pearlman, K. (1980) 'Job families: a review and discussion of their implication for personnel selection', *Psychological Bulletin*, 87, 1, 1–29.

Powell, G. N. (1988) *Women and Men in Management*, Sage, London.

Saville Holdsworth Ltd (1988) *Manual for the Work Profiling System*, Saville Holdsworth, Esher, Surrey.

Smith, J. M. and Robertson, I. T. (1986) *The Theory and Practice of Systematic Staff Selection*, Macmillan, London.

Stewart, R. (1967) *Managers and their Jobs*, McGraw-Hill, Maidenhead.

Stewart, R. (1982) *Choices for the Manager*, Prentice-Hall, Englewood Cliffs, N. J.

3

Selection in Organizations

MIKE SMITH
School of Management, UMIST

The People Make the Place

Once an organization has defined the roles and jobs it wishes to fill, the next task is to find the people to fill them. However, not all people are the same. In almost all circumstances it becomes necessary to select the best person for the job. The selection decisions are some of the most important choices any organization can make. If the wrong person is appointed to a job the organization will suffer reduced output and the person concerned may suffer worry and anxiety from being in a job where they are out of their depth.

The importance of selection has recently been highlighted by Schneider (1987). He argues that for years organizational psychologists have underestimated the importance of selection, retention and attrition. He points out that typical experiments in organizational psychology tend to under-estimate the importance of selection because, following the classic laws of experimental design, investigators randomly assign people to experimental groups or situations. Under these circumstances, where the effects of people are controlled experimentally, it is hardly surprising that the results show that the situations are the most important determinants of organizational behaviour. In essence, Schneider is arguing that the methodology of organizational psychologists causes us, unwittingly, to under-emphasize the importance of people.

Schneider goes on to argue that the big differences between organizations are caused by the fact that they **a**ttract different types of people, that they **s**elect different people and there is also the **a**ttrition of certain types of people from the organiza-

28

tion. The effect of the ASA processes is that different organizations end up with different types of people. These different types of people then construct around them or they maintain different types of organizational structures, goals and cultures. The people make the place rather than the place making the people.

The Selection Paradigm

Good methods of selection can help prevent organizational dry rot setting in. Good selection is based on a systematic approach to matching the characteristics of individuals to the needs of the organization. Many people believe that the selection process starts with placing an advertisement in a newspaper. As Figure 3.1 shows, good selection starts with the analysis of the jobs and the roles which people fill. Many of

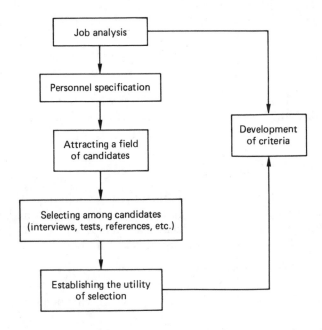

Figure 3.1 *The selection paradigm*

the points in producing a job analysis have been outlined in the previous chapter.

The Personnel Specification

Once the job has been defined the next phase is to describe the kinds of characteristics which would be seen in the ideal candidate. This second phase in the selection process is called the personnel specification. One of the best frameworks for devising a personnel specification is Rogers' Seven-Point Plan which suggests that requirements are organized under the following headings:

1. Physical make-up – including appearance and speech;
2. attainments – such as qualifications and licences;
3. general intelligence;
4. special aptitudes – such as numerical or verbal reasoning;
5. interests;
6. disposition and personality;
7. home circumstances.

In almost all cases, it is important that the specifications should not discriminate against women or any minority group.
Many personnel specifications differentiate between characteristics which are essential to the performance of the job and those characteristics which are desirable.

Attracting a Field of Candidates

Once the organization has defined the type of person it needs, the next step is to encourage appropriate people to make an application. Initially this means letting people know that a vacancy has arisen. The main media available to do this are:

Advertising within the organization;
vacancies boards outside the premises;
files of application forms from previous vacancies.

Government employment agencies;
private employment agencies;

headhunters (Executive Search Agencies);
unions and professional organizations;
University Appointments Boards ('the milk round');
careers conventions.

National newspapers;
local newspapers;
trade publications;
electronic media such as teletext.

More information on each of these methods is contained in Smith, Gregg and Andrews (1989). Whichever media is used two points are paramount. First, the media must not introduce inequality of opportunity. For example, relying on word of mouth to attract candidates is probably discriminatory because it tends to preserve the status quo: newly arrived minorities are less likely to have friends working in the organization. Second, the media must be appropriate to the type of person the organization wishes to attract.

It has been suggested that some media produce better recruits than other media. For example, it has been suggested that informal media tend to produce people who are less likely to leave the organization after a short time. However, such findings are contaminated by other biographical factors.

Demographic changes over the last few years have highlighted the importance of attracting a good field of candidates. As the numbers of school leavers in the population have declined employers have exerted greater efforts to attract their share. This has led to a change in focus for the selection system. It is now seen as a social process in which the employers and candidate go through a series of information exchanges which, hopefully, culminate in an offer, and an acceptance of, employment. Herriot (1989) has mapped out the sequence of these stages and some of the reasons why one party breaks the chain of events.

Choosing Among Candidates

Once a good field of candidates has been assembled, the next task is to choose the candidate that seems to hold most promise. Many methods can be used to aid this choice. The methods range from the traditional interview and references to tests or work samples and, perhaps, graphology. But which is the best method? If an expert on interviewing is consulted he is almost certain to recommend the use of interviews. If an expert on handwriting is consulted, they are almost certain to recommend graphology. Clearly expert opinion is of little use.

Perhaps the only way of settling on the best method of selection is to set out, in advance, the characteristics of good predictors (methods of selection). There are four main requirements: *practicality, sensitivity, reliability and validity.*

Practicality is the most basic requirement of a predictor. Unless a predictor is practical, it will simply not be used. Practicality covers things like cost, flexibility, time and convenience. It also involves the attitudes of the management and, to an increasing extent, the attitudes of the candidates themselves.

Sensitivity is the extent to which the candidates are given different scores. If a predictor gives the same score, or nearly the same score, to all candidates it is useless as a method for choosing between them. Some methods such as interviews give nearly all candidates the same score – usually average or a little better than average. Tests on the other hand usually give a wide range of scores.

Reliability refers to the consistency of the result. If a method of choosing candidates gives one score today and an entirely different score the next day, it can't be a very good method of selection. Reliability is usually expressed in terms of a correlation coefficient. Perfect consistency is shown by a correlation coefficient of 1.0. Chance consistency is shown by a correlation coefficient of zero. For a measure to be much use it must have a reliability coefficient of at least .7. Preferably it should be above .9.

Validity refers to the accuracy of the conclusions that are based on the measure. In the selection situation, validity boils down to the accuracy in identifying good workers. Many people characterize validity as the extent to which a measure gauges what it is supposed to measure. Unfortunately, the situation is more complex. To establish validity it is usually essential to conduct a study. Validity studies invariably involve three stages.

First, a large sample of over 200 applicants are selected in some way. The selection must yield a quantitative score for each member of the sample – say, on a 1 to 10 scale. *Second*, the productivity of each person in the sample is measured – again, say on a 1 to 10 scale. Ideally, all applicants are employed and their performance is assessed after a period of several months. In this case the study is called a predictive validity study. In many cases, however, predictive studies are impractical and concurrent studies are used. In a concurrent study the sample consists of existing employees whose productivity can be checked at the same time as the selection measure is used. Scientifically, predictive studies are the most desirable but they are also impractical in many situations. Fortunately, comparisons show that predictive and concurrent studies yield very similar results. In non-operative jobs productivity is hard to measure and it may be necessary to use other indexes such as an evaluation by a superior of tenure or promotion record. The *third* aspect of a validity study is to see if there is any relationship between the selection measure and job performance. The usual way of measuring the relationship between two things is to use a correlation coefficient. A perfect relationship has a value of $+1$. A chance relationship has a correlation of zero. An inverse relationship has a negative correlation.

In the 1950s and 1960s workers such as Ghisseli (1966) collected validity coefficients and found that the average validity was a disappointing .3. Since that time, industrial psychologists have learnt that this figure can be misleading because a proper study needs a large sample, an unrestricted range (that means, the figure should be based on all applicants not just those who passed the test) and the measure of productivity should be accurate. In most of Ghisseli's studies the sample size was about 65, only those who passed the selection process were included and the measures of performance, the criteria such as superior's evaluation, were often contaminated. Fortunately, it is possible by statistical means to correct for both the restriction of range and the contamination of the measures of performance. In the last decade a method of combining the results from several small studies has been devised. The method is called *meta-analysis*. Meta-analysis means that we can now base our conclusions on samples consisting of many hundreds if not thousands of cases (see for example Hunter and Hunter, 1984). Meta-analysis means that we can be much more confident of the results. The results of some meta-analyses can be seen in Figure 3.2.

Using Figure 3.2 we can scientifically evaluate some of the different methods of selection. These methods of selection can be divided into four groups: the chance methods, the poor methods, the reasonable methods and the good methods.

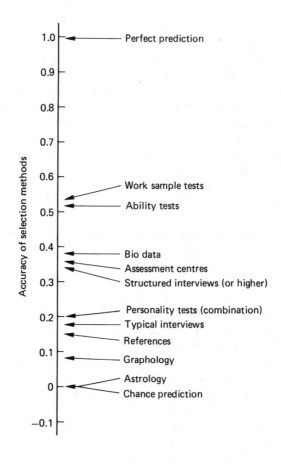

Figure 3.2   *Validity of some methods of selection*

The Chance Methods of Selection: Graphology and Astrology

Graphology and *astrology* seem to be as accurate at picking good employees as using a table of random numbers. Yet in continental Europe graphology is used surprisingly often. Graphology is usually very practical – it can differentiate between people and graphologists are fairly consistent in the results they produce. However, validity is the missing link. Properly conducted studies of graphology are rare. Much of the evidence is anecdotal and circumstantial. Everyone in selection, irrespective of the method they use, is able to quote their 'lucky hits'.

Astrology is used reasonably widely in the Far East. There is evidence that some aspects of astrology are better than chance. For example, some French investigators have produced fairly convincing evidence that *very* eminent sportsmen, medics and soldiers tend to be born under certain astrological configurations. This trend is very weak and is only apparent when large samples of very eminent people are used. The trend is almost certainly too weak to be used in practical selection situations. There are also two non-mystical explanations for a weak trend. First, the season of birth may be a factor: winter babies may have rather different experiences to summer babies during the first important months of their lives. Second, there may be some kind of self-fulfilling prophecy: enough Aquarians may read their personality analyses in the papers and they may then subconsciously tend to live up to them.

The Poor Methods of Selection: Interviews, References and Personality Tests

Interviews and references are probably the most frequently used methods of selection. It is ironic that they are also some of the worst. Both interviews and references are notably better than chance and can contribute to effective selection but they are much poorer than many people are prepared to admit.

Interviews in particular pose great problems to an efficient selection system. They are traditional. They are expected. They provide the selector concerned with powerful, interpersonal 'vibes' which seem to have great validity. These 'vibes' are often so strong that they overpower the information given by more controlled and accurate methods of selection. Indeed, one eminent industrial psychologist commented that 'the problem with interviews is how to stop them lousing up the rest of the selection process'.

We have known for decades that interviews are not very good at selecting the right people for the job. A famous study in the 1920s collected data when 12 experienced sales managers interviewed 56 applicants. He prevented the sales managers swapping notes and obtained their individual rankings of the candidates. If the interviews were any good, there should be *some* agreement between the interviews. There was very little. The results were appalling. One candidate was ranked second by one interviewer and 56th by another. The accuracy of interviews has been repeatedly reviewed since that time and each review has arrived at similar conclusions.

The detailed research on interviews has hardly been reassuring. One study demonstrated that a typical interviewer makes up his mind in the first four minutes of the interview and then spends the rest of the time looking for evidence to support his snap decision. In another study it was found that the *interviewer* spent 57 per cent of the time talking and the interviewee only 30 per cent. The remainder of the time was, presumably, spent in stony silence. Research suggests that at the end of the average interview the interviewer can't remember 50 per cent of the information that has been given to him by the interviewee. Other research shows that interviewees place disproportionate emphasis on anything that is unusual or unexpected – generally this is negative behaviour or information.

In essence, the problem with the interview is its unreliability. The unreliability of the interview has four main causes. First, different interviewers have different views of the job and the characteristics that are needed to perform the job. If they can't agree on such basic things there is little prospect of agreement at a later stage. Obviously, a good job description and a good personnel specification can do much to remove this source of unreliability. Second, interviewers are inconsistent in the questions they ask candidates. If one interviewer asks about hobbies and another interviewer asks about school, is it any wonder that in many cases they come to different conclusions? In most circumstances it is essential that interviewers work out a plan and then stick to that plan with all candidates. Third, interviewers are not consistent in the way that they ask questions. Some interviewers are aggressive and others are gushingly friendly. Consequently the reactions they evoke from interviewees are different and hence they come to different conclusions. Finally, interviewers judge and weigh the replies differently. Some interviewers are easy touches and give even a mediocre reply a high mark. Other – meaner – interviewers give the same answer a low mark. Putting these faults right can do much to improve interviews. But putting these faults right fundamentally alters the nature of the interview. As later paragraphs will show, these new structured or situational interviews are more accurate.

It has also been known for many years that *references* are not a good way of picking the best workers. Indeed, the average reference is more an indication of the literary skills of the person giving the reference than of anything else. Usually, the referee is nominated by the candidate. This gives rise to problems because only an idiot would nominate a referee who is likely to make an adverse comment. Indeed, most referees adopt the role of the candidate's champion and consequently most references are glowing tributes to the candidate. The nomination of the referee gives rise to other problems. The referees are usually chosen for their status when in fact they should be chosen for their knowledge of the job and their knowledge of the candidate: many a university tutor has provided a reference for a student he hardly knows and for a job which he did not know existed!

In commercial and industrial settings the motives of the referee add further complications. There are powerful motives to understate the achievements of a good subordinate who has applied for work elsewhere. There are even more powerful motives to laud even the most miserable accomplishments of a totally incompetent subordinate. In response to all these criticisms most organizations have reappraised their use of references. They still use references because it discourages candidates from lying during other phases of the selection process. However, they restrict the information they request to facts such as starting date, leaving date, job title and the exact nature of the job performed.

Personality Tests are one of the most controversial methods of selection. They are controversial in two ways: ethical and scientific. Many people feel that there is something wrong in testing personality – trespassing on forbidden areas or invading privacy. In fact, most personality questionnaires do not ask for personal or very sensitive information and they are probably less invasive than the average interview or reference check. Indeed, the ethical issues apply to all methods of selection not just personality tests.

The second area of controversy about personality tests is their validity. Meta-analyses tend to produce validities of .15 for individual scales on a personality test – which is less than impressive. However, the proponents of personality tests cry that this is unfair since many old fashioned and abandoned personality tests such as the 'inkblot test' are often included in the calculations. Furthermore, personality tests need to be interpreted with some sophistication. It may be that the relationship between some traits and success is curvilinear. For example, if tension and success are plotted on a graph the result might be an 'n' shape: little tension brings little success, moderate tension brings high success and high tension bringing little success. Traditional meta-analysis will therefore underestimate the validity of personality tests.

There is a further complication. Personality traits need to be judged in conjunction with each other. For example, on its own, a high level of energy and motivation will say little about someone's likely success. But when taken in conjunction with the trait of self-organization it could say a great deal – highly energetic and motivated people who are organized can achieve a great deal – highly energetic people who are disorganized and chaotic are often a menace to themselves and everyone in range! The techniques of meta-analysis have not yet developed to the level where these sophistications can be taken into account.

The discussion in the previous paragraphs has concerned accepted personality tests such as the Eysenck Personality questionnaire, the 16 PF test and the Organizational Personality Questionnaire, or McCrae and Costa's NEO FFI inventory. Unfortunately, many poorly designed personality tests are offered for sale. The question is how can these tests be identified? There are no foolproof rules but the following are reasonable guides:

1. Good tests are only supplied to trained users and they are *never* administered via the post.
2. Good tests have at least 10 questions per scale. This makes sure that random elements have a chance to cancel out – simply divide the number of questions in the test by the number of scores produced.
3. Good tests do not put people into watertight categories – people are simply not made in a few discrete types: they occupy all points along a continuum.
4. Good tests use questions that measure one thing at a time rather than questions where the questions ask you to choose between four or five fundamentally separate things (i.e. ipsative tests).

Ever since Whyte's *Organization Man* included suggestions to beat personality tests selectors have been worried about the possibility of faking personality tests. To some extent these worries have been exaggerated. In one study a group of subjects were schooled in Whyte's rules and then asked to complete a personality test. Another group were asked to complete the test without any such preparation. The two sets of results were randomized and submitted to a practising personnel officer and the practising personnel officer tended to prefer those who had not used the rules. Despite such reassurances, many test constructors now take the precaution of including a lie scale in their tests.

The Reasonable Methods of Selection: Biodata and Situational Interviews

Biodata are one of the most cost effective methods of selection and practically every adult has been subjected to this method – yet it is one of the least known methods of selection. Biodata involves selecting someone on the basis of biographical information such as age, number of jobs, qualifications etc. It is widely used in the insurance industry and in assessing the creditworthiness of people applying for loans and credit cards.

In essence, biodata is based on the beliefs that our characteristics are formed by our experiences or, that we choose our experiences because of our characteristics. In either event, there is a link between experiences and characteristics. If experiences are coded it should be possible to predict performance. A typical biodata questionnaire will ask candidates 20 or so questions such as: how many jobs have you had in the past 10 years?, what is the longest you have stayed in any one job?, what are your hobbies?, how many GCSEs have you obtained?, how many brothers and sisters do you have? These questions are examples of 'hard' biodata questions – questions that can be objectively verified. Some biodata questionnaires contain 'soft' items such as: what was your favourite subject at school or who is the person you most admire?. Biodata questionnaires using soft items are often hard to distinguish from personality questionnaires. A trial questionnaire is administered to a sample of, say, 300 people who are already in the job and whose performance is known. Weights are then calculated for each answer so that the best prediction is obtained.

Biodata typically obtains very high reliabilities and validities of .3 – .4. There are substantial set up costs because a study is needed to establish the appropriate weightings. However, once the study has been conducted the costs per individual are very low indeed. They are very suitable for use with occupations where large numbers of people need to be recruited in a very short time.

Unfortunately, biodata suffer from three potential disadvantages. *First*, they may fall foul of equal opportunities regulations. For example, a question may ask 'how far do you live from the place of work?' and the scoring system might give a low weighting to applicants living more than five miles away. However, this may be discriminatory against a minority who tend to live in a certain area just over the border. *Second*, biodata systems are not very transportable. A questionnaire and system of weightings which work in one organization rarely work in another organization. *Third*, biodata systems decay very rapidly and the questionnaire and its system of weightings need to be checked frequently – at least every three years.

Because traditional interviews have proved such a poor method of selection many attempts have been made to improve them. One of the most successful attempts has been Garry Latham and Associates' (1980) development of the *Situational Interview*. In the situational interview the candidate is asked how they would react to situations they would face in their work. The situations are carefully controlled and prepared. The responses are then carefully graded against carefully prepared specimen answers. Although this type of interview takes a great deal of preparation it is much more accurate than the traditional interview. Typically, validities of about .4 are obtained but some studies have reported validities as high as .7.

Good Methods of Selection: Ability Tests and Work Samples

Ability tests are some of the best methods of choosing workers. Some of the reasons are perfectly plain. In a good test a lot of the coincidental, random factors will be removed because each candidate will be given an identical task, identical instructions, identical conditions and his or her performance will be objectively scored. Furthermore, each question will have been carefully tested before being used.

The tests also work because they seem to measure things that are fundamental to all jobs: the ability to identify the key aspects of a problem, the ability to see how these aspects are linked to each other and the ability to deduce what comes next. Intelligent behaviour of this kind is important to job performance in two ways. First, it means that people can learn the job more quickly and more thoroughly. Second, it means that when novel problems occur people are more likely to think of a satisfactory solution. It has been suggested that the higher the job the better ability tests can predict performance.

Ability tests can take many forms. The biggest distinction is between tests of mental ability and tests of perceptual and physical ability. The results from physical and perceptual tests tend to give specific results. There is a strong tendency, however, for mental tests to give similar results. Consequently, the most frequently used ability tests are tests of general mental ability. However, in some specific circumstances such as the recruitment of a finance director, it may be necessary to measure a more specific ability such as numerical ability. In other circumstances, it may be necessary to measure spatial ability, verbal ability or mechanical ability.

One of the major advantages of these tests is that they can be obtained off the shelf by people who are qualified to use them. They also yield qualitative scores which apply to a wide variety of occupations. The main disadvantage is that the relevance of the test may not be apparent to the candidates.

Work samples are widely used. If someone applies for a job as a typist, it is almost inevitable that they will be asked to type a sample of work. Proper work samples are much more systematic than this example but it does serve to illustrate the essential features of a work sample – a representative part of the job that needs to be done. In technical terms, there is point to point correspondence between the task set for the applicant and the job. In practice a proper work sample requires the job to be analysed and the key points noted. These key points are then incorporated in a shortened task which is set for the applicant. The way that the applicant completes the task is observed or recorded and their efforts are compared to a standard set of examples. Good work samples usually obtain validities of about .5.

It is fairly easy to construct work sample tests for manual occupations. For example, a garage mechanic could be asked to repair a car which has a series of known faults. Work samples are also relevant to many managerial and professional positions. Intray exercises are work samples of how well a manager will handle the paperwork involved in his job. A presentation is a work sample of how well he will give a speech. A group discussion is a work sample of how well he will perform in meetings. It is possible to simulate other management activities such as a disciplinary interview or counselling a subordinate.

The big advantage of work samples is their apparent realism. Applicants come to believe that they are being judged on their ability to do the real thing and work samples are usually quite popular. The big disadvantage of work samples is their lack of transportability – if it is necessary to select for another job, an entirely new work sample must be constructed.

Composite Measures: Assessment Centres

None of the selection methods is perfect. So it might make sense to use a combination of methods so that the strengths of one method can compensate for the weaknesses of another. One particular type of combination is called the Assessment Centre. An essential feature of an Assessment Centre is that many methods are used to assess many features of an applicant.

A typical Assessment Centre lasts two days in which eight candidates are observed by four or five assessors as they complete a range of tasks such as:

a test of mental ability;
a personality test;
an interview;
an intray exercise;
a group discussion;
a counselling role play;
a business analysis exercise.

At the end of the two days, the assessors will meet to discuss the candidates and combine the various scores to arrive at an overall assessment of the candidates' suitability. Assessment Centres require a great deal of effort and resources so the question arises, how accurate are they? Certainly some impressive validities of about .65 have been obtained. However, these validities have been using promotion as the criteria. When studies have used actual performance on the job the validities are much lower – about .4.

It is interesting to speculate why the validities of Assessment Centres are so mediocre. Part of the reason is that the meta-analyses include some very bad Assessment Centres which were poorly constructed. Another part of the reason is the subjectivity involved in the final discussions among the assessors.

Alternatively, it could be an example of Gresham's Law that the bad drives out the good and that the inaccurate but powerful vibes of the interview drive out the accurate and logical predictions of the work samples and ability tests.

Fairness in Selection

Fairness is a consideration which must be borne in mind throughout the design of a selection system. *Fairness* means ensuring that the selection system is not biased against anyone on the basis of race, sex, age or handicap. Bias can creep in at all stages of the selection paradigm. For example, the personnel specifications can make stipulations in terms of height or age which are unfair to women. Similarly, discrimination can arise in the way that the job is advertised. Word of mouth tends to support the status quo and disadvantage newly arrived immigrant groups. Advertising in magazines read by one sex can also result in bias.

Bias at the stage of selecting a candidate can certainly take place and in the 1960s bias in tests was of great concern. Since that time a great deal of effort has been expended in trying to establish what constitutes adequate evidence of bias (see for example Cleary and Hilton, 1968).

Certainly the accusations of rejected candidates and the opinions of experts have proved to be very poor evidence. Statistics about the proportions of minorities employed are better evidence but they are not conclusive evidence. It may be, for example, that only the least suitable members of a minority choose to apply for a job in, say, a police force. Consequently, in such cases an employer is perfectly justified in rejecting a greater proportion of applicants from a minority group. However, a great disproportion in the numbers employed in majority and minority groups is a clear signal that something *might* be wrong.

The best evidence of bias in selection is to collect data for a sample of applicants and plot a trend line to show the relationship between the scores at selection and subsequent performance. A method of selection is clearly biased if this trendline over-predicts the job performance of the majority group and under-predicts the performance of the minority group. Subsequent research in the USA has investigated bias using this method (see Schmitt and Noe, 1986). The results indicate that bias is less of a problem than expected. Tests seem to be very fair methods of selection and, if anything, they introduce a very slight bias in favour of the minority group. It is impossible to give an authoritative statement of the bias of interviews because the results are rarely recorded in a quantitative form. But the subjectivity of most interviews certainly allows plenty of room for bias to occur.

Estimating the Utility of Selection

One of the most important developments in the last decade has been the improvements in ways of calculating the benefits of selection. Industrial psychologists typically talk about the accuracy of selection in statistical terms such as correlation coefficients or standard deviations. But decision-makers in organizations are used to making decisions in monetary terms such as return on investment or payback period. Decision-makers have found it hard to understand the psychologists and have consequently often given priority to other functions who were able to phrase their arguments in money terms.

Work by Boudreau (1984) and others has reversed this situation and the basic utility formula is:

$$utility = (O/P \times R \times SD) \times N \times T - costs$$

P is the proportion employed. If there are three applicants per job p = .33. O is the ordinate of the normal curve at point $1 - p$. O is usually obtained from statistical tables which show that the ordinate at .66 is .36. R is the validity coefficient. SD is the value of a standard deviation of performance. It is best to establish this value empirically but it may also be estimated as 40 per cent of salary. N is the number of people selected using the selection system and T is the average length of service (tenure) of the people who are selected.

Using this formula – or formulae incorporating sophistications such as interest rate, taxes and the tendency for better employees to use more resources – the value of a selection system can be calculated. For example, it is possible to calculate the advantages to an organization of replacing interviews with ability tests. The firm has 10 vacancies and about one in three applicants are suitable. The average salary is £10,000 and the average new hire remains in post for 1.5 years. Meta-analyses suggest that interviews have a validity of about .19 while ability tests have a validity of about .53. The equations are:

$$\begin{aligned}
\textit{interview utility} \;&=\; (.36/.33 \times .19 \times £4000) \\
&\quad \times 10 \times 1.5 - 4500 \\
&=\; £792
\end{aligned}$$

$$\begin{aligned}
\textit{ability test utility} \;&=\; (.36/.33 \times .53 \times £4000) \\
&\quad \times 10 \times 1.5 - 9000 \\
&=\; £25620
\end{aligned}$$

From these figures it is clear that even the much maligned interview is worthwhile and for an expenditure of £4,500 brings increased performance worth almost £8,000 – a rate of return of 17 per cent p.a. and a payback period of about 10 months. However, despite the fact that tests are twice as expensive they are a much better investment and result in improved performance worth about £26,000. The rate of return is 89 per cent p.a. and the payback period is about six months. Such high rates of return are by no means uncommon – especially when three conditions are met:

1. A more valid method of selection is used;
2. there are many applicants per job;
3. it is a difficult job where some candidates do well and others do badly.

The main point which repeatedly emerges from utility analyses is that selection is one of the best investments that any organization can make.

Outplacement

It is apposite to end this chapter on the darker side of selection – outplacement. Organizations grow. They also decline. Even great organizations at some stage arrive at the point where they need to lose staff. It is usually an intensely unpleasant decision which is likely to have a severe impact on the livelihood of many innocent people. Often the decision is imperative in order to safeguard the livelihoods of even greater numbers of innocent people.

Proper management of the reduction in staff is as important as the proper management of recruitment of staff. Badly managed outplacement can have horrendous impact on the people concerned. It can also have a horrendous impact on the organization for two main reasons. First, in a poorly managed outplacement, it is the more able and talented people who tend to leave. A 'last in first out' policy or the tendency for the most talented to get alternative job offers can result in a haemorrhage of talent at the very time when an organization needs all the talent it can conserve. Second, a poorly managed outplacement can have a negative impact on those that remain. They may rationalize their experience in the terms 'Joe worked hard for 20 years yet look how callously and unfairly he was treated – why should I work hard?'

The proper management of outplacement situations involves two main elements: support for the individuals in finding new jobs, and the fair and accurate assessment of ability. The methods described earlier in this chapter can be easily adapted to help with the second of these requirements.

References for Chapter 3

Boudreau, J. W. (1983) 'Economic considerations in estimating the utility of human resource productivity improvement programs', *Journal of Applied Psychology*, 36, 551–57

Cleary, T. A. and Hilton, T. L. (1968) 'An investigation of item bias', *Educational and Psychological Measurement*, 28, 61–75.

Ghiselli, E. E. (1966) *The Validity of Occupational Aptitude Tests*, Wiley, New York.

Herriot, P. (1989) 'Selection as a social process', in Smith, J. M. and Robertson, I. T. (eds.), *Advances in Selection and Assessment*, Wiley, Chichester.

Hunter, J. E. and Hunter, R. (1984) 'Validity and utility of alternate predictors of job performance', *Psychological Bulletin*, 96, 72–98.

Latham, G. P. *et al.* (1980) 'The situational interview', *Journal of Applied Psychology*, 65, 422–47.

Smith, J. M. (1988) 'Calculating the sterling value of selection', *Guidance and Assessment Review*, 4,1, 6–8.

Smith, J. M., Gregg, M., and Andrews, R. (1989) *New Horizons in Selection and Assessment*, Pitman, London.

Schmitt, N. and Noe, R. A. (1986) 'Personnel selection and equal employment opportunity', in Cooper, C. L. and Robertson, I. T. (eds.), *International Review of Industrial and Organizational Psychology*, Wiley, London.

Schneider, B. (1987) 'The People Make the Place', *Personnel Psychology*, 40, 3, 437–53.

4

Training in Organizations

MIKE SMITH
School of Management, UMIST

Selection is by no means perfect. When new recruits join an organization they are unlikely to have all the skills and competencies which are needed to do the job. Conditions also change. Even if employees once perfectly fit a job, changes will tend to erode the match between the person and their work. The way to increase or maintain skills is investment in training. Training is thus one of the most vital activities of any organization but it is important to recognize that training has its limits. No amount of training can increase someone's intelligence. Only exorbitantly costly or unethical training is likely to produce fundamental changes in someone's personality or thinking style. Because training is such an important business activity many agencies play an active role in its provision.

Agencies involved in Training

The agency most involved in training is the trainees. They will feel the greatest impact of training on their career prospects and their satisfaction with their working lives. Trainees usually undergo training in order to equip themselves for a new and better job.

Training has its next greatest impact on the trainee's superior. Indeed, one of a manager's most fundamental responsibilities is to ensure that subordinates are fully trained.

One of the most commonly accepted definitions of a manager is 'someone who gets work done through other people'. The other people will not be able to do that work unless they are fully trained. Many managers are simply ignorant of this responsibility. Other managers allow training to go by default – there is always some urgent production problem which either prevents them from coaching and training their staff or prevents staff being released for training. In the short run such expedients may be effective. In the long run, the quality of staff is degraded and they are able to attempt a narrower range of work at a lower level of efficiency.

The impact of training on the organization is important. Without training a workforce will be less efficient. In a commercial setting, poor training usually involves a loss in profitability. The role of the organization centres upon providing a system which should help individuals and managers meet their responsibilities. The system usually involves four main components. First, it must procure resources that can be invested in training. Usually this involves making a budget allocation. The size of the allocation varies enormously but the 'going rate' is about 1 per cent of payroll costs. The most advanced organizations have specific training policies and at graduate level they budget for five weeks of training per year for the first two years after recruitment and two weeks training per year thereafter. Second, the organization needs a system for making sure that those who need the training are the ones that receive it. This may involve some formal assessment of training needs. The third component is the actual training to meet these needs. In large firms this will often involve establishing a training centre. In smaller organizations it will involve 'buying in' training from consultants or colleges. The final stage is to evaluate whether the training has been effective. Although there are notable exceptions, both the manager and the organization tend to focus on training as an aid to improve performance in the employee's present job.

There are agencies at industry level who are active in training. There are industry training boards such as the Engineering Industry Training Board. Sometimes, industry research associations such as HATRA (Hosiery and Allied Trades' Research Association) also undertake training activities. These organizations try to make sure that a whole industry has a supply of well-trained workers. Often their major role is to forecast likely shortages of trained workers and to alert and stimulate the individual organizations into taking action. Often they also play a co-ordinating role such as trying to ensure that companies and colleges have facilities which are • complementary rather than competitive.

At national level, Government is involved in training. Sometimes this involvement is no more than a cynical attempt to manipulate some index such as unemployment figures. In most cases, however, the concern is a genuine one arising out of the knowledge that training can help promote national wellbeing by improving the quality of the workforce. The Government's perspective is very long term. The Government's role is to provide an infrastructure such as colleges and universities, to monitor long term trends and to stimulate action. Governments usually set up an agency or commission of some kind to co-ordinate its work.

With such differing perspectives, the topic of training is inevitably complex. In order to provide a manageable description, the remainder of this chapter will focus upon the viewpoint of the organization. Figure 4.1 sets out the basic training paradigm which many organizations adopt.

Establishing Organizational Goals

The first stage of the training paradigm is to establish the organization's objectives. A great deal of training effort is wasted because this stage is overlooked. For example, one large retailing company wasted hundreds of thousands of ecus (European Currency Units) training its cashiers in arithmetical skills when it knew that within six months it would be installing automated cash registers. Similarly a helicopter manufacturer wasted a fortune in training technicians to manufacture one machine when it had already taken the decision to withdraw from that sector of the market.

Organizational goals are affected by Government legislation and the business environment. For example, the privatization of utilities such as gas and electricity meant that these

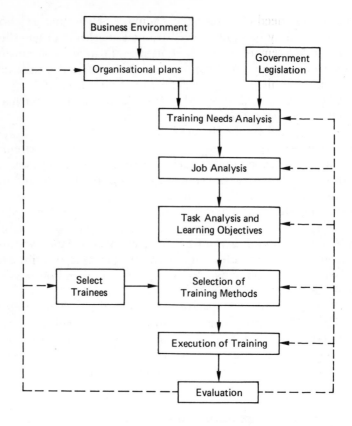

Figure 4.1   *The training paradigm*

organizations needed to retrain their staff in terms of the legal requirements and accountancy practices of private companies. During the 1980s quality and reliability became important features in the marketability of goods and many manufacturers needed to spend millions of ecus on quality training. The decline in the number of school leavers in the 1990s means that companies are having to train other categories of worker to do the jobs usually performed by school leavers.

Once the organizational goals have been established it is necessary to decide which of these needs are best met by training. Training specialists have a tendency to see all manpower needs in terms of some training activity. In practice it may be more efficient to meet these needs by using other management techniques such as recruitment or job design. In many circumstances, it is more effective to buy new equipment which makes the job simpler and easier.

Training Needs Analysis

The second stage in the training paradigm is to specify the training need in terms of the tasks people perform. An audit of the workforce's present abilities is made. The training need is the gap between the present abilities and the required abilities. A Training Needs Analysis is closely associated with an organization's manpower plans. In any event, the training needs should be directly derived from the organization's goals.

For example, a firm may intend to expand its output of a new type of fixing for the construction industry by 40 per cent. It might find that it needs to retrain 100 existing operatives in the specific new skills; improve the knowledge of its 10 sales staff in the new product and completely train 40 new operatives. In addition, it might need to train several office staff in 'export procedures' and it may even need to train a new assistant marketing manager.

For convenience, many organizations group their training needs according to the categories of workers. The main categories are:

1. operative
2. clerical
3. sales
4. technical
5. administrative
6. professional/technological
7. managerial

In recent years, a great deal of attention has been paid to the training needs of managers. Two recent and very important reports surveyed management education in USA, West Germany, France, Japan (Handy, 1987) and in the UK (Constable and McCormick, 1987).

Some types of training are relevant to all categories of employee and they are categorized according to the subject matter involved. The main ones are:

1. induction training
2. safety training
3. industrial relations training
4. pre-retirement training
5. interpersonal skills
6. booster training
7. versatility training

Usually, this type of analysis results in a training plan that consists of a large matrix with the various occupations or training categories listed down the side and the tasks listed across the top. At a glance, the matrix will then show the numbers of employees who need to be trained in each task. The training needs which emerge are then prioritized.

Task Analysis

Once the tasks have been identified, they must be analysed in finer detail into the form of training objectives. Training objectives should be written in a way that is not subjective. It should be clear and unambiguous whether or not these objectives have been met. Often, training objectives are woolly-minded such as, 'the trainee will understand export procedures'. The problem is that we can never open up a trainee's mind and check their understanding. The phrase 'export procedures' is also woolly-minded – does it mean the customs clearance forms or does it include making arrangements for shipping and insurance?

A more objective statement would be, 'Given four different types of customs, insurance and freight forms, the trainee will be able to identify and complete, without assistance or reference books and without more than one error, the appropriate customs shipping and insurance forms for type 47 wall fixings for export to Liechtenstein.' Objectives of this kind are usually called *behavioural objectives* and at the end of training it is clear to everyone – including the trainee – whether or not they have been achieved. Good descriptions of how to produce behavioural objectives are given in Gagne and Briggs (1979) and Davies (1971).

A vital part of a behavioural objective is the statement of the competency involved. Identification of these competencies is a crucial part in producing good training. Competencies are so important that several people have tried to classify them. In operative training, they often boil down to job knowledge and skills (see Seymour, 1966). The CRAMP alogorithm (ITRU, 1986) divides competencies into five types: Comprehension, Reflexes, Attitudes, Memory, and Procedures. Probably the best classification of competencies is that devised by Gagne and Briggs (1979).

According to Gagne and Briggs competencies are divided into five categories.

Intellectual skills are particularly important in training. They involve learning how to *do* some kind of mental operation such as *identifying* a metaphor, *calculating* an insurance premium or *creating* a new system. Intellectual skills make the individual able to respond to conceptualizations of their environment. Intellectual skills are so important that they have been subdivided and arranged in a hierarchy of skills as shown in Figure 4.2.

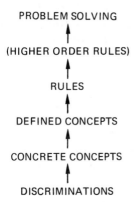

PROBLEM SOLVING

↑

(HIGHER ORDER RULES)

↑

RULES

↑

DEFINED CONCEPTS

↑

CONCRETE CONCEPTS

↑

DISCRIMINATIONS

Figure 4.2 *Gagne's hierarchy of intellectual skills*

Perceptual and motor skills involve the abilities to physically do something rather than think something. Classic examples of perceptual and motor skills are the competencies to drive a lorry, use a typewriter, adjust optical instruments. Handwriting and drawing are also perceptual motor skills. Exotic examples of perceptual motor skills are manoeuvring a space buggy or cutting diamonds. Fuller descriptions of perceptual motor skills are given by Fitts and Posner (1967) and Holding (1981).

Information or knowledge concerns the number of facts that a person can remember. Gagne and Briggs refer to this as verbal information but it is clear that numerical and spatial information should also be included. The learning of facts is often derided by educationalists but it is clear that the learning of facts is an essential part of training. Without facts other types of learning become irrelevant and cease to have continuity. The facts to be learned vary enormously from job to job.

Attitudes are an important aspect of many training programmes. An attitude is a relatively persistent tendency to react favourably or against a certain object or situation – they represent peristent choices in the direction of behaviour. For example most sales staff are expected to have a positive attitude towards customers. In certain occupations it is vital that employees have a very positive attitude towards safety procedures.

The final type of competency is rather different from the rest and concerns *cognitive strategies*. These refer to the way that trainees go about learning new things. Some trainees go about learning things in a very methodological and logical way while others seem to be almost random in their learning efforts. Some trainees focus on the practical aspect while other focus on theory. Some trainees start with the detail and build up to the main points while others start with the main points and then tackle the detail. From these examples it can be seen that a cognitive strategy is a process whereby trainees control the way they learn. Of course, some of these strategies are more effective than others and one of the most fundamental aspects of any training is to get the trainees to adopt an efficient cognitive strategy.

Choice of Training Methods

Once the task has been analysed in terms of competencies, the next stage is to choose training methods which impart these competencies. The following section will aim to describe the main training methods. For the sake of convenience each method will only be described under its main category but, in fact, a training method may be applicable to two or more competencies. For example, lectures may be used to develop intellectual skills and give information. Further details of many of these methods is given by the ITRU (1977) paper.

Training Methods for Intellectual Competencies

Classes are, perhaps, the most traditional method of developing intellectual competencies. In a class a teacher first describes the intellectual skill and then uses that skill on several examples. Student understanding is then checked by a question and answer session in which the teacher re-explains points which have been misunderstood. The advantages of classes are that they are relatively cheap to provide and they can be very good in ensuring that specific intellectual skills are developed. Unfortunately, class size must be restricted to a relatively small number (say, under 18) otherwise an effective question and answer session cannot take place. Classes also tend to make fairly slow progress and can only cover quite limited ground. Important disadvantages of classes are that they are necessarily teacher-centred and for large periods of time an individual trainee will be inactive.

Discovery learning is an approach to training in which instead of telling trainees how to process information they are placed in a situation where they discover by their own actions how to process it. Discovery learning is particularly effective when the material is very theoretical and when trainees have little previous experience of the subject. For example, with the electrification of the railways, railway workers needed to be able to apply the principles of electro-circuit theory. This could have been attempted by using classes but the classroom method seemed quite inappropriate for mature employees. Consequently a safe, low-voltage circuit board was developed and the railmen were asked to solve a graded series of problems using the circuit board. As they solved the problems they discovered for themselves the main principles of electro-circuit theory. Discovery learning is considered to be particularly appropriate for use with older trainees.

Programmed instruction is an effective method of developing some intellectual skills. The skills are broken down into discrete sections about the length of a short paragraph. The sections are called frames. After each frame, the trainee makes a response to a question by choosing one of the alternative answers A to E. If the trainee understands the principles and selects the correct answer a congratulatory message is received and a frame containing the next principle is presented. If the wrong answer is selected, the programme works out the most likely cause and presents a frame of further explanation before returning the trainee to the original question. Trainees do not proceed to the next principle until they have understood the previous one.

Initially, the hardware involved in programmed instruction was a scroll of paper which moved behind a window set in a specially designed machine. These machines were displaced by computers and became known as computer aided instruction (CAI). Recent advances in technology have incorporated the use of video discs in order to make the training very realistic. For example, one bank uses video discs to train its staff in the principles of assessing client's suitability for loans. Trainees first view a sequence in which the loan applicant introduces himself and explains the reason for requesting a loan. At the end of the sequence, the trainee is asked what question he would pose to the applicant and on pressing a button the applicant's answer to that question is viewed. The process is repeated in a way which closely simulates a typical loan interview. At the end of the session, the trainee's decision and the processes used to arrive at the decision are printed out and are available for discussion with a tutor.

Programmed instruction has the advantage of incorporating many aspects of the psychology of learning: the trainee receives accurate and effective feedback and is able to proceed at his or her own pace. Instruction is available at times which suit the trainee and hence it is less disruptive of normal work.

However, programmed instruction involves very high set-up costs and bright trainees often find the method tedious.

Training Methods for Perceptual and Motor Skills

The discrimination method teaches trainees to detect the difference between items that are very similar. The basis of the technique is very straightforward. At the beginning of training trainees are asked to make choices between objects that are very different from each other and as training progresses the differences are reduced until they are minimal. For example, it is vital that radar operators on missile ships are able to discriminate between the echos from enemy bombers and fighters and commercial passenger aircraft. Training to make this discrimination could first start by asking them to make discriminations between small, fast, low-flying fighter planes and slow large jumbo jets flying at 10,000 metres. Once these discriminations had been achieved, they would be asked to make discriminations between fighters and small 'feeder' commercial aircraft. Finally, the radar operators would be asked to discriminate fighters from small, low-flying executive jets.

In many perceptual motor tasks operatives are required to make fine discriminations. For example, when banknotes are printed at the Bank of England they have to be checked for imperfections which may be as slight as a faulty watermark or a faulty wavy line. The checking has to be done at high speed and trained operatives are expected to flick through a wad of banknotes and identify those containing faults. One of the best methods in training people in this skill is the method of *cueing and fading*. Special wads of banknotes are prepared containing known faults. At the start of training banknotes containing a fault will have a coloured dot in the top corner – a pink dot will mean a watermark fault, a blue dot will mean a printing fault for example. These coloured dots act as cues indicating that somewhere on the note there is a fault. All the trainee has to do is locate it. When proficiency has been achieved a second wad is prepared in which there is merely a grey dot in the corner. Here the trainee has to locate the fault and classify it.

In the final stages of training, the cue is completely withdrawn and there are no dots on the faulty notes.

The magnification method is an alternative to cueing and fading in teaching people to make fine discriminations. As its name implies the object to be perceived, especially the faults to be perceived, are made bigger. The magnification is then gradually reduced until the trainee can deal with material of the normal size. For example, mending weaving faults on worsted cloth requires operatives to see individual fibres and to reweave that patch of cloth. Trainee menders find this a difficult task and at the start of training they are given a large high-powered magnifying glass. When they can copy at this level a lesser-powered glass is substituted and so on until they can manage to mend worsted using only the naked eye. *Slow motion techniques*, using video, ciné film or specially adapted machinery that runs at a slower rate is really a version of the magnification method – except that it is time rather than light waves that are magnified.

The progressive part method is really a schedule for organizing the practice of complex motor skills such as typing. It assumes that the task can be broken down into, say, four or five parts. The progressive part method suggests that part A should be learned to perfection. Then part B should be learned. Next parts A and B should be practised together before learning part C in isolation. When part C has been mastered, parts A, B and C should be practised together. In essence, the cumulative part method means that each new part is learned thoroughly in isolation and then it is practised in conjunction with the other parts which have already been mastered. A classic example of the progressive part method is learning to touch type. Trainee typists first practise the home row keys. When they have mastered the home row, they practise the upper row keys. Then they practise the home and upper row together. Next they practise the bottom row keys before practising all three rows.

In some circumstances the responses to be learned cannot be broken down into separate parts because in some jobs three or four basic movements must be executed in a smooth continuous sequence. In these circumstances, *the simplified tasks method* of training is usually appropriate. In this method, trainees are presented with simplified abstractions of the tasks where all inessential details are omitted. The task is then sufficiently simple for a beginner to master after only a short period. The details can be reintroduced at a later stage of training. The danger with this method is that the task is simplified so much that it becomes artificial and no longer resembles the work done by operatives.

Training Methods for Imparting Knowledge and Information

Lectures are probably the most frequently used method of imparting knowledge and skills. Although they are often much maligned they have outlived other methods because they have formidable advantages. Firstly, they are very cheap. The cost of a lecture per student to, say, a group of 200 students is about equal to the cost of a daily newspaper. They are very flexible and only require a few days' notice before they are available whereas the lead time for videos and computer aided instruction can be many months. Unfortunately lectures also have formidable disadvantages. They are essentially teacher centred methods in which the learner remains passive. Passivity inevitably induces boredom and after about 25 minutes the concentration of most trainees falls very dramatically. Boredom is also increased if the lecture involves tedious detail. These factors mean that lectures are only suitable for use with intelligent and highly motivated students. Because there is little scope to deal with individual objections and queries, lectures on controversial topics have little effect. However in the hands of a skilled lecturer the lecture can serve very useful functions. They can give a panorama of the domain to be studied and they can give students an enthusiasm for the subject matter so that they become motivated to follow up the information elsewhere.

Books are an old technology but still retain formidable advantages over other kinds of instruction. They are cheap, can be used in a flexible way and they are convenient to use at different times and in different places. One of the great advantages of books is that they allow the trainee to proceed at his or her own pace and if something is misunderstood it can be read and reread until a satisfactory level of knowledge is obtained. The big disadvantage of books is that the reader usually takes a fairly passive approach to reading and hence books are likely to become boring. The passivity of books can be overcome by readers making notes and actively questioning themselves about the material. Some books are in the form of programmed texts. Inevitably, books tend to be slightly out of date and they tend to deal with general situations rather than the specific situation facing the trainee.

As every student knows, mnemonics and jingles are useful ways of remembering short material. Most people remember the colours in the rainbow by the mnemonic 'Richard of York Gave Battle In Vain', French verbs taking *être* are remembered with 'Mrs Van de Tramp' and who would remember the year Columbus discovered the West Indies without the jingle 'In fourteen hundred and ninety-two Columbus sailed the ocean blue'? A variation on mnemonics and jingles are to devise rules which help reduce the load of remembering specific pieces of information. A classic example is the rule to help poor spellers – 'I before E except after C'. The difficulty with rules of this kind is that it is difficult to devise rules which cater for all eventualities and the learner is left with the task of remembering the exceptions to the rule.

The cumulative part method is a system which can be used when a lot of closely integrated information has to be learnt. The danger is that the material will be broken up into smaller units and the units learned separately. Whilst the trainee will be able to remember the various parts, there is a great danger that the parts will be reproduced in the wrong order – rather like being able to receite accurately the verses of a poem but to get the verses in the wrong order. Research shows that whenever possible, it is better to learn a task as a whole rather than split it into parts. However, some tasks are too big to learn at one go. The cumulative part method aims to overcome this difficulty. Part A is learned, then parts A and B are learned together. Next part A, part B and part C are learned together and so on until all the material is known. It is important to note the difference between the cumulative part method and the progressive part method: in the progressive part method, the additional material is always practised on its own before being incorporated with the material that is already known; with the cumulative part method the new material is always integrated with the existing material.

A great deal can be done to reduce the load on the trainee's memory by also using *checklists, simple instructions,* and *algorithms* (tree diagrams) but in themselves these are not actually training techniques.

Training Methods for Developing Attitudes

Seminars and informal groups are probably the most frequently used methods of changing attitudes. Usually, a group of five or six trainees meet to discuss a topic such as safety or customer care. The meeting is usually led by a skilled tutor who introduces the topic and then invites discussion. Hopefully, the desired attitude will emerge during the discussion otherwise the desired attitudes will be carefully introduced by the tutor. Trainees will be encouraged to air their objections to the desired attitude and the objections will be gently countered. Finally, when a group consensus in favour of the desired attitude has formed, the group leader will get each trainee to say publicly that they intend to adopt the desired attitude. There are many variations on this model but, in essence, they adopt Lewin's three phases of unfreezing, changing and refreezing attitudes. These techniques are very effective and they utilize the powerful forces of group conformity and public commitment. However, they raise ethical considerations since they involve an element of manipulation and indeed, they are similar to the techniques of brainwashing.

Role play is also an effective method of changing trainees' attitudes towards groups of people they are likely to meet in their work. A trainee receptionist can be asked to play the role of a member of the public and an instructor can play the role of a rude, inattentive and inefficient receptionist. The trainee is then asked to recall their own reactions and feelings and to suggest ways that the behaviour of the receptionist could be improved. This role play could be repeated using different scenarios. The scenarios need to be as realistic as possible and the role plays need to be followed up with exercises to ensure that conclusions are drawn and remembered.

T-groups or encounter groups were very much in vogue during the 1960s and early 1970s as methods of improving attitudes and skills towards other people. The idea behind these methods is that in our day to day dealings with other people we often, and perhaps for very good reasons, conceal from them the true impact of their behaviour. Because the feedback is attenuated, people are unaware of the reactions of others. As a consequence, mistrust or some form of maladaptive behaviour may arise. T-groups and encounter groups aim to improve the accuracy of the feedback and so encourage greater sensitivity and group cohesion. Sometimes this kind of training is called sensitivity training. Typically a group of six people and a tutor meet in a fairly unstructured situation without any specific task to perform. They focus upon the relationships in the group and the impact they have upon each other. There is usually an agreement to give open and honest feedback. Thus in a non-threatening situation people learn how others perceive them and they also feel free to try out new ways of interacting.

Training Method for Improving Cognitive Strategies

Case studies and simulations are frequently used in management training. The trainee, or a group of trainees, are presented with a scenario and they are asked to respond as they would in a real life situation. At various stages they are required to make various decisions or a plan. They are then given appropriate additional information and asked to make further responses. In this way several years' experience can be compressed into a fairly short time. Often the outcomes and the reasons are then discussed with a tutor in order to gain a real understanding of the dynamics which underpin the case study. In itself, participation in case studies usually improves self-insight into the way that trainees learn new things: they see others learning and they are also aware of their own learning process. However, the greatest benefit is derived if time is set aside at the end of the case study for the trainees and the tutor to focus on the way that individuals in the group set about learning. The tutor will try to get each participant to identify those attitudes and behaviours which inhibited them from finding an acceptable solution. Time will then be devoted to thinking of more appropriate ways of learning. In an ideal situation there will be other case studies where trainees can develop and practise these new strategies of learning.

Projects and mentoring are other ways of encouraging trainees to develop efficient ways of benefiting from experience. First an organization will identify employees with the potential to develop to a senior level. The progress of each of these employees will be tracked and at appropriate points they will be given assignments or projects which provide new experience and a chance to develop new skills. In order to get the maximum benefit from this experience each employee is allocated a mentor. It is the mentor's job to hold regular meetings, discuss the progress of the project and to suggest ways in which the employee might derive more benefit from them. This type of training can incorporate many varieties. One particular variety is Action Learning in which the projects are usually undertaken in an outside organization. Thus the trainee gains wider experience. They are not constrained by habitual roles and feel freer to experiment with different strategies of learning.

The Psychology of Learning

The type of competency to be developed is an important but not the only consideration in deciding upon the training method which should be used. Findings from the psychology of learning need to be taken into account too.

The basic factors in the psychology of learning are the principles of *attention and motivation*. Many trainers forget that unless the trainee is awake, attending and wanting to learn, very little training will actually take place. Attention is partly a function of the physical environment. Stuffy, warm environments tend to produce poor attention. The absence of distraction will help maintain attention. Timing is also an important determinant of maintaining attention. It becomes progressively harder to maintain attention as time progresses. Indeed there is evidence that after 25 minutes a trainee is absorbing material at only 5 per cent of the rate it was absorbed during the first few minutes.

Motivation is a more complex phenomenon than attention. Generally, motivation is divided into two aspects: extrinsic motivation and intrinsic motivation. Extrinsic motivation is the external pressure that is applied to trainees in order to make them learn. Typical examples of extrinsic motivators in training are course marks, bonuses for passing exams, the threat of dismissal for failing exams, self-esteem in relation to other trainees. Extrinsic motivators should not be ignored and can play an important role in trainee motivation. However, there is research which suggests that extrinsic motivators are less powerful than intrinsic motivators. Intrinsic motivators concern the appeal and interest of the training itself. Generally, training which has high intrinsic appeal will be training which is varied, meaningful, where the trainee has some freedom to decide how to tackle the work and where the trainee gets some feedback on his or her progress.

A second, blatantly obvious, requirement for training is that *the trainee should be able to receive the training information*. At its most banal this means that the trainee should be able to see and hear what is shown and said. Although this is an obvious requirement of good training it is a principle that is breached every day. Often too many apprentices are huddled around a demonstration for all to see clearly. Often, students are crammed at the back of large rooms where they have difficulty in hearing the voice of a tutor or lecturer. It is arguable that the efficiency of training could be improved by 10 per cent if only instructors and teachers would ensure that all trainees could see and hear the instruction.

A third important principle in the psychology of learning is that trainees should receive *good knowledge of results*. Sometimes this is called feedback and it is linked with the idea of reinforcement. A simple experiment involving drawing lines the length of a block of wood demonstrated this. Subjects were blindfolded and never saw the block of wood but they could feel it at any time they wished. One group was given feedback in terms of whether they were right or wrong. The other group received no feedback. The performance of the feedback group quickly improved from a 'hit rate' of 12 per cent to a 'hit rate' of over 60 per cent while the hit rate of the no feedback group remained at about 12 per cent. (Baker and Young, 1960).

This experiment demonstrates two important points concerning knowledge of results. First, it should be as specific as possible and second, it should be given as soon as possible – preferably within a few seconds.

Some psychologists emphasize the need for reinforcement. In other words, at the end of each piece of behaviour a trainee should be rewarded if the behaviour is correct and punished if the behaviour is incorrect. Food or money or some privilege are examples of positive reinforcements and unpleasant noises, sarcastic comments and electric shocks are examples of negative reinforcement. Fortunately, human beings respond to quite subtle reinforcements and praise or disapproval are all that is needed in most training situations. An important point which has repeatedly emerged from research on reinforcers is that positive reinforcement is much stronger than negative reinforcement. If negative reinforcement is frequently used it reduces trainee motivation and the trainees learn to avoid punishment rather than learn the task (that is, they learn to avoid getting caught doing the wrong thing rather than learning to do the right thing!). Consequently, it is said that training schemes should include much positive reinforcement and little negative reinforcement.

Other psychologists suggest that reinforcement is not essential for learning to take place. They say that reinforcement is only important because it is one way of giving knowledge of results.

The fourth major aspect of the psychology of learning is the concept of *transfer of training*. In other words, what is learnt in training should also be useful when actually doing the job itself – in theory, if someone is 100 per cent successful in training, they should also be 100 per cent successful in practice. This rarely happens and there are two main reasons: the training situation does not accurately reflect the job, and social factors. Transfer of training is usually good to the extent that the training situation mirrors the job. Suppose a job involves responding to four lights A, B, C, D by pressing four buttons W, X, Y, Z respectively. If training involved learning the responses A – W, B – X, C – Y and D – Z we would expect very good transfer of training which approaches 100 per cent. If training involved the responses A – W, B – X, C – S, D – T only 50 per cent transfer of training would be expected and if training involved responses A – Q, B – R, C – S and D – T then there will be no transfer and training will have been a waste of time. Unfortunately, transfer of training can be negative and training can actually reduce job performance. This usually occurs when the same signals and responses are involved but in different combinations. In the above example there would be negative transfer of training if the trainees were taught A – Y, B – Z, C – W and D – X: it would be like learning to drive a car in which the left to right order of the pedals was brake – accelerator – clutch instead of accelerator – brake – clutch.

Often, training fails to transfer to the workplace for social reasons. The trainee may learn the correct procedure but is then placed to work alongside colleagues who are accustomed to doing things in the wrong way. The trainee will face strong and probably irresistable pressure to adopt the wrong way of doing things. For example, one police force taught its trainee constables to be thoughtful, unprovocative and sensitive when enforcing the law and they were successful in getting the trainees to adopt this approach. However, when the trainees were put on the beat alongside experienced constables, they soon absorbed and adopted the canteen culture of 'if you give them an inch they will take a mile' and 'it pays to show them who's the boss'.

Attention and motivation, reception of information, knowledge of results and transfer of training are probably the most basic and important aspects of the psychology of learning. However, it is also necessary to be aware of four other aspects, the learning cycle, learning curves, overlearning, and massed *vs* distributed practice. It is also worth being aware of the reasons why trainees forget.

Learning is usually controlled by learning strategies (see Glaser and Bassok, 1989). *Kolb and Fry's (1975) model* of these strategies has become almost a cult in its own right. They start by saying that a good learning style is a cycle of four states. The *concrete experience state* can be thought of as the start of the cycle – it is the events we actually perceive and can be thought of as a straight forward perception of the objective world. After we have experienced something we enter the *reflective observation* state where we take a more measured and reflective view of what has happened to us – we start to internalize the experience in our long term memory. The third state is *abstract conceptualization* where we step back from the reality of a specific situation and draw general conclusions which apply to a range of similar situations and we may develop hunches or theories to explain what has happened. The final state is the state of *active experimentation* where we try to check out these theories and hunches by seeking out other situations that generate concrete experiences yielding data on the correctness of our theories.

According to Kolb, individuals rarely develop all aspects of the learning cycle to an equal extent. The states we tend to favour give us our characteristic learning style. For example, 'a converger' is someone who does best in solving traditional problems at an objective level – they tend to operate in the abstract conceptualization state. An 'assimilator' is someone who is good at building up theoretical models and is good at inductive reasoning – they tend to operate in both the abstract conceptualization and the reflective observation stage. The 'accommodator' is someone who is best at doing things and who operates largely in the concrete experience and the active experimentation stage. Finally, the 'diverger' is good in situations which involve generating different ideas – they tend to operate in the reflective experience stage.

Learning curves are a graph showing the progress of trainees. The time in training is shown on the bottom axis and the performance of the trainees is shown up the side. The performance of the trainee is plotted day by day or perhaps week by week. Most people would expect that the graph of learning rises fairly constantly. This is rarely true. Usually, there is a fairly pronounced increase in learning. Then the graph levels off to a plateau before starting to rise again. Learning plateaux are not uncommon and they seem to represent areas where the trainee is not making any progress. Learning plateaux can be explained in two ways. First, they can represent periods of assimilation where the trainee is consolidating (or overlearning) the material they have just mastered. Second, learning plateaux may represent intervals before the trainee has learnt to integrate material. Learning plateaux were first documented by Bryan and Harter who, in the early 1900s, were teaching telegraph operators to send messages in morse code. They noticed that there was a period of rapid learning as the trainee operators learnt the dot–dash combinations for the individual letters for example, 'T – H – E'.There was then quite a long plateau where they seemed to be learning nothing. Then, there was a rapid rise in performance to the level of competent operators as the trainees learnt to combine the individual letters and send the dot–dash combinations for whole words, in other words 'THE'.

Sometimes, learning curves show falls in the level of performance and these falls represent *forgetting*. It was once believed that forgetting was a direct function of the time that elapsed since the material had been learned. However, it was noticed that this explanation cannot be true because if we learn something and then immediately fall asleep for 12 hours, when we wake we can remember the material almost as well as when we went to sleep. It would appear that most forgetting occurs because learning new material interferes with the retention of old material. For example, if one person is asked to learn a list of words in the morning and then engages in an leisure activity for several hours he is likely to be able to recall the original list. If someone else learns the same list in the morning and then a similar list in the afternoon, it is highly likely that they will make a lot of mistakes when trying to recall the original list. Learning the second list interferes with the remembering of the first list. This phenomenon is known as retroactive inhibition and there is a similar pheno-menon known as proactive inhibition.

It is vital to bear retroactive and proactive inhibition in mind when planning training courses. Many stupid training managers prefer intensive courses. Training costs a lot of money and in an effort to get the best value they arrange courses which start at 8.00 in the morning and, with the occasional break, continue to 8.30 in the evening. Such courses polish the image of the training manager as a hard-driving and hard-headed manager but the laws of retroactive inhibition mean that, in fact, the trainees remember less.

Often the situation is compounded by the second major reason we forget – the emotional repression of unpleasant memories. There is quite a lot of evidence that we tend to push things we dislike out of our consciousness. This is called repression. Technically it is not forgetting but the practical effects are the same. Often, training managers of the 'macho' ilk who insist on very intensive courses also engender a tense and unpleasant atmosphere. The combined effect of the two processes means that trainees on intensive courses often remember less than those on more reasonable programmes.

There are two major ways to minimize the effects of forgetting: *overlearning* and the use of *distributed practice*. It has been repeatedly demonstrated that material that is overlearnt is much less likely to be forgotten. Indeed, as a general rule of thumb, overlearning of 50 per cent is recommended. For example, if trainees, on average, need to repeat an exercise 10 times before they get it completely right, a training scheme should allow time for the exercise to be repeated 15 times so that it is overlearned to the point where it will not be forgotten.

If two hours is available to overlearn some material, the question arises 'how should this two hours be organized?' There are two main possibilities. The two hours could be used in a single session or it could be broken up into, say, six 20-minute sessions. The evidence from experiments is clear: whenever possible the time available should be split up into sessions which do not last longer than 20 or 30 minutes – in that way, attention and motivation is retained and the effects of retroactive inhibition are minimized.

Delivering Training

Once the tasks to learn have been analysed and the appropriate method of instruction has been chosen, the next stage is to organise the instruction into a course or some other system which will deliver the actual training. In fact, the choice of delivery system needs to balance carefully the practical constraints which apply to the individual and their organization.

On-the-job training is probably the most ubiquitous form of training and merely involves asking an experienced worker to show the trainee how to do things. This type of training is usually called 'sit by Nellie' or 'stand by Sid' training. It is a very flexible way of delivering training and only requires a few moments' thought about who would be the most appropriate experienced worker. It also has the advantage of being realistic and avoiding problems of transfer of training. 'Sit by Nellie' training has the added allure that it involves few additional out of pocket costs. However, in most cir- cumstances, on-the-job is a very bad way of delivery training. It almost totally ignores the principles of learning. The best person at doing the job is not necessarily the best person to teach the job to others. Nellie may well teach the trainee bad habits. Furthermore, training usually takes longer and the experienced worker's output usually falls. When these factors are taken into account, on-the-job training is very expensive. Delivering training by on-the-job methods should only be used when all else fails – even then it should only be used when Nellie or Sid have themselves received some training in the psychology of instruction

The main alternative to on-the-job training is *vestibule training*. Here a special area or training centre is set aside and appropriate staff are selected and trained to give proper instruction to trainees. Jobs will be analysed, proper training plans prepared and proper training records maintained. Pro- vided there is a proper throughput of trainees, vestibule training will be cheaper because normal production is main- tained and trainees learn the job quicker. Unfortunately, vestibule training may encounter problems of transfer of training, it is often inflexible because there is a substantial lead time in providing appropriate facilities and the initial set-up costs are high so it can only be used where there is a substantial throughput of trainees.

Often the throughput of trainees is too small or there is insufficient expertise within the organization to provide train- ing centre facilities. Probably the best alternative is to send trainees once a week to a local college or central training school. *Day release* is usually very cheap because it is usually subsidized. It is also good at providing trainees with a perspective which is wider than that which could be provided by many organizations. On the other hand, this delivery system, involving the trainee's absence from the workplace, can be highly disruptive of production. Furthermore, it is inevitable that a centralized facility can only teach the more general skills and procedures rather than the specific skills and procedures of a particular organization. There is also a tendency for day release training to encounter severe transfer of training problems – especially since resource limitations often prevent colleges buying up-to-date equipment.

Block release is very similar to day release and it is most useful for firms located in outlying areas where it would be impractical for trainees to make daily journeys to a college. Day release is also suitable for specialized training which needs to be offered on a national basis. A typical block release module lasts four or five days and there may be several modules spaced over a period of months. A particular disadvantage with block release is that the training is usually intensive and does not allow much time for consolidation in between sessions. Consequently, block release places considerable strain on slow learners. In addition prolonged absences from home may be very unwelcome to some employees.

Evening classes are cheap and are used by firms who are too mean to provide better forms of training. They are not particularly effective since both the students and the tutors have usually already completed a day's work and may not be at the peak of learning readiness. A high drop out rate is to be expected and typically less than one in 10 people who start a course of evening classes complete them. Consequently evening classes should only be used with very highly motivated students.

Distance learning has developed enormously since the days of 'correspondence courses'. A good distance learning package will start with questionnaires or some other means of assessing the individual's level of competence. Then an appropriate combination of sound cassettes, worksheets, videos and laser discs will be used to provide information. Laser discs are particularly useful since they can adapt the presentation according to the detailed needs of the trainee and they can test the progress of the trainee 'en route'. A good distance learning package will also include the materials or instructions for practical exercises. Finally, a good distance learning package will use tests to check that learning has actually taken place. The big advantage of distance learning packages is that they can be used at any location or time that suits the trainee and consequently they do not interfere with the normal flow of work. But, the set-up costs of distance learning packages are hideously high and are only justified when a large and recurrent training need is involved. A fuller description of the use of technology in training is given by Kearsley (1984).

Evaluation of Training

The final stage in the training paradigm is the evaluation of training. It can be argued that 2 or 3 per cent of the training budget should be reserved for evaluation. The object of evaluation is to decide whether the training is in fact meeting the training need. Good evaluation will identify those aspects which should be left alone and those aspects which should be improved. In principle, there are three ways of evaluating training.

The worst and most frequently adopted method of evaluation is to use *trainee reaction*. This can be achieved by talking to individuals, holding group discussions or by using questionnaires which are often called 'reactionnaires' and 'happiness sheets'. On their own, happiness sheets are of dubious value – they produce a climate in which tutors aim to obtain high ratings by transforming themselves from trainers to entertainers and the trainees have a thoroughly enjoyable and interesting time learning nothing.

A better method of evaluating training is to measure trainee's competence at the start and the end of training. The difference should then be compared to any improvements in a control group. Often this is known as *evaluating the immediate outcomes* of training. In many senses this is the fairest method of evaluation *if* it can be assumed that the training needs analysis is correct. Evaluating the immediate outcomes is fairly easy in operative and technician training – the number of widgets made or the number of circuits wired can be counted. But in professional and managerial training it is difficult to measure increased competence. Despite its great superiority over the reaction level of evaluation, the evaluation of immediate outcomes is rarely attempted because many firms are reluctant to provide suitable control groups.

The final level of evaluation is to assess training's impact on the employee's performance. Often this is called the *ultimate level of evaluation* – it is, after all, the main reason for doing almost all training. However, it is very difficult to separate the effects of training from inadequacies of management: the training may be great but performance may be poor because supplies may be of poor quality and the scheduling of work may be bad. In these circumstances it would be wrong to say that training did not offer value for money.

Probably one development in the very near future will be to follow the lead of selection and develop ways of estimating the monetary value of training. In this way human resource managers will be able to weigh the benefits from different types of training so that training resources can be deployed in such a way that the maximum benefit is obtained. A detailed discussion of how to measure training effectiveness is given by Rae (1986).

References for Chapter 4

Baker, C. H. and Young, P. (1960) 'Feedback during Training and Retention of Motor Skills', *Canadian Journal of Psychology*, 14, 257–64.

Constable, J. and McCormick, R. (1987) *The Making of British Managers*, British Institute of Managers, London.

Davies, I. K. (1971) *The Management of Learning*, McGraw-Hill, London.

Fitts, P. M. and Posner, M. I. (1967) *Human Performance*, Brooks/Cole, Belmont, Ca.

Gagne, R. M. and Briggs L. J. (1979) *Principles of Instructional Design*, Holt, Rinehart and Winston, New York.

Glaser, R. and Bassok, M. (1989) 'Learning Theory and the Study of Instruction', *Annual Review of Psychology*, 40, 631–66.

Handy, C. (1987) *The Making of Managers*, National Economic Development Office, London.

Holding, D. H. (1981) *Human Skills*, Wiley, Chichester.

ITRU (1976) *CRAMP: A Guide to Training Decisions. Research Paper TR1.* Industrial Training Research Unit, Cambridge.

Kearsley, G. (1984) *Technology and Training*, Addison-Wesley, Reading, Mass.

Kolb, D. A. and Fry, R. (1975) 'Towards an applied Theory of Experiential Learning', In C. Cooper (ed.) *Theories of Group Processes*, Wiley, Chichester.

Rae, L. (1986) *How to Measure Training Effectiveness*, Gower, London.

Seymour, W. D. (1968) *Skills Analysis Training*, Pitman, London.

5

Motivation in Organizations

PETER L. WRIGHT
University of Bradford Management Centre

Introduction

In general terms, motivation is concerned with the forces which instigate, give direction to and sustain behaviour. In other words, motivation is what arouses people into action, determines the goals towards which these actions are channelled and influences the vigour and persistence with which such goals are pursued. It is one of a number of factors which influence performance at work (see Taylor and Wright, 1982; Wright and Taylor, 1984). Undoubtedly, such factors not only influence work behaviour directly, but can also influence levels of motivation. Having clear goals to aim at, believing that one has the ability to succeed, obtaining accurate feedback on one's standard of performance, for example, are all likely to affect motivation. These other factors differ from motivation in one important respect. They put the individual in a position where he or she *can* perform a task well. Unless we have a clear idea of what we should be achieving, the necessary ability to do the task, feedback concerning our level of performance, and appropriate resources and working conditions, it will be difficult to perform the task well. Motivation is concerned with whether the individual *wants* to perform the task well. For this reason, Wright (1987) defines motivation more narrowly within the organizational context as: 'The willingness to expend effort on a particular task in order to attain an incentive or incentives of a certain type.'

Levels of work motivation vary considerably both within and between people. Thus an individual may be willing to expend a great deal of effort on one task, but very little on another. Similarly, one individual may be willing to expend effort on a particular task to attain certain incentives, whilst another may not think it worth while to do so. In order to explain such variations in levels of motivation, two main types of motivation theory have been developed. First, there are the *content theories* which are concerned with the forces which arouse motivated behaviour in the first place. Secondly, there are the *process theories* which are concerned with the factors which influence the direction which motivated behaviour takes. An understanding of both is necessary to be able to use motivation theory to influence levels of work motivation.

Content Theories of Motivation

Central to most content theories of work motivation is the concept of need. Needs provide the force which arouses motivated behaviour in the first place. In content theories, the motivation to work tends to be explained in terms of the desire to satisfy unfulfilled needs. It is therefore assumed that, if we can discover what are peoples' most important needs and how they can be fulfilled within the working environment, then this will tell us how to motivate people.

Early content theorists tended to argue that employee behaviour was motivated by a relatively narrow set of needs. For example, F. W. Taylor, founder of the 'scientific management' movement, placed great emphasis on money as a motivator. One of his early 'successes' was his study of labourers loading pig iron on to railway wagons at the Bethlehem Steel Company in the USA in the 1890s. By redesigning the job to eliminate all unnecessary movement, introducing rest pauses to eliminate fatigue and introducing an incentive pay system, Taylor so increased the productivity of the wagon loaders that the firm were able to reduce their numbers from 400 to 140 at the expense of a 60 per cent increase in wages.

Later research has confirmed the importance of monetary rewards as a source of work motivation. Lawler (1971) claimed that even the most conservative studies of individual incentive schemes suggest that they can increase productivity by between 10 and 20 per cent. Even greater increases were later found in Locke *et al.*'s (1980) survey of 15 different studies of pay incentive plans. The median improvement in performance was 35 per cent, with a range of 3 per cent to 75 per cent.

Nevertheless, during the 1930s, work motivation theorists began to suggest that the importance of money as a motivator had been grossly over-rated, and that other factors, primarily social needs, were more important. This change in emphasis was largely the result of the famous series of studies carried out at the Hawthorne Plant of the Western Electric Company during the 1920s and 30s (Roethlisberger and Dickson, 1939).

One study examined the behaviour of the workers in the company's Bank Wiring Room. It was found that, despite the existence of a group incentive scheme, the workers used social pressure to ensure that each person's output conformed to a group norm, which was lower than they could have produced by working harder at the job. In another investigation, the Relay Assembly Room study, a separate work room was set up for six workers to examine the effects of changes in their working conditions, for example, rest pauses, a shorter work-ing day, and so on. The result of such changes, introduced in consultation with the workers, was to increase productivity in each case. Finally, the investigators removed all changes and returned the working conditions to those which had existed at the beginning of the study. To their surprise, output rose yet again, reaching 30 per cent above the level which had been achieved at the beginning of the study.

Faced with this evidence, Roethlisberger and Dickson concluded that it had not been the changes themselves, but their social meaning, which had produced the increase in output. Because the changes had been introduced 'carefully and with regard to the actual sentiments of the workers', they had developed a spontaneous informal organization which not only expressed their own values but was more in harmony with the aims of the management.

Undoubtedly, employees' social needs have a major impact on their work motivation. However, this is not to say that other needs do not also have an influence. In the Relay Assembly Room study, for example, the pay system was changed at the beginning of the study, and evidence from other investigations carried out during the Hawthorne Studies suggests that this may have accounted for almost half the increase in output achieved. Similarly, it could be argued that the workers in the Bank Wiring Room were attempting to safeguard future earnings, because they were afraid that their bonus might be cut if they demonstrated that they could easily achieve higher levels of productivity. Furthermore, it is possible that, because they were consulted about the changes made, the workers in the Relay Assembly Room were able to fulfil what later motivation theorists were to call 'higher order' or 'growth' needs.

During the late 1930s and early 1940s, two clinical psychologists, H. A. Murray and A. H. Maslow, attempted independently to produce a comprehensive list of human needs. Based on clinical observations, Murray *et al.* (1938) identified 12 physiological needs, such as the needs for air, water, food and sex and 28 psychological needs, including the needs for achievement, affiliation, recognition, dominance, autonomy, play, and so on. Murray's work has had little direct application in the field of work motivation, probably because his list of needs was so long and complex that it defied easy presentation to practising managers. Nevertheless, it did influence later researchers, particularly McClelland, whose findings do have more direct relevance to the world of work.

Rather than studying motivation in general, McClelland and his associates decided to examine single motives in depth. They began by studying one of Murray's 28 psychological motives, the need for achievement. Since then McClelland has extended his studies to other psychological motives, such as the need for power, the need for affiliation and the avoidance motive (McClelland, 1987).

The need for achievement *(n Ach)* may be defined as the desire to perform well in relation to a standard of excellence. Research by McClelland and others has shown that people who are high in *n Ach* are interested in excellence for its own sake, rather than for rewards of money, prestige or power (McClelland and Winter, 1969). They tend to seek out challenging tasks, where success can result from the exercise of their own effort and skills and like concrete short term feedback on their performance so that they can tell how they are doing. Research has shown that the development of *n Ach* during early childhood is influenced by methods of childhood upbringing, particularly the expectation of independent behaviour at an early age (Winterbottom, 1958). However, McClelland has also shown that motivation training can be used to develop *n Ach* in adults and that this can lead to higher levels of entrepreneurial activity and success (McClelland and Winter, 1969).

McClelland also suggests that high *n Ach* should lead to success in small businesses and sales, where the key people do most of the work for themselves. However he questions whether people with high *n Ach* will make good managers in large complex organizations, where it may be impossible to do things for oneself and get immediate feedback. In large organizations, he argues, the leadership pattern which is associated with managerial effectiveness is one which combines being at least moderately high in the need for power, lower in the need for affiliation, and high in self-control. High *n Power* is important because it means that the person is interested in the 'influence game', in having an effect on others; low *n Affiliation* is important because it enables the manager to make difficult decisions without worrying unduly about being disliked; and high self-control is important because it means that the person is likely to be more concerned with maintaining organizational systems and following orderly procedures (McClelland and Burnham, 1976, McClelland and Boyatzis, 1982). Research by McClelland and his associates has provided some evidence to support this theory (House and Singh, 1987).

Maslow's (1943) list of human needs contained many of those previously identified by Murray. Unlike Murray, however, Maslow classified these needs into five major groups – physiological, safety, social, esteem and self-actualization (see Figure 5.1). He further suggested that these needs formed a hierarchy, with physiological needs at the

Need Level	Examples of Needs
Self-Actualization	Realizing one's potential, continuing self-development, creativity
Esteem Needs	*Self-esteem*: self-respect, self-confidence, autonomy, achievement. *Reputation*: status, recognition, prestige.
Social Needs	Feeling of belonging, good social relations.
Safety Needs	Freedom from danger, secure, orderly and predictable environment.
Physiological Needs	Hunger, thirst, sex, sleep, air, etc.

Figure 5.1 *Maslow's need hierarchy*

bottom and self-actualization at the top. Thus, if the lowest needs are unfulfilled, he argued, they will dominate behaviour, but once they are fulfilled, they no longer motivate, and people will work their way step by step up the hierarchy to the higher order needs for esteem and self-actualization. This theory was later used by other writers to draw far-reaching and largely unjustified conclusions about work motivation. However, the research evidence provides little support for Maslow's hierarchical theory, and in any case, the original theory was hedged about with so many qualifications and exceptions that it is difficult to see how any clear cut conclusions could be drawn from it. Maslow himself was well aware of this. He commented later (1965) that he was 'a little worried about this stuff which I consider tentative being swallowed whole by all sorts of enthusiastic people who really should be a little more tentative in the way I am.'

Nevertheless, Maslow's work remains influential. Although the hierarchical aspect of his theory is now largely discredited, his classification scheme still provides a useful way of demonstrating the wide variety of needs which can motivate human behaviour. Furthermore, the broad distinction between Maslow's higher order needs (self-actualization and esteem) and lower order ones (social, safety and physiological) has been an important part of many later theories of work motivation.

A similar distinction, for example, can be found in Herzberg's Two-Factor theory of job satisfaction (Herzberg,

Mausner and Snyderman, 1959). Herzberg argued that job satisfaction and job dissatisfaction were caused by two entirely different sets of factors, which he called motivators and hygiene factors, respectively. Hygiene factors, such as supervision, salary, interpersonal relations and working conditions, he said, did not influence job satisfaction. Improving them would decrease job dissatisfaction, but would not produce job satisfaction in a positive sense. Conversely, improving motivators, such as the job itself and opportunities for achievement, recognition, responsibility and advancement, would increase job satisfaction, but would not affect job dissatisfaction. Herzberg therefore argued that the only way to bring about job satisfaction, and thus increase motivation, was to improve the motivational factors. This process of actually building into people's jobs greater scope for personal achievement and its recognition, more challenging and responsible work, and more opportunity for individual advancement and growth, Herzberg (1968) called job enrichment.

The theoretical and practical aspects of Herzberg's work have fared quite differently as far as subsequent research is concerned. The Two-Factor theory has been evaluated in a great many research studies and the majority have failed to support it (Smith and Cranny, 1968; Locke, 1975). It appears that the factors causing job satisfaction and dissatisfaction do not neatly divide into two separate categories, as Herzberg suggests. On the other hand, it has been shown that job enrichment can have beneficial effects on job performance. Locke *et al.* (1980) reviewed 13 studies of the effects of job enrichment and found a median improvement in performance of 17 per cent, with a range of 1 per cent to 63 per cent. In other words, the major weakness of Herzberg's theory was not in claiming that job enrichment could improve performance, but in claiming that it was the *only* way to increase motivation.

Indeed, from the mid-1960s, there was a growing acceptance of the view that early motivation theorists had greatly underestimated the complexity of human motivation. Not only are people motivated by a wide variety of different needs, but they are also highly variable. Whilst each individual may have his or her own hierarchy of needs, arranged in his or her own particular order of importance, this order will vary from individual to individual, and even within the same individual over time and in different situations (Schein, 1965). What this means is that no theory of human needs can tell us what motivates a particular individual or group of individuals. People differ, and what motivates one individual or group may not motivate another. Content theories of motivation are undoubtedly useful in that they draw attention to the wide variety of different needs which can affect human behaviour. However, if a manager wishes to know what motivates a particular individual or group, there is no substitute for studying that individual or group and finding out what is important to them.

The importance of individual differences is clearly recognized in current approaches to job design. For example, Hackman and Oldham's (1976, 1980) Job Characteristics Model suggests that Growth Need Strength (the extent to which the individual values the fulfilment of higher order needs) will influence the extent to which people will want and be motivated by enriched jobs. According to the model (see Figure 5.2), certain core job characteristics will typically produce certain favourable psychological reactions on the part of employees, leading to beneficial work and personal outcomes. However, this effect will be greater, Hackman and Oldham argue, the higher the growth need strength of the worker concerned. This model has proved difficult to subject to rigorous validation, but a recent review of the research evidence by Fried and Ferris (1987) provides considerable support for the model as a whole, and in particular for the differential effect of growth need strength.

However, the theory does have two limitations. Firstly, it does not tell us what to do if workers on the same job have widely differing growth need strength. As research by Graen, Scandura and Graen (1986) has shown, enriching jobs can result in a dramatic increase in performance for those with high growth need strength, but actually decrease the performance of those with low growth need strength. Providing separate enriched and non-enriched production lines, as was done at Motorola (Lawler, 1974), would simply not be practical in the vast majority of cases. Secondly, the model does not tell us what to do to increase the satisfaction and

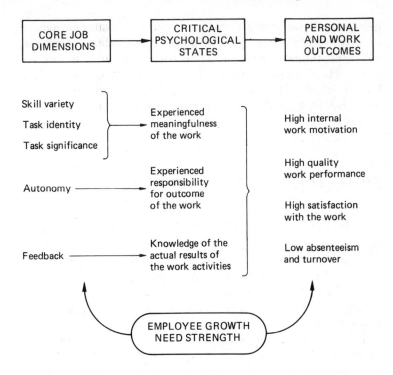

Figure 5.2 *Hackman and Oldham's job characteristics model*
Source: J.R. Hackman and G.R. Oldham (1976) 'Motivation through the design of work: Test of theory', *Organizational Behavior and Human Performance*, 2, 250–79.

motivation of those who have low growth need strength. As in Herzberg's earlier theory, their needs are ignored.

In summary, content theories of motivation have provided evidence of the wide variety of different needs which can motivate human behaviour, and more recently have drawn attention to the critical influence of individual differences on the way such needs affect work performance and satisfaction. Nevertheless, the study of human needs can at best provide only a partial explanation of motivated behaviour. Knowing that someone has a need for money, for example, will not in itself tell us what he or she will do in an attempt to fulfil this need. The response may be to work harder (if pay is related to performance), put in for promotion, look for another, better-paid job, relapse into apathy because there does not appear to be any way of earning more money, and so on. Predicting which particular course of action will be selected in any one particular situation requires more than an understanding of human needs. It requires an understanding of the *processes* whereby these needs are converted into motivated behaviour. It is this subject which is taken up in the next section.

Process Theories of Motivation

The portrait of human motivation presented by content theories of motivation is largely an emotional rather than an intellectual one. People are motivated to fulfil their needs without apparently devoting too much thought to the process. Process theories of motivation represent an attempt to redress this balance. The emotional aspects are not ignored, but greater emphasis is placed upon the role of cognition than in content theories.

Locke, for example, takes the view that motivation can best be described in terms of a striving to attain goals, intentions and purposes. He and his colleagues have carried out extensive research into the effectiveness of goal-setting as a means of influencing work performance. Their findings show that higher performance can result from gaining employees' commitment to the achievement of goals which are both difficult and precisely defined, rather than simply asking them to 'do their best'. The research further suggests that to gain maximum benefit from goal-setting, not only should specific goals be set, but feedback should also be provided to show performance in relation to these goals (Locke *et al.*, 1981). Seventeen studies of goal-setting were reviewed by Locke *et al.* (1980). They found a median improvement in performance of 16 per cent, with a range of 2 per cent to 57 per cent.

Adams' equity theory is concerned with the effects of perceived fairness of rewards on work behaviour. According to Adams (1963, 1965), people who believe that their rewards are unfair in relation to those received by other people will take steps to restore a sense of equity. Based on this theory, it has been suggested that people who believed that they were underpaid would feel resentful and decrease the quantity or quality of their output, whereas those who believed that they were overpaid would feel guilty and increase the quantity or quality of their output. The research evidence firmly supports the first contention, and this has obvious implications for those concerned with the motivation of employees. However, people who are overpaid do not always react as the theory predicts (Mowday, 1987). Some may feel guilty and improve their performance, but others may restore their feelings of equity in more convenient ways, such as changing their perception of their contribution or finding a more favourably rewarded group with which to compare themselves.

Both Locke's goal-setting theory and Adams' equity theory are partial theories of work motivation, in that they attempt to explain only one aspect of the motivational process. There is, however, one process theory which attempts to provide a comprehensive framework, within which it is possible to explain most aspects of work motivation. This is expectancy theory and the remainder of this section will be devoted to describing this theory in some detail.

The first major expectancy theory of work motivation was put forward by Vroom (1964), although later writers, such as Porter and Lawler (1968), have both added to and modified the theory in certain respects. The main principles of the theory are shown in Figure 5.3. Variables in solid boxes represent those included in expectancy theory itself. Those in 'dotted' boxes show how other concepts, particularly those from other motivation theories, can be incorporated within an expectancy theory framework.

According to expectancy theory, the level of work motivation is determined by two main factors, value of outcomes and effort–outcome expectations.[1] Value of outcomes represents the individual's preferences with respect to the various outcomes which may result from performing a particular task. Two broad classes of outcome may be distinguished, intrinsic and extrinsic. Each may be positive or negative. Intrinsic outcomes are those which are derived directly from the task

---

1. These terms are often given different names in different versions of expectancy theory. Valence, value of rewards, expectancy, and effort–reward expectations are common alternatives.

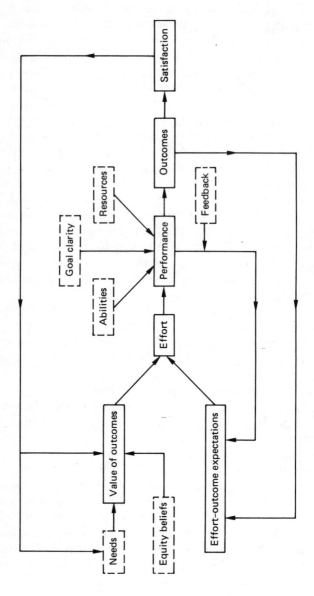

Figure 5.3 *An expectancy model of motivation and job satisfaction*

itself. Typically, they are outcomes which we award ourselves, depending upon how well we feel we have performed the task. Thus, if we feel we have performed well, we may experience a sense of achievement, feelings of pride and accomplishment, enhancement of self-esteem and the satisfaction of a job well done. If we have performed badly, we may experience shame, guilt, embarassment, frustration and so on. Extrinsic outcomes, on the other hand, are those given to us by other people. Within the organizational context, they include such things as more money, promotion, recognition from one's boss, good social relations, 'perks', such as a bigger office or a named car parking space, and so on. Alternatively, they may include loss of pay, a reprimand, being sent to Coventry, loss of leisure time, and so on.

These intrinsic and extrinsic outcomes may be regarded as the things which fulfil or prevent us from fulfilling our needs. Just as needs vary between people, so will the value of outcomes. For example, some people may place a high value on money and be willing to take risks to increase their earnings, whilst others would prefer a more secure job. Similarly, some people may be keen to be promoted or to have a more challenging job, whilst others may prefer to avoid extra responsibility or place a higher value on good relations with colleagues.

Effort–outcome expectations, on the other hand, represent the individual's beliefs concerning the probability that such outcomes will result from expending a certain amount of effort on a particular task. This is made up of two components. The first, effort–performance expectations, refers to the individual's beliefs concerning the level of performance he or she is likely to achieve by investing a certain amount of effort in the task. The second, performance–outcome expectations, refers to the individual's beliefs concerning the outcomes which are likely to result from achieving that level of performance. According to expectancy theory, if either of these variables is zero, then motivation will be zero.

For example, suppose an employee is told that the main criterion for promotion is productivity and that any employee who can increase his or her productivity by 10 per cent will greatly enhance his or her promotion prospects. This will not increase the employee's level of motivation if any of the following apply:

1. The employee has no wish to be promoted.
2. The employee does not believe that it is possible to achieve a 10 per cent increase in productivity no matter how hard he or she tries.
3. The employee does not believe that he or she will actually be promoted even if an increase in productivity of 10 per cent is achieved.

In addition, there are negative outcomes to be considered. Obtaining a 10 per cent increase in productivity may result in increased friction with subordinates, resentment from colleagues, less opportunity to do more rewarding work, loss of leisure time, and so on. Thus the employee will only be motivated if all three variables are above zero, and the probable positive outcomes outweigh the negative ones. Providing this is the case, the more the positive outcomes outweigh the negative ones, the more motivated the individual will be, and the more effort he or she will be willing to put into the task in question.

The amount of effort the individual puts into the task is one of the factors which will determine his or her level of performance. Other factors include:

1. *Goal Clarity*: the extent to which the individual has a clear understanding of the objectives which he or she should be achieving in relation to the task in question.
2. *Ability*: the extent to which the individual has the knowledge and skills required for the task.
3. *Resources*: the extent to which the individual has the equipment, raw materials, support staff, etc., required to perform the task.

These factors, together with effort, will determine the level of performance which the individual achieves. As a result of achieving this level of performance, the individual will experience certain outcomes, which in turn produce feelings of satisfaction or dissatisfaction, depending upon the extent to which such outcomes match the individual's aspirations.

It will be seen that, in expectancy theory, satisfaction is an end–result variable. That is, it results from job performance and the type of outcomes which ensue, but does not itself have a direct influence on job performance. The research evidence provides considerable support for this view. Vroom (1964) reviewed 20 studies of the relationship between job satisfaction and work performance, and found a median correlation between the two of only 0.14, a figure which as he pointed out is so low as to have little theoretical or practical significance. Similarly, Iaffaldano and Muchinsky (1985) reviewed 70 studies of the relationship between job satisfaction and work performance some 21 years later and found an average correlation of 0.17.

So far, we have assumed tht the individual is performing the task for the first time. However, there are many tasks which we do over and over again. In so doing, we obtain first hand information about how easy it is to achieve different levels of performance, what outcomes result from achieving these levels of performance, and how satisfying these outcomes are. Such additional information may in turn affect our effort–outcome expectations or our feeling about the value of outcomes, thus modifying our initial level of motivation. To complete the model, therefore, it is necessary to build in various feedback loops to show that in many cases we are dealing with a cyclical process.

Feedback can also be either intrinsic or extrinsic. In some cases, it is possible to obtain feedback directly from the task itself. For example, when typing a document, one can inspect what one is typing as one carries out the task, and identify mistakes which require correction. Such intrinsic feedback can obviously affect our beliefs about the amount of effort required to achieve a satisfactory level of performance, and this is shown in the solid feedback line from performance to effort–outcome expectations in Figure 5.3.

In some cases, however, it may be difficult to judge for ourselves how well we are performing or have performed a task. For example, the manager of a well-run hotel may not realize how successful he or she is because the majority of guests do not comment on the quality of the service. Similarly, the author of a badly-worded memo may not realize that it has offended the majority of those who have received it. Under these circumstances, we may not know whether we have reached the required standards of performance, and if not, which aspects of performance require most improvement. Thus we might change something which is actually successful or continue doing something which is ineffective, because we mistakenly believe that we have achieved a satisfactory level of performance. Furthermore, even where intrinsic feedback is available, we may not necessarily make use of it. We may, for example, overlook a typing error or spell a word incorrectly because we do not know how to spell the word in question. In such circumstances, feedback from an external source can be very useful. In the organizational context, this may be provided informally by the individual's superior or colleagues, or may take the form of a specially designed feedback system, such as customer surveys. Such extrinsic feedback is shown separately in the dotted box in Figure 5.3.

One of the major advantages of expectancy theory, from the practical point of view, is that it provides a method of analysing the effects of different outcomes on work performance and explaining why they have the effects they do. For example, the effectiveness of money as a motivator can be explained in terms of its value as an outcome and the ease with which it can be linked to performance. Where a job has an output which can be counted (for example, amounts produced or amounts sold), then this can be linked to specified amounts of additional pay, as in a piece-work system. Thus there can be high expectations that improved performance will lead to increased earnings, resulting in higher levels of motivation for those people who place a high value on money as an outcome.

Many jobs, however, do not have a single output which is easily measured. A Personnel Manager is one example. Alternatively, the output may not be under the sole control of the job holder. For example, a Production Manager whose department has a decline in output of 10 per cent could be a poor performer or someone who is coping magnificently with the adverse effects of a strike by certain key workers. In such circumstances, performance cannot be measured directly.

Organizations wishing to relate pay to performance therefore tend to give merit increases based on superiors' assessment of performance in an annual appraisal system. This makes the link between performance and monetary rewards much more tenuous. If the appraisees trust the judgement and objectivity of the appraisers, then the system may have the desired effect. On the other hand, if the appraisees believe that the appraisers are incapable of recognizing good performance, or give merit increases based on criteria other than standard of work performance, then this will undermine their effort–outcome expectations and their faith in the appraisal system. Thus, instead of motivating employees, the system may well produce dissatisfaction, resentment and frustration. This view is amply supported by a review of research into payment by results systems carried out by Thierry (1987). In studies of merit rating, unfavourable outcomes were reported in 13 cases and favourable outcomes in only one. The main complaints were that the relationship between assessment and bonus was unclear, the time gap between performance and bonus too long, and the differences in amount of bonus awarded too small. By contrast, studies of piece-rate systems produced favourable outcomes in 44 cases and unfavourable ones in only three.

Turning now to social relations, this is an outcome which has high value for many employees, but it is not one which organizations can easily link to performance. The main source of such outcomes as a feeling of belonging, social support, and so on is the work group to which the employee belongs. They, not management, will decide what behaviours will be rewarded by social acceptance or punished by rejection, and as we have seen from the Hawthorne Studies, the work group may equally well use social control to hold down performance as to increase it. Thus attempting to improve social relations at work, for example by providing better social facilities, will not necessarily improve performance. On the other hand, it may well improve job satisfaction, and this can have other beneficial organizational effects, such as decreasing labour turnover (Vroom, 1964).

Finally, there are the outcomes which fulfil higher order needs. Some of these, such as promotion and verbal recognition, are extrinsic; that is, they are within the power of the organization or individual manager to give or withhold. Thus they can be linked to performance, and when used in this way can act as a powerful source of motivation for people who value such outcomes.

Many of the outcomes which fulfil higher order or growth needs are, however, intrinsic. It is impossible to give someone a sense of achievement or the stimulation of a challenging job. Such outcomes arise directly from the job itself. Thus, all an organization or manager can do is to provide an opportunity to experience such things by redesigning the individual's job so that *it* offers challenge, responsibility, interest, and so on. In such jobs, however, there is a strong natural link between performing well and experiencing such outcomes. We can only feel a sense of achievement by actually achieving something, experience a sense of responsibility by behaving responsibly, or enjoy the stimulation of an interesting job by taking an interest in it. Thus, in intrinsically motivating jobs, employees with high growth needs will monitor their own performance and award themselves such outcomes when they believe that they have achieved a satisfactory level of performance. For this reason, they develop strong expectations that good performance will lead to the attainment of valued outcomes, which explains why job enrichment can be an effective motivational technique for employees with high growth needs.

Research into expectancy theory has provided some support for its basic principles. Mitchell (1974) reviewed 22 studies in which an attempt had been made to predict job effort from a combination of what we have called value of outcomes and effort–outcome expectations. He found that the average correlation between expectancy theory predictions and actual job effort was about 0.35. This is high enough to suggest that value of outcomes and effort–outcome expectations do have a significant effect on effort. Nevertheless, it still leaves a large amount of the variation in effort still to be accounted for. Part of the problem is undoubtedly methodological. Such variables as expectations, values and effort are difficult to measure precisely and accurately, and so there could be large amounts of error involved in attempts to test the model.

However, it is unlikely that methodological problems alone are responsible for expectancy theory's failure to predict job effort more accurately. Another contributory factor is almost certainly the fact that the basic expectancy model does not contain all the variables which influence effort. Expectancy theorists therefore began to develop more and more complex versions of the theory, often incorporating concepts and processes from other motivation theories, in an attempt to provide a more comprehensive explanation of the motivation to work. Unfortunately, these additional concepts also tend to be difficult to measure and their precise relationship with expectancy theory variables difficult to establish, which in turn makes it difficult to carry out a rigorous test of the model. This led Lawler and Suttle (1973) to comment rather sadly that 'At this point in time, it seems that the theory has become so complex that it has exceeded the measures that exist to test it.'

Furthermore, even the more complex versions of the theory do not include all the variables which influence human motivation. Expectancy theory is based on the assumption that human beings, consciously or unconsciously, assess their preferences and expectations in a rational manner in order to decide how much effort to put into a task. As Locke (1975) points out, however, human beings often do not make their decisions in this way. Much of human behaviour is impulsive, emotional, neurotic or habitual, rather than calculated in the way in which expectancy theory appears to suggest.

Whilst Locke's criticism is justified, it must be pointed out that this is also a problem for other cognitive theories, including his own goal-setting theory. Irrational behaviour is by its very nature unpredictable. Admittedly, there are theories, such as psychoanalysis, which can provide an explanation of irrational behaviour after it has happened, but even they are unable to predict what irrational behaviour will occur before the event. It is arguable, therefore, that it is more useful to concentrate, as expectancy theory does, on the more rational aspects of human motivation, which are at least to some extent predictable, and thus capable of being influenced, rather than attempting to deal with the irrational aspects, which are by their nature virtually impossible to predict.

In summary, then, expectancy theory cannot provide a final answer to the problem of work motivation. It does not include all the variables involved, nor, due to the measurement problems, can it provide precise predictions of levels of work motivation. What it does do, however, is to provide a framework within which it is possible to incorporate virtually the whole of motivation theory, including needs, goals, equity beliefs and feedback as well as other factors which influence performance, such as abilities and resources. This makes it an extremely useful tool for the analysis of motivational problems. In effect, it provides a list of the factors which need to be taken into account when attempting to influence levels of work motivation. There may well be other factors involved, but unless *at least* these factors are taken into account, there is a danger that one of the key variables in a particular situation will be overlooked, and consequently an attempt to influence motivation will misfire. In the next section, we will show in more detail how the concepts of expectancy theory and those of the other motivation theories described in this chapter can be incorporated into a checklist for the analysis of motivational problems.

Implications of Motivation Theory for the Practising Manager

The motivation theories we have examined have a number of practical implications for the manager who wishes to influence levels of work motivation. These can be expressed in the form of a checklist of steps which can be taken whenever the manager feels that he or she is faced with a motivational problem or simply wishes to maintain levels of motivation amongst staff who are already performing at a satisfactory level.[1]

1. *Check Goal Clarity.* Establish whether the individual or group is aware of precisely what they are supposed to achieve in the job and to what standard of performance. If

---

1. This checklist is based on previous work in Taylor and Wright (1982), Wright and Taylor (1984) and Wright (1987).

they are not, then a variety of steps can be taken. With some individuals a quiet word stressing the importance of some aspect of the job may be enough. With other, a more rigorous goal-setting approach, with precise targets and deadlines, may be necessary. If lack of clarity concerning goals is widespread, then an attempt to solve the problem at the organizational level may be appropriate. This could take the form of making goal-setting an explicit part of the performance appraisal system, making existing goal-setting procedures within the appraisal system more rigorous, or introducing a separate management by objectives system.

2. *Check Ability and Resources.* Establish whether the individual or group has the necessary knowledge, skills, equipment, support staff and raw materials to do the job well. If deficiencies in these areas are contributing to the problem, then there is a limit to the extent to which the problem can be solved by tackling it simply in motivational terms, and other steps may be necessary, such as staff development, training, improved selection techniques and so on.

3. *Check Needs and Value of Outcomes.* Find out what it is that the individual or group wants most, which lies within the power of the organization or the immediate superior to grant. There is little point in attempting to motivate people by offering them things which they do not want. It can even make things worse.

4. *Link Valued Outcomes to Performance.* Simply providing people with valued outcomes will not necessarily motivate them. It will probably increase their job satisfaction, but, as we have seen, increased job satisfaction does not necessarily lead to improved performance. To increase motivation, it is necessary to link the attainment of valued outcomes to performance, so that good performance results in attaining valued outcomes, whilst poor performance does not. Exactly how this is done will depend upon whether the outcomes in question are intrinsic or extrinsic.

   Intrinsic Outcomes: Redesign the person's job so that it provides such outcomes as challenge, stimulation, feelings of responsibility, a sense of achievement and so on.

Extrinsic Outcomes: Monitor the person's performance and award such positive outcomes as pay increases, promotion, recognition, perks, and so on, in relation to level of performance achieved. Wright and Taylor (1984) suggest that a simple 2 x 2 diagram, such as that shown in Figure 5.4, can be an aid to linking extrinsic outcomes to performance. If organizations or individual managers wish to motivate good performance, then obviously there should be a great many more items in quandrants 1 and 4 than in quadrants 2 and 3. Good performers should obtain many positive outcomes and few negative ones. Conversely, poor performers should obtain few positive outcomes and, where appropriate, negative ones. If this is not the case, then there is clearly something very wrong with the motivational system.

Surprisingly often, one hears employees complain that in their jobs it does not pay to be a good performer. Good performers are given the most unrewarding tasks to do, because they are the only people with the ability and the sense of responsibility to do them well. 'Difficult' employees, on the other hand, are given more rewarding tasks to do in the hope that they will not then make trouble. Similarly, poor performers are given easy tasks to do, because their incompetence would cause too many

	good performance	poor performance
positive outcomes	1	2
negative outcomes	3	4

Figure 5.4   *Extrinsic outcomes and work performance*
Source: P.L. Wright and D.S. Taylor (1984) *Improving leadership performance*, Prentice-Hall, Hemel Hempstead.

problems if they were given the same work as other people, but receive the same positive outcomes as other employees. If pay is linked to performance, poor performers may even be better paid than good performers, because it is easier to exceed production targets on easy jobs than dificult ones. Of course, many managers will be extremely reluctant to give poor performers difficult jobs to do, knowing that they will probably do them badly. Nevertheless, if analysis of the reward system shows that positive outcomes typically go to the poor performers and negative ones to the good ones, then it will hardly be surprising if the organization or individual manager has motivational problems.

5. *Check Effort–Outcome Expectations.* Check whether people actually believe that positive outcomes will result from good performance. If their beliefs are incorrect, attempt to persuade them that such a link exists.

6. *Provide Feedback.* Give people information about the standard of work performance which they achieve. This may relate to their day to day performance or to specific incidents which have had a significant effect on the organization, people within it and so on. It should be noted that this is easier to do if performance goals have been agreed beforehand.

7. *Check Equity.* Make sure that the outcomes are fair in relation to the person's contribution, and that they will also appear fair to other people in relation to their contribution and outcomes.

The aim of the above checklist is to help managers to analyse motivational problems and to generate hypotheses concerning their possible causes and potential solutions. As we have stressed throughout, it will be necessary to check out such hypotheses with the employees concerned, because it is their needs and perceptions which will determine their level of motivation, and the manager's assumptions about these may not be valid. Thus, the checklist is intended not so much to provide solutions to motivational problems, but to encourage managers faced with such problems to consider a wider range of options than they might otherwise have taken into account.

It must also be stressed that the checklist is not intended as a panacea, capable of solving all motivational problems. Some motivational problems may be difficult or impossible to solve. Job enrichment may be prohibitively expensive for some products, particularly if competitors can produce much the same goods at significantly lower prices using conventional production methods. It may be extremely difficult to provide a clear link between extrinsic outcomes and performance or there may be such a lack of trust between superiors and subordinates that the latter cannot be convinced that such a link exists. The employee may have needs which the organization cannot fulfil or can only be fulfilled by paying more than his or her performance is worth. In such cases, the solution, if there is one, may lie outside the realms of motivation theory. It may involve, for example, transferring or dismissing the employee concerned and recruiting someone whose needs can be fulfilled by the organization or changing the organizational climate by some form of organizational development. However, these are quite drastic steps. They can be unpleasant for the individuals concerned or disruptive for the organization as a whole. Thus, if instead some way can be found to solve the problem, using the motivational principles outlined in this chapter, then this could be of considerable benefit in both organizational and human terms.

References for Chapter 5

Adams, J. S. (1963) 'Toward an understanding of inequity', *Journal of Abnormal and Social Psychology*, *67*, 5, 422–36.

Adams, J. S. (1965) 'Inequity in social exchange', in L. Berkowitz (ed), *Advances in experimental social psychology*, vol 2, Academic Press, New York, 267–99.

Fried, Y. and Ferris, G. R. (1987) 'The validity of the job characteristics model: A review and meta-analysis', *Personnel Psychology*, *40*, 2, 287–322.

Graen, G. B., Scandura, T. A. and Graen, M. R. (1986) 'A field experimental test of the moderating effect of Growth Need Strength on productivity', *Journal of Applied Psychology*, *71*, 3, 484–91.

Hackman, J. R. and Oldham, G. R. (1976) 'Motivation through the design of work: Test of a theory', *Organizational Behaviour and Human Performance*, *16*, 2, 250–79.

Hackman, J. R. and Oldham, G. R. (1980) *Work redesign*, Addison-Wesley, Reading, Mass.

Herzberg, F., Mausner, B. and Snyderman, B. (1959) *The motivation to work*, Wiley, New York.

Herzberg, F. (1968) 'One more time: How do you motivate employees?' *Harvard Business Review, 46*, Jan/Feb, 53–62.

House, R. J. and Singh, J. V. (1987) 'Organizational behaviour: Some new directions for I/O psychology', *Annual Review of Psychology, 38*, 669–718.

Iaffaldano, M. T. and Muchinsky, P. M. (1985) 'Job satisfaction and performance: A meta-analysis', *Psychological Bulletin, 97*, 2, 251–73.

Lawler, E. E. (1971) *Pay and organizational effectiveness: A psychological view*, McGraw-Hill, New York.

Lawler, E. E. (1974) 'For a more effective organization – Match the job to the man', *Organizational Dynamics*, Summer, 19–29.

Lawler, E. E. and Suttle, J. L. (1973) 'Expectancy theory and job behaviour', *Organizational Behaviour and Human Performance, 9*, 3, 482–503.

Locke, A. E. (1975) 'Personnel attitudes and motivation', *Annual Review of Psychology, 26*, 457–80.

Locke, A. E., Feren, D. B., McCaleb, V. M., Shaw, K. N. and Denny, A. T. (1980) 'The relative effectiveness of four methods of motivating employee performance', in K. D. Duncan, M. M. Gruneberg and D. Wallis (eds.) *Changes in working life*. Wiley, New York, 363–88.

Locke, A. E., Shaw, K. N., Saari, L. M. and Latham, G. P. (1981) 'Goal setting and task performance: 1969–1980', *Psychological Bulletin, 90*, 1, 125–52.

McClelland, D. C. (1987) *Human motivation*, Cambridge University Press, Cambridge.

McClelland, D. C. and Boyatzis, R. E. (1982) 'The leadership motivation pattern and long term success in management', *Journal of Applied Psychology, 67*, 6, 737–43.

McClelland, D. C. and Burnham, D. H. (1976) 'Power is the great motivator', *Harvard Business Review, 54*, March/April, 100–10.

McClelland, D. C. and Winter, D. G. (1969) *Motivating economic achievement*, Free Press, New York.

Maslow, A. H. (1943) 'A theory of human motivation', *Psychological Review, 50*, 370–96.

Maslow, A. H. (1965) *Eupsychian management*, Dorsey Press, Homewood, Illinois.

Mitchell, T. R. (1974) 'Expectancy models of job satisfaction, occupational preference and effort: A theoretical, methodological and empirical appraisal', *Psychological Bulletin, 81*, 1053–77.

Mowday, R. T. (1987) 'Equity theory predictions and behaviour in organizations', in R. M. Steers and L. W. Porter (eds.) *Motivation and work behaviour*, McGraw-Hill, New York, 89–110.

Murray, H. A. *et al.* (1938) *Explorations in personality*, Science Editions, New York.

Porter, L. W. and Lawler, E. E. (1968) 'What job attitudes tell about motivation', *Harvard Business Review*, 46, Jan/Feb, 118–26.

Roethlisberger, F. J. and Dickson W. J. (1939) *Management and the worker*, Harvard University Press, Cambridge, Mass.

Schein, E. H. (1965) *Organizational psychology*, Prentice-Hall, Englewood Cliffs, N.J.

Smith, P. C. and Cranny, C. J. (1968) 'Psychology of men at work', *Annual Review of Psychology*, 19, 467–96.

Taylor, D. S. and Wright, P. L. (1982) 'Influencing work performance: The development of diagnostic skills', *Journal of Management Development*, 1, 44–50.

Thierry, H. (1987) 'Payment by results systems: A review of research 1945–1985', *Applied Psychology: An International Review*, 36, 1, 91–108.

Vroom, V. H. (1964) *Work and motivation*, Wiley, New York.

Winterbottom, M. R. (1958) 'The relation of need for achievement to learning experiences in independence and mastery', in J. W. Atkinson (ed) *Motivation in fantasy, action and society*, Van Nostrand, Princeton, N.J., 453–78.

Wright, P. L. (1987) 'Motivation and job satisfaction', in C. Molander (ed) *Personnel management: a practical introduction*, Chartwell Bratt, Bromley, Kent, 65–83.

Wright, P. L. and Taylor, D. S. (1984) *Improving leadership performance*, Prentice-Hall, Hemel Hempstead.

6

Communication in Organizations

RICHARD S. WILLIAMS
Birkbeck College, University of London

We saw in Chapter 2 how communication is an important part of the manager's job. Many studies of managerial work have shown that managers, on average, spend a large proportion of their time working with others. So, if only because of the amount of time the typical manager spends interacting with people, we have to conclude that communication in organizations is important. Though it is clear that managers have an almost over-riding preference for oral communication they do spend some of their time, albeit a small proportion, generating or reading written communications.

The various studies of managerial work also reveal something of the nature of the interaction and the parties involved. For example, Rosemary Stewart's (1967) work showed that of the time spent interacting with others around 41 per cent of it was with subordinates, 12 per cent with bosses, and the remaining 47 per cent with others, such as managerial peers. From this we can see that some communication within organizations is *vertical – upwards* or *downwards* – and some of it is *lateral*.

All this talk at work is not confined just to managers. For example the study of car workers by Goldthorpe *et al.* (1968) showed that workers on the shop floor are active talkers; 47 per cent said they spent 'a good deal' of their time talking with others with a further 39 per cent saying 'now and then'.

Such interpersonal communication is, however, just one way of viewing communication in organizations. There is another: this is termed *employee communication* which is usually

103

taken to mean the systems by which management and employees communicate with each other. Here, by contrast to managers' preferences for oral methods, written means of communication predominate.

The Purposes of Communication in Organizations

Let us first consider employee communication and the reasons why managements communicate with their workers.

Because it is the Law

Various statutory provisions require employers to convey certain information to their staff. This might be information about conditions of service, about health, safety and welfare, or about what the company has done to further employee involvement. A useful summary of the legislative require-ments is to be found in Townley (1989). More generally, some organizations take the moral view that employees have a right to receive company information. At one level then employee communication is concerned simply with informing staff because the organization is obliged to do so, whether legally or morally.

For the Good of the Staff

Here we are concerned with employee morale and wellbeing. Amongst the several characteristics of jobs identified by Warr (1987) as being associated with good mental health are such factors as the opportunity for interpersonal contact and environmental clarity. This refers to the provision of informa-tion about the results of behaviour, the future, and required behaviour – in other words, the sorts of things covered by an appraisal system. Communication is an inherent aspect of these characteristics. However, it hardly seems likely that employers are being wholly altruistic in their motives for fostering positive morale. Quite apart from this one has to wonder whether a formal communication scheme is neces-sarily the best way of achieving this purpose. For example, an

appraisal scheme can contribute to morale but the effectiveness of appraisal is often dependent on the day to day
communication which takes place between appraiser and
appraisee (Fletcher and Williams, 1985).

This points to the necessity for managers to have good
communication skills; for example, giving feedback and invit-
ing subordinates to discuss performance problems are
amongst the competencies associated with managerial effectiveness (Boyatzis, 1982). It is also appropriate just to note here
the importance attached to communication skills in some
contemporary models of leadership (see for example Sashkin,
1988).

For the Good of the Organization

Perhaps most of the reasons why employee communication
schemes exist are to further the interests of the organization in
some way. A survey carried out for the Institute of Personnel
Management (Arnott *et al.*, 1981) shows the importance of
reasons to do with organizational effectiveness and efficiency,
as summarized in Figure 6.1. In effect, the underlying aim
here is to change employee attitudes and behaviour.

Interestingly, the importance of the different types of reason
has varied over time. During the 1970s there were several

Reason	(%)
Make organization work better	64
Improve morale	48
Employees have a right to know	47
Improve productivity	46
Gain acceptance of change	44
Make managers manage	35
Reduce industrial disputes	19
Moderate wage claims	15
Increase flexibility	14
Legal requirements	14
Trade union pressure	5
General social trends	4
Pre-empt expected legislation	4
Employee pressure	3

Figure 6.1 *Employers' reasons for communicating to employees*

legislative initiatives which prompted increased interest in communication schemes (Townley, 1989). Today, there is not the same legislative push but there has been a resurgence of interest in employee communication. This has been particularly in the context of employee involvement programmes which some organizations have introduced as part of their response to the increasingly competitive climate in which they now find themselves.

Communication and Employee Involvement

To consider what is meant by employee involvement it is helpful first to examine participation at work. One kind of participation is called immediate (or direct) participation: 'This term refers to employees' involvement and influence in decisions of direct relevance to their day to day work activities, such as job, work group and departmental matters. . . [It] emphasizes the interaction between individuals and their immediate supervisors in reaching decisions. . .' (Wall, 1978). A second kind is called distant (or indirect) participation: 'This concerns employee involvement in higher levels of organizational decision-making which, for practical reasons, usually occurs through forms of representation such as worker directors or a works council. Decisions made at this level ultimately affect everyone within the organization and provide the framework within which more immediate participation takes place' (Wall, 1978).

Today, employee involvement is most commonly equated with a broadened conception of direct participation. Wall (1978) excludes discretionary forms of job redesign (such as job enrichment or autonomous group working) from his definition of direct participation on the grounds that the individual (or group) is given delegated responsibility for specific matters. In other words, these practices do not need the interaction between employees and supervisors which Wall regards as a characteristic of participation. Nowadays, however, job enrichment (individual or group) is usually seen as a form of employee involvement with the delegation that it entails being at one end of a continuum of involvement.

Why Involve Employees?

In general terms, many organizations have introduced employee involvement programmes in an effort to secure their employees' commitment. Crises, stemming from such factors as increased competitiveness, have led organizations to realize that they must carry their workforces with them if they are to survive and grow. White (1987) summarizes the rationale underlying the desire for employee commitment:

1. That committed employees will devote most of their energies to their work for the company rather than to their private affairs;
2. that they will favour the company in which they work rather than others, even at some financial loss;
3. that they will be ready to give additional time and effort when this is needed;
4. that they will give priority to the company when its values and interests seem to be in conflict with those of, for example, a professional body or trade union.

Clearly, these four points reinforce the view that a central aim of employee communication programmes is to modify employees' attitudes and behaviour towards organizational interests. A legitimate organizational endeavour or manipulative propaganda? The answer to this question must largely be a matter of opinion but it does highlight the political aspect of employee communication schemes.

How to Involve Employees and Secure their Commitment

The sorts of practices which we see in organizations today include direct involvement in the job as in participative decision-making and forms of job enrichment, performance appraisal, quality circles, and incentive payment systems. All of these practices involve communication in some way or another. Take pay, for example. Incentive payment systems are a means of involving employees to the extent that the broader-based schemes, such as profit sharing, may foster a sense of identification with the organization. The logic is easy to understand: if you wish your employees to be concerned about the success of the organization then their financial reward needs to be related to the organization's financial success. All well and good, but there are a lot of implications in this for communication within the organization, such as reporting on the organization's financial success and doing so in a way which is understandable to the whole of the workforce.

That communication is important for employee involvement and commitment has received some recognition, as evidenced by the use of two-way methods such as regular meetings or employee surveys. But one recent British survey (Marginson and Sisson, 1988) suggests that communication is much more likely to be one-way, using the management chain, than two-way, with suggestion schemes and surveys being the least common. The survey also suggested that those companies more likely to make use of two-way methods were those having extensive systems of employee involvement.

Mohrman *et al.* (1986) make the point that employee involvement means much more than changing the design of jobs or communications policy: 'It needs to change every thread of its fabric, including its human resource practices.' Some evidence about the reality of employee involvement in the UK comes from Marginson and Sisson (1988). A majority of the organizations surveyed claimed to have an overall policy for the management of employees yet in less than half was the policy written down and in still fewer was the policy statement given to employees. In the light of this it is hardly surprising to discover such survey findings as are reported by Hutton (1988):'Employees often felt inadequately informed about the reasons for major business decisions, that they had too little to say in major decisions affecting them personally and they had too little opportunity to express their view to the company'. So much for employee communication!

The reasons for interpersonal communication depend to a large extent on who is communicating to whom. For example, Katz and Kahn (1978) categorize communications down the line, from manager to subordinate, into five types:

1. Specific task directives: *job instructions.*
2. Information designed to produce understanding of the task and its relation to other tasks: *job rationale.*

3.   Information about organizational *procedures and practices*.
4.   *Feedback* to the subordinate about his or her performance.
5.   Information of an ideological character to inculcate a sense of mission: *indoctrination of goals*.

Katz and Kahn (1978) point out that many tasks require co-ordination in order to get done, a function that is served by lateral communication. They also draw attention to the social and emotional support which it may be provide. Argyle and Henderson (1985) report further evidence about this and Figure 6.2 lists the nature of communication activities engaged in by work colleagues. Hence, at the personal level, communication is important for its contribution to the satisfaction of individual needs, for helping to establish and maintain interpersonal relationships, for entertainment, for the creation of understanding amongst people and, as indicated above, for promoting employee morale and wellbeing. Communication upwards will often serve a control function: it is a means of reporting progress, and it can provide a check on the effectiveness of downward communication (that is a *feedback* mechanism). Thus, in these senses upward communication has a managerial purpose for the recipient of the information. But there are also functions to be served for the sender of the message, such as seeking help or providing a channel for frustrations to be vented. Upward communication is particularly important for fostering employee participation, involvement and commitment.

Helping each other with work
Discussing work
Chatting casually
Having an argument or disagreement
Teaching or showing the other person something about work
Joking with the other person
Teasing him/her
Discussing your personal life
Discussing your feelings or emotions
Asking or giving personal advice
Having coffee, drinks, or meals together
Committee work, or similar discussion at work

Figure 6.2   *Types of communication activity amongst work colleagues*
Source: Argyle and Henderson 1985.

Methods of Communication in Organizations

Written and Oral Methods

There exists a large number of methods of communication and the list in Figure 6.3 is far from exhaustive. As well as being vertical or lateral, one-way or two-way communication within an organization can be *formal* or *informal* and we can infer this from the Figure. So, for example, employee councils and annual reports are formal methods of communication and such methods as these are often part of the bureaucracy of an organization. The grapevine, on the other hand, is highly informal. The inclusion of industrial action and absenteeism might come as a surprise but they can legitimately be regarded as means of communication. Communication is partly about sending a message and these actions do precisely that, but whether the message is received and understood is quite another matter. This indicates that there are two sides to communication – the *sender* and the *receiver*.

Figure 6.3 also reveals that communication in organizations appears to be dominated by written and oral methods. But

Two-way: Upwards and Downwards	*One-way: Downwards*
	Mass meetings
Briefing groups	Notices, posters and public address systems
Interviews	Briefing meetings
Walking the floor	House journals and newspapers
Employee councils	Bulletins
Consultative committees	Staff handbook
Collective bargaining negotiations	Annual report to employees
Induction programmes	Pay packet inserts
The grapevine	Personal letters
Response systems	Exhibitions and films
Horizontal or Sideways	*One-way: Upwards*
Reports	Suggestion scheme
Memos	Union newsletter
Telephone	Response to surveys
House journals	Industrial action
Quality circles	Labour turnover
	Absenteeism and lateness
	Quality circles

Figure 6.3 *Methods of communication*
Source: Stanton, 1986

there is little doubt that a great impact is being made today by various forms of new technology, including audio-visual methods (video being the prime example) and electronic means, such as electronic mail, fax and teleconferencing.

Electronic

The electronic means bring with them the prospect of increased organizational efficiency and effectiveness. Information from the head office can be sent to all branches rapidly and simultaneously. This is likely to be very good for the organization but for the users and operators of these sophisticated communication systems the consequences may not always be positive. In particular there is the danger of more isolation as there may be less of a need for people to move about and interact with each other directly in the collection and transmission of information (Frese, 1987). Against this, there is the possibility that the computer itself may become a subject of discussion and hence engender social interaction.

Non-verbal Communication

We should also note the importance of non-verbal communication (NVC), such as gestures, facial expressions, eye contact, and the like. Argyle (1989) describes how non-verbal communication conveys emotional states and information about the sender of a message. Interpersonal attitudes, he suggests, are conveyed mainly by non-verbal language which also serves to support speech.

One-way vs Two-way Communication

Many of the methods of communication listed in Figure 6.3 are one-way. There is nothing absolutely wrong with such communication but there is certainly one major problem – the sender cannot be completely sure that the message has been received and understood. If reception and understanding do not take place then properly effective communication has not occurred. One-way methods deny the recipient the opportunity to ask questions, to comment or to check understanding, and these are similarly denied to the sender.

On the other hand, one-way communication is likely to be quicker than two-way and it appears to be efficient: a message over the company's loudspeaker system can be sent to all and sundry in just a few minutes. A video of the chief executive introducing a corporate plan can be shown to staff in all the branches. But what do people think and feel about the message that has been sent? Unless there is some *feedback mechanism* the sender will not know. This is why two-way communiction is important.

With two-way communication the sender is able to check that the recipient understands. In giving job instructions the supervisor will be able to ask questions to ensure that the clerk knows how to operate the new procedure. The clerk too will be able to ask what exactly the supervisor wishes to have done. Worries, anxieties and frustrations may be voiced – on both sides. But all this takes time and is sometimes seen as a disadvantage of two-way communication. Though there undoubtedly is this cost there is the more substantial benefit of greater comprehension and retention.

What is Communicated

The Confederation of British Industry (1977) in its booklet *Communication with People at Work* classified what should be communicated to employees into five major categories:

1. Progress
2. Profitability
3. Plans
4. Policies
5. People

Progress includes not only the organization's progress, as might be communicated in a company's newspaper or in a briefing meeting, but also that of the individual as might be conveyed in an appraisal interview or on a more frequent basis by the line manager. Profitability is part of some organizations' progress but is listed separately so as to emphasize the importance of providing information about the company's financial performance. Whereas communications about progress and profitability are often about the past, information about policies and plans may well be about the future. A staff handbook will contain details of policies, for example about conditions of service, as they are today but such policies change over time and these changes need to be communicated to staff. Also, company plans will often affect employees directly and so they should be kept informed of new developments. Information about people will include details of staff changes, vacancies, social and sporting activities, and the like.

Some evidence of what actually is communicated within organizations comes from the Institute of Personnel Management survey of employee communication schemes (Arnott *et al.* 1981). Figure 6.4 shows the information most commonly provided to employees by the organizations taking part.

We should note however that such surveys reveal only part of the picture. What is communicated informally on a day to day basis? What do subordinates communicate up the line? On this latter point Katz and Kahn (1978) suggest vertical communication upwards falls into four categories: '. . . what people say (1) about themselves, their performance, and their problems, (2) about others and their problems, (3) about organizational practices and policies, and (4) about what needs to be done and how it can be done.' And bearing in

Type of information	(%)
Organizational change	89
Profits	84
Sales	77
Short term employment prospects	69
New technology	68
Productivity	57
Profits by unit(s)	56
Quality	53
Competitors and their activities	51
Market share	50
Investment	50
Costs, materials, etc.	49
Orders	46
Market behaviour	44

Figure 6.4 *Information most commonly provided by employers*
Source: Arnott *et al.*, 1981.

mind its social and emotional functions we might expect quite a lot of interpersonal communication to be about non-organizational matters – the weather, family and domestic matters, holidays, sexual exploits, social gatherings, politics, and so on.

Assessing the Effectiveness of Communication in Organizations

We saw earlier that labour turnover and absenteeism can be regarded as methods of communication because they send a message. One of the messages that they could be sending is about the state of communication in the organization – ' I'm leaving because no-one ever tells me what is going on around here' or 'I don't feel like going in today because there's never a word of praise from the boss.' Of course, there may be other reasons for absences and resignations but surveys have shown that there is at least an association between inadequate communication (as seen by the workforce) and labour turn-over. For example, Hutton's (1988) findings described earlier came from a survey in a rapidly changing organization which was experiencing a high level of turnover.

The grapevine or 'walking the floor' offer the potential for revealing communication problems but these are not wholly reliable methods. If the boss is the source of the communication problem the chances are he is not going to be sensitive to the problem so walking about won't help him very much. And the effectiveness of the grapevine depends very much on the particular network(s) of which you are a member. Organizations which are concerned to investigate more rigorously and systematically the effectiveness of their communications sometimes use a survey.

Surveys as a Means of
Assessing Communication Effectiveness in Organizations

Hutton (1988) makes the point that

> In one sense all employee surveys are concerned with communications since they are designed to increase un-

derstanding of the beliefs, perceptions and attitudes of one party (perhaps the whole workforce) by another (normally management). But some employee surveys are concerned just with the processes of communications within a company. Such research can range from a detailed examination of the main communications channels operating within a company, with analysis of informational needs and assessment of source credibility, to highly focused inquiries into the nature and effectiveness of one specific communication channel.

Hutton's management checklist reveals the sorts of things which might be investigated in a communications audit:

1. How effective are your communications – upwards and downwards?
2. What channels are used for communications within the company?
3. Which channels are preferred for communications?
4. Which are the least/most effective?
5. What information is communicated?
6. What information would employees like to be communicated?
7. How credible do they find company communications?

From this list we see that in general terms at least two sets of functions are served: evaluative and diagnostic. Thus, as well as assessing the adequacy of communication systems as they are today employee surveys can also help in improving those systems or in designing new ones. Reeves (1980) refers to the value of surveys for the design of communication schemes but draws attention to the limitations stemming from the disadvantaged position of those being communicated to: they often are low down in the hierarchy with management being in control of the communication channels.

There is, nonetheless, value in asking employees what they would like to know: this may reveal a mismatch between what is desired and what is being provided. Consider the CBI's list of five 'Ps'. Do employees want to know about all of these things? Townley (1989) summarizes surveys which reveal that they are more concerned with what is directly relevant to them – matters concerning job and financial security for example. That employees appear to be less interested in more distant matters does not mean that information about these should not be provided. As Townley (1989) points out once people have the basic information about policies which directly affect them they may then want to know more about how those policies were determined. And how and from whom do employees like to receive information? If they prefer to receive it from their immediate supervisors should the organization be putting a lot of money into producing a glossy newspaper? Surveys can help organizations to answer such questions.

Reeves (1980) notes the difficulty of assessing the impact of employee communication systems. He draws a distinction between employee-oriented aims and company-oriented ones. The former, he believes, are easier to assess: 'If employees know more about the company this can usually be attributed to any improvement 'in communications'. Townley (1989) reports mixed responses by employees to communication schemes. Sometimes there is initial suspicion followed later by a greater acceptance. Scepticism, particularly about the credibility of the information disclosed, seems to be more strongly felt by manual workers than by managers.

But what of the objectives that organizations wish to achieve, such as making the organization work better or improving productivity? The first of these is vague and ill-defined and so would be difficult to measure. Even where it is possible to specify the objective in, say, quantitative terms such as a 5 per cent improvement in productivity, there would still be problems in showing a link between the communications practices and increased productivity. (This is just one illustration of the more general problem of assessing organizational effectiveness.) Reeves (1980) sums up the position thus: 'To a large extent, employee communications may have to be an act of faith for management, a belief that they are ultimately worthwhile even though this cannot be readily demonstrated.'

Barriers to Communication

Barriers to communication fall into two main groups; those which are external to the communicators and those which are internal, whether within the sender or receiver.

Barriers External to the Communicators

One external barrier is the culture of the organization; for example, cultures vary in the extent to which they value communication. Then there are physical barriers. In a noisy environment means of communication such as loudspeaker systems will be of reduced effectiveness. Fax machines or electronic mail may suffer from electrical interference and so the message may get distorted. Distortion can take place in human systems just as easily, as we shall see below. Perhaps the nature of the individual's job gives only limited opportunity for communication. Or the network of contacts is so extensive that communication overload results. Smith *et al.* (1982) list possible responses to overload, whatever its cause: ignore the additional information, queue the information dealing with it on a first come first served basis, reduce the quality of response, delegate, assign priorities.

Barriers Internal to the Communicators

1. The manager, the secretary or the clerk may fail to see a need to communicate a particular item of information.
2. The need may be seen but the sender decides not to communicate at all or to convey only certain information, perhaps out of some political motivation or anxiety.
3. The need is seen, the sender decides to communicate, but the message is not expressed clearly. The sender misjudges the recipient and uses too complex language and a lot of jargon. The sender chooses an inappropriate channel: a memo is sent whereas a quick chat would have given the needed personal touch.
4. Distortion may take place. If a message is passed from one person on to another, and then another, and so on the meaning can very easily get distorted. We mis-hear or

mis-read something, or forget something else. Important details may get missed out; irrelevancies and embellishments may get added. Even the apparently simple act of recording a telephone call is subject to distortion, especially if there is no paper and pencil handy to record the call as it is being received.

5. The attitudes, opinions, beliefs or expectations of the sender or receiver may get in the way. 'The boss says we can go and talk to him any time. I don't believe him, he's just saying that.' 'The company newspaper – it's a load of propaganda; they're only trying to pull the wool over our eyes.' 'I don't like her; everyone knows women don't make good managers.' 'He's from Barcelona. He won't understand.' So, our expectations as receivers may influence us and we will hear only what we want to hear. Our own characteristics may influence how we perceive others; we project our characteristics onto the sender of the message.

These examples illustrate some of the obstacles to communication; many of them can be looked on as a kind of psychological noise analogous in its effects to physical noise. There are many other barriers and a summary of the main ones is shown in Figure 6.5

Communication as a Psychological Process

Better communication seems to be something of a panacea when it comes to improving organizational performance. But before this universal medicine can be applied it is necessary to be clear about what is meant by communication. As we have seen sometimes the term is used to denote some kind of formal organizational system, such as briefing groups or the use of notice boards. Sometimes it is used to refer to the informal conversations that take place between manager and staff or between colleagues, whether face-to-face or by telephone, one-to-one or in a group. But underlying both these aspects of communication is a more basic psychological process.

The earlier section on barriers shows something of the psychological nature of the communication process. We have already seen that communication requires at least two par-

	Sender	Recipient	Social/environmental
Barriers in sending a message	Unaware message needed Inadequate information in message Prejudgements about message Prejudgements about recipient		
Barriers to reception		Needs and anxieties Beliefs and values Attitudes and opinions Expectations Prejudgements Attention to stimuli	Effects of other environmental stimuli
Barriers to understanding	Semantics and jargon Communication skills Length of communication Communication channel	Semantic problems Concentration Listening abilities Knowledge Prejudgements Receptivity to new ideas	
Barriers to acceptance	Personal characteristics Dissonant behaviour Attitudes and opinions Beliefs and values	Attitudes, opinions and prejudices Beliefs and values Receptivity to new ideas Frame of reference Personal characteristics	Interpersonal conflict Emotional clashes Status differences Group frame of reference Previous experience of similar interactions
Barriers to action	Memory and retention Level of acceptance	Memory and attention Level of acceptance Flexibility for change of attitudes, behaviour etc. Personal characteristics	

Figure 6.5 *A summary of the main barriers to communication*
Source: Torrington and Hall, 1987.

ties – the sender and the receiver – and this is true even when the communication is one-way. The company newspaper is likely to be read by at least some employees but whether they receive and understand the messages it conveys will depend upon a number of factors. Some have to do with the presence or absence of the barriers just listed and others involve different aspects of the psychological nature of communication.

A Simple Model of Communication

Smith *et al.* (1982) presented a simple information-processing model of the communication process, as shown in Figure 6.6.

The Sender

In this model the communication process begins with some information that needs to be conveyed to another or others. But whether or not the information in fact is communicated is a matter of choice for the sender who needs to be clear about what exactly is to be communicated.

If the sender decides to send the message it needs to be *encoded*. In other words, the idea in the sender's mind needs to be translated by the central nervous system into speech patterns, some form of written message, or a visual message. Once encoded the message is then sent by one or another of the means discussed above. As well as choosing the 'medium' of communication – verbal or non-verbal – we also have to choose the 'channel', for example, in writing, by telephone, face-to-face, and so on.

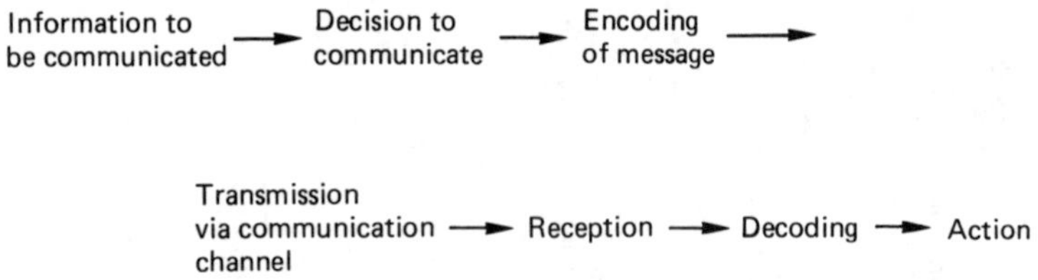

Information to be communicated ⟶ Decision to communicate ⟶ Encoding of message ⟶

Transmission via communication channel ⟶ Reception ⟶ Decoding ⟶ Action

Figure 6.6   *An information-processing model of communication*
Source: Smith *et al.* 1982.

But all of this does not add up to effective communication because it is only half the story; the other half is the receiver.

The Receiver

The person(s) to whom the message is sent then perceives it. Though perception is undoubtedly a physiological process to view it solely in these terms is too narrow and simplistic. We interpret what we perceive in the light of our past experience and in terms of our current mood. So, perception is a cognitive and emotional process as well as being a physiological one. Smith *et al.* (1982) define perception as the 'process by which we become aware of, and make meaning out of, the world around us'.

So far as communication is concerned for most people the eyes and ears are the principal sensory organs but for some the sense of touch is particularly important, as for example is the case in reading Braille.

We are constantly bombarded by stimuli of many different kinds; in fact too many impinge upon us for us to be able to perceive all of them. Hence perception is a selective process. Two main sets of factors influence selectivity in perception. On the one hand, some are within the perceiver – our past experience and how we feel at the time. Hence barriers to effective communication may intrude at this stage through tiredness, bad temper, over-excitement, or some other state of the recipient, as we have seen above. On the other hand, our attention may be caught by characteristics of what is being perceived – the message itself or the sender (or both). This points to a special aspect of the perceptual process and communication, namely that it is also a process of person perception. So, the charismatic managing director commands our attention simply on grounds of personality alone quite apart from what is being said. And in selection interviews the appearance of the interviewee and their non-verbal behaviour have an effect on the judgements made by the interviewer, albeit less of an influence than what the interviewee actually says (Keenan, 1989).

Selectivity is a two-edged sword; because there are so many stimuli selective attention serves to protect us from overload.

Humans have only limited capacity for processing information and the selectivity of attention helps to reduce what is further processed in the brain. Selectivity therefore acts as a filtering mechanism but it does not always work to our advantage for at times, perhaps often, we may also fail to attend to the important.

There is next a process of *decoding* comparable (but in reverse) to that of encoding. The message received by the sensory organs is transmitted via the central nervous system to the brain. This process of decoding is partly a process of organization and interpretation. A sender may have sought to introduce meaning into the message by careful choice of words, choice of illustrations, tone of voice, facial expression, and such like, but whether the same meaning will be received depends on the recipient. Our past experiences, personality, mood, thoughts and feelings all influence our organization and interpretation of what would otherwise be a jumble of sensory information.

More variability now enters the perceptual aspect of the communication process. Two or more people may receive the same message – say, an announcement about staff promotion – but they respond to it in very different ways. One is pleased that Joe has been promoted; he's a good chap and deserves it. Another, a rival, is filled with resentment.

Again, this highlights that communication, particularly interpersonal communication, is very much a process of social perception. Our interpretation of a message will be influenced by several factors related to the sender of the message rather than the content of the message itself:

1. the credibility of the source, for example experts are generally more persuasive than non-experts;
2. the intentions of the sender (rather, intentions as perceived by the receiver);
3. the halo effect – we may be so seduced by some physical characteristic of the sender, such as their attractiveness, that this blinds us to their weaknesses and we end up giving them an overly favourable assessment in, say, a selection interview;
4. stereotyping – an over-generalization about someone based on their membership of some social category.

The final link in this model is for the recipient to take some action. The first person goes out of his way to congratulate Joe; the second ignores him as they pass by in the corridor.

Some models have one more step, that of feedback. As we have seen this is necessary to be sure that the message has been comprehended by the receiver. It also emphasizes the interactive nature of communication.

Improving Communication Effectiveness

What should be done in order to improve the effectiveness of communication within organizations?

To judge from books published on the subject and from catalogues of training courses it seems that most of the attention is paid to the sender of the message. There are many books (see for example Stanton, 1986) which give practical tips on a wide range of communication skills such as writing, listening, conducting meetings, and so on. Other books focus more particularly on interpersonal skills; yet others are still more specific and deal with just one communication skill such as selection interviewing. Then there are various audio and video packages which individuals can work through in their own time or which might form the basis of a training course. There seems to be rather less material for the receiver, with what there is mostly being about listening skills and rapid reading. Though such materials have a place, evidence as to their effectiveness is lacking.

Removal of the barriers to communication needs to be addressed if communication is to be improved. Here, of course, we are concerned not just with the communicators but also with aspects of the organization. How does the structure of the organization inhibit effective communication? Are there certain role positions within the organization which help or hinder communication? Clearly, it is necessary to know what the barriers are before they can be removed and surveys have a part to play in answering such questions. More generally, we should note Steers' (1977) advice about improving communication effectiveness, as summarized in Figure 6.7.

There are also various publications which give advice on employee communication schemes. For example, Bucking-

Downward Communications
1. Job instructions can be presented clearly to employees so they understand more precisely what is expected.
2. Efforts can be made to explain the rationale behind the required tasks to employees so they understand why they are being asked to do something.
3. Management can provide greater feedback concerning the nature and quality of performance, thereby keeping employees 'on target'.
4. Multiple communication channels can be used to increase the chances that the message is properly received.
5. Important messages can be repeated to ensure penetration.
6. In some cases, it is desirable to bypass formal communication channels and go directly to the intended receiver with the message.

Upward Communications
1. Upward messages can be screened so only the more relevant aspects are received by top management.
2. Managers can attempt to change the organizational climate so subordinates feel freer to transmit negative as well as positive messages without fear of retribution.
3. Managers can sensitize themselves so they are better able to detect bias and distorted messages from their subordinates.
4. Sometimes it is possible to use 'distortion-proof' messages, such as providing subordinates with report forms requiring quantified or standardized data.
5. Social distance and status barriers between employees on various levels can be reduced so messages will be more spontaneous.

Horizontal Communications
1. Efforts can be made to develop interpersonal skills between group members and departments so greater open-ness and trust exist.
2. Reward systems can be utilized which reward interdepartmental co-operation and minimize 'zero-sum game' situations.
3. Interdepartmental meetings can be used to share information concerning what other departments are involved in.
4. In some cases, the actual design of the organization itself can be changed to provide greater opportunities for interdepartmental contacts (e.g. shifting from a traditional to a matrix organizational design).

Figure 6.7 *Strategies for improving communication effectiveness*

ham (1981) presents a six-point framework for communications policy and practice:

1. A clearly defined policy on communications to which top management is committed;
2. such a policy should embrace all employees systematically;
3. communications are a responsibility of line management;
4. information must be relevant and easy to understand;
5. the emphasis should be on face-to-face communication, supported by other channels;
6. good communications require managerial time, effort and resources and a highly professional approach.

However, it is questionable that even this is enough. There are the various communication barriers to contend with and we should be mindful of the earlier-quoted comment of Mohrman *et al.* (1986) about the need for an organization to change 'every thread of its fabric'. All this points to the subject of Chapter 12, in other words organizational change.

References for Chapter 6

Argyle, M. (1989) *The Social Psychology of Work*, 2nd edn, Penguin, Harmondsworth.

Argyle, M. and Henderson, M. (1985) *The Anatomy of Relationships*, Heinemann, London and Penguin, Harmondsworth.

Arnott, M. M., Minton, C. C. and Wilders, M. (1981) *Employee Communication in the 1980s*, Institute of Personnel Management, London.

Boyatzis, R. E. (1982) *The Competent Manager*, Wiley, New York.

Buckingham, G. (1981) 'Communications in Practice – Conclusions', in Institute of Personnel Management, *Practical Participation and Involvement: Communication in Practice*, IPM, London.

Confederation of British Industry (1977) *Communication with People at Work*, CBI, London.

Fletcher, C. and Williams, R. (1985) *Performance Appraisal and Career Development*, Hutchinson, London.

Frese, M. (1987) 'Human-Computer Interaction in the Office', in C. L. Cooper and I. T. Robertson (eds.), *International Review of Industrial and Organizational Psychology – 1987*, Wiley, Chichester.

Goldthorpe, J. H., Lockwood, D., Bechofer, F. and Platt, J. (1968) *The Affluent Worker: Industrial Attitudes and Behaviour*, Cambridge University Press, Cambridge.

Hutton, P. (1988) *Survey Research for Managers*, Macmillan, Basingstoke.

Katz, D. and Kahn, R. L. (1976) *The Social Psychology of Organizations*, 2nd edn, Wiley, New York.

Keenan, T. (1989) in C. L. Cooper and I. T. Robertson (eds.), *International Review of Industrial and Organizational Psychology – 1989*, Wiley, Chichester.

Marginson, P. and Sisson, K. (1988) 'The Management of Employees', in P. Marginson, P. K. Edwards, R. Martin, J. Purcell, and K. Sisson, *Beyond the Workplace*, Basil Blackwell, Oxford.

Mohrman, S. A., Ledford, G. E., Lawler, E. E., and Mohrman, A. M. (1986) 'Quality of Worklife and Employee Involvement', in C. L. Cooper and I. T. Robertson (eds.), *International Review of Industrial and Organizational Psychology – 1986*, Wiley, Chichester.

Reeves, T. K. (1980) 'Information Disclosure in Employee Relations', *Employee Relations*, 2, 1–39.

Sashkin, M. (1988) 'The Visionary Leader', in J. A. Conger, R. N. Kanungo and Associates, *Charismatic Leadership*, Jossey Bass, San Francisco.

Smith, M., Beck, J., Cooper, C. L., Cox, C., Ottaway, D., and Talbot, R., (1982) *Introducing Organisational Behaviour*, Macmillan, Basingstoke.

Stanton, N. (1986) *What do you Mean 'Communication'?* 2nd edn, Pan, London.

Steers, R. M. (1977) *Organizational Effectiveness: A Behavioural View*, Goodyear, Santa Monica.

Stewart, R. (1967) *Managers and their Jobs*, Macmillan, London.

Torrington, D. and Hall, L. (1987) *Personnel Management: A New Approach*, Prentice-Hall, Hemel Hempstead, Herts.

Townley, B. (1989) 'Employee Communication Programmes', in K. Sisson (ed), *Personnel Management in Britain*, Basil Blackwell, Oxford.

Wall, T. D. (1978) 'Job Redesign and Employee Participation', in P. B. Warr (ed) *Psychology at Work*, 3rd edn, Penguin, Harmondsworth.

Warr, P. B. (1987) 'Job Characteristics and Mental Health', in P. B. Warr (ed) *Psychology at Work*, 3rd edn, Penguin, Harmondsworth.

White, G. (1987) *Employee Commitment: Work Research Unit Occasional Paper 38*, Work Research Unit, London.

7

Stress in Organizations

CARY L. COOPER
Manchester School of Management, UMIST

The complexity of industrial organizational life is a source of stress for managers. Brummett, Pyle and Framholtz (1968) suggest that managers are suffering extreme physiological symptoms from stress at work, such as disabling ulcers, or colitis, or coronary heart disease (CHD), which force them to retire prematurely from active work before they have had an opportunity to complete their potential organizational life. These and other stress-related effects (such as tension or poor adjustment) also affect the family. Thus, stress pervades the whole quality of managerial life (Cooper, Cooper and Eaker, 1988). The mental and physical health effects of job stress are not only disruptive influences on the individual managers, but are also a 'real' cost to the organization, on whom many individuals depend: a cost which is rarely, if ever, seriously considered either in human or financial terms by organizations, but one which they incur in their day to day operations. In order to do something positive about sources of stress on managers at work, it is important to be able to identify them. The success of any effort to minimize stress and maximize job satisfaction will depend on accurate diagnosis, for different stresses will require different action. Any approach to the management of stress in an organization which relied on one particular technique (for example, organization development, job enrichment or transcendental meditation), without taking into account the differences within workgroups or divisions, would be doomed to failure. A recognition of the possible sources of management stress may help us to arrive at suggestions of ways of minimizing its negative consequences.

With this in mind, the research literature in the field of management and organizational stress is brought together in a framework that helps us identify more clearly the sources of managerial satisfaction and stress.

But first, what is stress? Stress is a word derived from the Latin word 'stringere', meaning to draw tight, and was used in the seventeenth century to describe hardships or affliction. During the late eighteenth century, stress denoted 'force, pressure, strain or strong effort', referring primarily to an individual, or to the individual's organs or mental powers. One of the first scientific attempts to explain the process of stress-related illness was made by physician and scholar Hans Selye, who in 1946 described three stages an individual encounters in stressful situations (Selye, 1946).

1. *alarm reaction*, in which an initial shock phase of lowered resistance is followed by countershock during which the individual's defence mechanisms become active;
2. *resistance*, the stage of maximum adaptation and, hopefully, successful return to equilibrium for the individual. If, however, the stressor continues or the defence does not work, he will move on to the third stage;
3. *exhaustion*, when adaptive mechanisms collapse.

Since Selye first postulated this process of environmental stressor and bodily reaction, a great deal of research work has been undertaken in the field of occupational stress. From the growing research literature, it is felt that the available data can be organized into the following model (Figure 7.1).

Most research indicates that depending on the particular job and organization, one or some combination of the sources of stress in Figure 7.1, together with certain personality traits, may be predictive of a variety of stress manifestations, such as coronary heart disease, mental ill-health, job dissatisfaction, marital disharmony or excessive alcoholic intake or other drug taking. The six major sources of occupational stress will here be discussed: factors intrinsic to the job; role in the organization; career development; relationships at work; organizational structure and climate; and home:work interface.

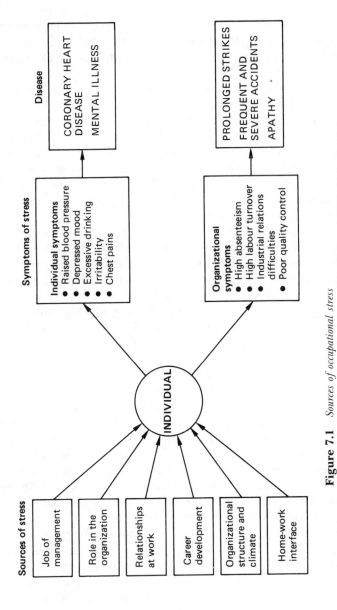

Figure 7.1 *Sources of occupational stress*
Source: C.L. Cooper, R.D. Cooper and L. Eaker (1988) *Living with stress*
Penguin Books: London.

The Job of Management

Factors intrinsic to the 'job of management' were a first and vital focus of study for early researchers in the field (Stewart, 1976), and in shopfloor (as opposed to management) studies they are still the main preoccupation (Cooper and Smith, 1985). Stress can be caused by too much or too little work, time pressures and deadlines, having too many decisions to make, working conditions, excessive travel, long hours, having to cope with changes at work and the expenses (monetary and career) of making mistakes (Cooper and Payne, 1988). It can be seen that most job descriptions include factors which for some individuals at some time will be a source of pressure. As Chapter 2 has shown, many of these factors are inevitable parts of the job of management.

One of the most important sources of stress on managers is their tendency to work long hours and to take on too much work. Research into work overload has been given substantial empirical attention. French and Caplan (1973) have differentiated overload in terms of quantitative and qualitative overload. Quantitative refers to having 'too much to do', while qualitative means work that is 'too difficult'. Miller (1960) has theorized that 'overload' in most systems leads to breakdown, whether we are dealing with single biological cells or managers in oganizations. In an early study, French and Caplan (1970) found that objective quantitative overload was strongly linked to cigarette smoking (an important risk factor or symptom of CHD). Persons with more phone calls, office visits and meetings per given unit of work time were found to smoke significantly more cigarettes than persons with fewer such engagements. In a study of 100 young coronary patients, Russek and Zohman (1969) found that 25 per cent had been working at two jobs and an additional 45 per cent had worked at jobs which required (due to work overload) 60 or more hours' work per week. They add that although prolonged emotional strain preceded the attack in 91 per cent of the cases, similar stress was only observed in 20 per cent of the controls. Breslow and Buell (1960) have also reported findings which support a relationship between hours of work and death from coronary disease. In an investigation of mortality rates of men in California, workers in light industry under the age of 45 who worked more than 48 hours a week have twice the risk of death from CHD compared with similar workers working 40 or less hours a week. Another substantial investigation on quantitative work load was carried out by Margolis *et al.* (1974) on a representative national US sample of 1,496 employed persons, of 16 years of age or older. They found that overload was significantly related to a number of symptoms or indicators of stress: escapist drinking, absenteeism from work, low motivation to work, lowered self-esteem, and an absence of suggestions to employers.

In another investigation of stress among British senior police officers, Cooper, Davidson, and Robinson (1982) found that work overload was a major stressor among the lower managerial ranks, particularly police sergeants. In particular, sergeants who scored high on the depression scale of the Middlesex Hospital Questionnaire tended to be older operational officers who believed they were overloaded and who perceived a number of bureaucratic and outside obstacles to effective police functioning. They complained about the long hours and heavy work load, as well as the increased paperwork, lack of resources and the failure of the courts to prosecute offenders.

Overload can also reflect itself in fatigue and the inability to relax, as was found by Cooper and Sloan (1985) in their large scale study on job and domestic stress among commercial airline pilots.

The results from these and other studies (Cooper and Melhuish, 1980) are relatively consistent and indicate that quantitative overload is indeed a potential source of managerial stress that adversely affects both health and job satisfaction.

There is also some evidence that 'qualitative' overload is a source of stress for managers. French *et al.* (1965) looked at qualitative work overload in a large university. They used questionnaires, interviews and medical examinations to obtain data on risk factors associated with CHD for 122 university administrators and professors. They found that one symptom of stress, low self-esteem, was related to work overload, but that this was different for the two occupational groupings. Qualitative overload was not significantly linked to low self-esteem among the administrators but was significantly correlated for the professors. The greater the 'quality' of work expected of the professor, the lower the self-esteem. Several other studies have reported an association of qualitative work overload with cholesterol level: a tax deadline for accountants (Friedman *et al.*, 1958), and medical students performing a medical examination under observation. French and Caplan (1973) summarize this research by suggesting that both qualitative and quantitative overload produce at least nine different symptoms of psychological and physical strain: job dissatisfaction, job tension, lower self-esteem, threat, embarassment, high cholesterol levels, increased heart rate, skin resistance, and more smoking. In analysing these data, however, one cannot ignore the vital interactive relationship of the job and manager, where the work of Rosemary Stewart and Henry Mintzberg are apposite; objective work overload, for example, should not be viewed in isolation but relative to the manager's capacities and personality.

Such caution is sanctioned by much of the American and some UK literature which shows that overload is not always externally imposed. Many managers (perhaps certain personality types, such as those with high achievement motivation, more than others) react to overload by working longer hours. For example, in reports on an American study (Uris, 1972) it was found that 45 per cent of the executives investigated worked all day, in the evenings and at weekends, and that a further 37 per cent kept weekends free but worked extra hours in the evenings. In many companies, this type of behaviour has become the norm to which everyone feels they must adhere (Wood, 1984).

The Manager's Role in the Organization

Another major source of managerial stress is associated with a person's role at work. A great deal of research in this area has concentrated on role ambiguity and role conflict, since the seminal investigations of the Survey Research Center of the University of Michigan (Kahn *et al.*, 1964).

Role ambiguity exists when a manager has inadequate information about his work role, that is, where there is *lack of clarity* about his work objectives, work colleagues' expectations and, about the scope and responsibility of his job. Kahn *et al.* (1964) found that men who suffered from role ambiguity experienced lower job satisfaction, high job-related tension, a greater sense of futility, and lower self-confidence. French and Caplan (1970) found, at one of NASA's bases in a sample of 205 volunteer engineers, scientists and administrators, that role ambiguity was significantly related to low job satisfaction and to feelings of job-related threat to one's mental and physical wellbeing. This also related to indicators of physiological strain such as increased blood pressure and pulse rate. Margolis *et al.* (1974) found a number of significant relationships between symptoms or indicators of physical and mental ill-health with role ambiguity in their representative national sample (n = 1,496). The stress indicators related to role ambiguity were depressed mood, lowered self-esteem, life dissatisfaction, job dissatisfaction, low motivation to work, and intention ot leave job.

Role conflict exists when an individual in a particular work role is torn by conflicting job demands or doing things he really does not want to do or does not think are part of the job specification. The most frequent manifestation of this is when a manager is caught between two groups of people who demand different kinds of behaviour or expect that the job should entail different functions. Khan *et al.* (1964) found that men who suffered more role conflict had lower job satisfaction and higher job-related tension. It is interesting to note that they also found that the greater the power or authority of the people 'sending' the conflicting role messages, the more role conflict produced job dissatisfaction. This was related to physiological strain as well, as the NASA study (French and Caplan) illustrates. They recorded the heart rate of 22 men for a two-hour period while they were at work in their offices. They found that the mean heart rate for an individual was strongly related to his report of role conflict. A larger and medically more sophisticated study by Shirom *et al.* (1973) found similar results. Their research is of particular interest as it tries to look simultaneously at a wide variety of potential work stresses. They collected data on 762 male kibbutz members aged 39 and above, examined the relationships between CHD, abnormal electrocardiographic readings, CHD risk factors (systolic blood pressure, pulse rate, serum cholesterol levels, etc.), and potential sources of job stress (work overload, role ambiguity, role conflict, lack of physical activity). Their data were broken down into occupational groups: agricultural workers, factory groups, craftsmen and managers. It was found that there was a significant relationship between role conflict and CHD (specifically, abnormal electrocardiographic readings), but only for the managers. In fact, as we moved from occupations requiring great physical exertions (such as agriculture) to those requiring less (managerial for example), the greater was the relationship between role ambiguity and conflict and abnormal electrocardiographic findings. It was also found that as we go from occupations involving excessive physical activities to those with less such activity, CHD increased significantly. Drawing together these data, it might be suggested that managerial and professional occupations are more likely to suffer occupational stress from role-related stress and other interpersonal dynamics and less from the physical conditions of work.

Another aspect of role conflict was examined by Mettlin and Woelfel (1974). They measured three aspects of interpersonal influence – discrepancy between influences, level of influence, and number of influences – in a study of the educational and occupational aspirations of high-school students. Using the Langner Stress Symptom questionnaire as their index of stress, they found that the more extensive and diverse an individual's interpersonal communications network, the more stress symptoms he showed. A manager's role which is at a boundary – which means, between departments or between the company and the outside world – is, by definition, one of extensive communication nets and of high role conflict. Kahn *et al.* (1964) suggest that such a position is potentially highly stressful. Margolis and Kroes (1974) found, for instance, that foremen (high role-conflict-prone job) are seven times as likely to develop ulcers as shop-floor workers.

The problems that role conflicts can generate were amply demonstrated by Cooper, Mallinger and Kahn (1988) in their investigation into dentists. It was found that the variables which predicted abnormally high diastolic blood pressure among dentists were factors related to the role of the dentist, that is, that he/she considers him/herself to be 'an inflictor of pain' rather than 'healer'; that he/she has to carry out non-clinical tasks such as administrative duties, sustaining and building a practice; and his/her role also interferes with his/her personal life, primarily in terms of time commitments.

Another important potential source of stress associated with a manager's role is 'responsibility for people'. One can differentiate here between 'responsibility for people' and 'responsibility for things' (equipment, budgets, and so on). Wardwell *et al.* (1964) found that responsibility for people was significantly more likely to lead to CHD than responsibility for things. Increased responsibility for people frequently means that one has to spend more time interacting with others, attending meetings, working alone and, in conse-quence, as in the NASA study (French and Caplan, 1970), more time in trying to meet deadline pressures and schedules. Pincherle (1972) also found this in a UK study of 2,000 executives attending a medical centre for a medical check-up. Of the 1,200 managers sent by their companies for their annual examination, there was evidence of physical stress being linked to age and level of responsibility; the older and more responsible the executive, the greater the probability of the presence of CHD risk factors or symptoms. French and Caplan support this in their NASA study of managerial and professional workers; they found that responsibility for people was significantly related to heavy smoking, raised diastolic blood pressure, and increased serum cholesterol levels – the more the individual had responsibility for 'things' as opposed to 'people', the lower were each of these CHD risk factors.

Having too little responsibility (Brook, 1973), lack of participation in decision-making, lack of managerial support, having to keep up with increasing standards of performance and coping with rapid technological change are other poten-tial role stressors mentioned repeatedly in the literature but with little supportive research evidence. Variations between organizational structures will determine the differential distri-bution of these factors across differing occupational groups.

Kay (1974) does suggest, however, that (independent of employing organizations) some pressures are to be found more at middle than at other management levels. He depicts today's middle manager as being particularly hard pressed

1. by pay compression, as the salaries of new recruits increase;
2. by job insecurity – they are particularly vulnerable to redundancy or involuntary early retirement;
3. by having little real authority at this high level of responsibility; and
4. by feeling 'boxed' in.

Relationships at Work

Relationships at work, which include the nature of relationships and social support from one's colleagues, boss and subordinates, have also been related to job stress (Payne, 1980). According to French *et al.* (1982), poor relationships with other members of an organization may be precipitated by role ambiguity in the organization, which in turn may produce psychological strain in the form of low job satisfaction. Moreover, they found that strong social support from peers relieved job strain and also served to condition the effects of job stress on cortisone levels, blood pressure, glucose levels and the number of cigarettes smoked, as well as cessation of cigarette smoking. It is interesting to note that among air traffic controllers, greater help and social support (as assessed by the repertory grid) was provided by friends and colleagues than by those in supervisory positions at work (Crump, *et al.* 1981).

In addition, where male executives had problems they were associated with problems in relationships, as Cooper and Melhuish (1980) discovered in their study of 196 very senior male executives. It was found that male executives' predispositions (outgoing, tough-minded, and so on) and their relationships at work were central to their increased risk of high blood pressure. They were particularly vulnerable to the stresses of poor relationships with subordinates and colleagues, lack of personal support at home and work, and to the conflicts between their own values and those of the organization.

Relationships with the Boss

Buck (1972) focused on the attitude and relationship of workers and managers to their immediate boss using Fleishman's leadership questionnaire on consideration and initiating structure. The consideration factor was associated with behaviour indicative of friendship, mutual trust, respect and a certain warmth between boss and subordinate. He found that those managers who felt that their boss was low on 'consideration' reported feeling more job pressure. Managers who were under pressure reported that their boss did not give them criticism in a helpful way, played favourites with subordinates, 'pulled rank' and took advantage of them whenever they got a chance. Buck concludes that the 'considerate behaviour of superiors appears to have contributed significantly inversely to feelings of job pressure'.

Relationships with Subordinates

Officially one of the most critical functions of a manager is his supervision of other people's work. It has long been accepted that an 'inability to delegate' might be a problem, but now a new potential source of stress is being introduced in the manager's interpersonal skills – he must learn to 'manage by participation'. Donaldson and Gowler (1975) point to the factors which may make today's zealous emphasis on participation a cause of resentment, anxiety and stress for the manager concerned. It may produce the following stressors:

1. a mismatch of formal and actual power;
2. the manager may well resent the erosion of his formal role and authority (and the loss of status and rewards);
3. he may be subject to irreconcilable pressures – e.g. to be both participative and to achieve high production; and
4. his subordinates may refuse to participate.

However, for those managers with technological and scientific backgrounds (a 'things orientation'), relationships with subordinates can be a low priority (seen as 'trivial', 'petty', time consuming and an impediment to doing the job well) and one would expect their interactions to be more a source of stress than those of 'people-oriented' managers.

Relationships with Colleagues

Besides the obvious factors of office politics and colleagues' rivalry, we find another element here: stress can be caused not only by the pressure of poor relationships but also by its opposite – a lack of adequate social support in difficult situations (Lazarus, 1966). At highly competitive managerial levels it is likely that problem-sharing will be inhibited for fear of appearing weak; and much of the (American) literature particularly mentions the isolated life of the top executive as an added source of strain (see Cooper and Marshall, 1978).

Morris (1975) encompasses this whole area of relationships in one model – what he calls the 'cross of relationships'. While he acknowledges the differences between relationships on two continua – one axis extends from colleagues to users and the other interesting axis from senior to junior managers – he feels that the focal manager must bring all four into 'dynamic balance' in order to be able to deal with the stress of his position. Morris's suggestion seems 'only sensible' when we see how much of his work time the manager spends with other people. In a research programme to find out exactly what managers do, Mintzberg (1973) showed just how much of their time is spent in interaction. In an intensive study of a small sample of chief executives he found that in a large organization a mere 22 per cent of a manager's time was spent in desk-work sessions, the rest being taken up by telephone calls (6 per cent), scheduled meetings (59 per cent), unscheduled meetings (10 per cent) and other activities (3 per cent). In small organizations basic desk-work played a larger part (52 per cent), but nearly 40 per cent was still devoted to face-to-face contacts of one kind or another (see Chapter 2).

The Managerial Career

The idea of career progression is often of over-riding importance to the individual manager. However, the managerial career has several dimensions and consequent sources of stress. Cooper and Marshall (1978) identified two main clusters of potential career stressors:

1. Lack of job security, fear of redundancy and obsolescence due to changing technology.
2. Status incongruity. This refers to under/over-promotion or frustration at having reached one's career ceiling.

Numerous studies have shown these factors to have deleterious health consequences (Cooper, 1983). Studies have also suggested the dysfunctional effects on organizations. This is particularly the case with status incongruity (Hall, 1976).

Recent studies also point to the importance of 'the career' in terms of stress outcomes. Martin (1984) found with hospital workers that 'inability to leave' was related to acute and chronic mental health probelms. Keenan and Newton (1984) found that 'frustrations in organizations' was frequently reported by young graduate engineers in industry. These authors reported frustration as related to a variety of stress outcome variables such as job dissatisfaction and work related anxiety. Despite these studies, the significance of the career as a life-long developmental process has been neglected. Sources of stress will be contingent on this process.

Indeed, as Chapter 13 will show, career development research has identified at least three distinctive career stages (Hall, 1976) that are relevant to the experience of stress: (1) establishment, (2) advancement, and (3) maintenance. The *establishment* stage refers to the early years of the career. Hall and Nougain (1964) found in a study of young managers, that in the first year of employment there were strong needs for 'safety', 'gaining recognition' and 'establishing oneself' in the organization. By the end of the fifth year, however, the need for safety had declined significantly.

The next stage they found was one of *advancement*. The individual is less concerned with 'fitting in' than with moving

up and mastering the organization. Once established, however, there follows a levelling off period, eventually reaching a
managerial plateau. In short, the manager reaches a point of
maintenance, often adopting a guidance role for new organizational entrants (Hall, 1976).

While perhaps of more relevance to managerial and professional workers, the central point is that different career stages
may emphasize different stressors. In the early years, 'relationships', particularly with superiors, may be of paramount
concern. This will relate to both feelings of security and also
provision of information about the company and the
employee's own performance. The individual experiences
'reality shock', moving through a socialization process by
learning and acquiring the values and orientations of the
organization (Van Maanen and Schein, 1979). Indeed, role
ambiguity could also be a major stressor during this phase.
Hall and Nougain (1964) found early experiences to affect a
manager's future attitudes, expectations and performance.

During the stage of advancement, 'promotion' and 'personal future plans' may begin to dominate. Also, since
individuals may have gained higher status, the need for
support from colleagues and subordinates may be vital for
good performance. Thus, stable positive relationships with
these 'support agencies' may be crucial.

Another potential stress source at this stage is from the
work:family interface. Preoccupation with the job during
advancement years is likely to have disruptive effects on
family life during important developmental years (Cooper,
1981b).

At the stage of *maintenance*, different factors may become
sources of stress. Career frustrations, fears of obsolescence or
even negative organizational attitudes could dominate his/her
concerns. A study of police inspectors (a rank equivalent to a
first line manager) by Glowinkowski and Nicholson (1984)
found the middle-aged group to hold considerable negative
attitudes towards the organization (that is, the constabulary),
in terms of their own careers. They also revealed a series of
superstitious beliefs and feelings of uncertainty, regarding the
workings of the promotion system itself. These authors emphasized the importance of the culture of the organization,

which encouraged the idea of promotion as a reward system, and yet provided no feedback or guidance regarding promotion chances.

Organizational Climate

A major source of managerial stress can arise from the organisation itself. These factors include, lack of participation in decision-making, low organizational trust, office politics, poor communications or even restrictions on behaviour. The main thrust of research in this field has tended to concentrate on lack of participation and stress-related outcomes.

In the French and Caplan (1970) study it was found that greater participation was related to higher job satisfaction, low job-related threat, and higher self-esteem. Buck (1972) found that managers and workers most under pressure tended to have more autocratic leadership. Margolis *et al.*'s (1974) national US sample found that non-participation was a significant predictor of several negative health indices. These included poor physical health, escapist drinking, low job satisfaction, low motivation, propensity to leave the organization and absenteeism. Wall and Clegg (1981) provide evidence from longitudinal data that when substantial increases in group autonomy and work identity were achieved, they were followed by increased work motivation, performance, job satisfaction and mental health. The authors discounted a Hawthorne effect because the changes were maintained over a period of at least 18 months. Also, while performance and motivation increases occurred quickly, the job satisfaction and mental health improvements took several months to appear. This study strongly suggests a causal effect of 'increased participation' on subsequent psychological strain.

Despite the studies mentioned above, most research into participation has emphasized blue-collar groups. However, it was suggested earlier that a manager's relationship with the organization may have become a highly significant source of stress. Some recent studies support this assumption.

A study of senior managers by Cooper and Melhuish (1980) analysed a broad range of stressors. They found that the 'relationship within the organization', 'job insecurity' and 'poor organizational climate' predicted of lower mental health and physical health among executives. This study showed that 'poor organizational climate' was no longer the preserve of blue-collar workers. Also, they found the absence of 'role-based stress' in the stress outcome equation. A study from the career development field by Alban-Metcalfe and Nicholson (1984) found similar results. Among a sample of British managers, 'challenge', 'creative work' and 'good quality management' were valued as highly important. Clearly specified work roles were rated as relatively unimportant.

A further point to consider is that movement towards greater worker participation (within society as a whole) can itself become a source of stress. Gowler and Legge (1975) pointed to four main factors which can make participation a source of stress for managers:

1. mismatch of formal and actual power;
2. the manager may resent the erosion of his formal role;
3. increased role conflict due to the need to be both participative and achieve high production;
4. subordinates may refuse to participate.

Home:Work Interface Stresses

The sixth 'source' of managerial stress is more of a 'catch-all' category for all those interfaces between life outside and life inside the organization that might put pressure on the manager: family problems (Pahl and Pahl, 1971), life crises (Dohrenwend and Dohrenwend, 1974), financial difficulties, conflict of personal beliefs with those of the company, and the conflict of company with family demands (Cooper, 1981b).

The area which has received most research interest is that of the manager's relationship with his wife and family. (It is widely agreed that managers have little time for 'outside activities' apart from their families. Writers who have examined their effects on the local community [Packard, 1975] have pointed to the disruptive effects of the executive's lack of involvement.) The manager has two main problems *vis-à-vis* his family:

1. That of 'time management' and 'commitment management'. Not only does his busy life leave him few resources with which to cope with other people's needs, but in order to do his job well the manager usually also needs support from others to cope with the 'background' details of house management, etc., to relieve stress when possible, and to maintain contact with the outside world.
2. The second is often a result of the first, namely the spillover of crises or stresses in one system which affect the other.

As these two are amost inseparable, we discuss them together.

Marriage Patterns

The 'arrangement' the manager comes to with his wife will be of vital importance. Pahl and Pahl (1971) found that the majority of wives in their middle-class sample saw their role in relation to their husband's job as a supportive, domestic one; all said that they derived their sense of security from their husbands. Barber (1976), interviewing five directors' wives, finds similar attitudes. Gowler and Legge (1975) have dubbed this bond 'the hidden contract', in which the wife agrees to act as a 'support team' so that her husband can fill the demanding job to which he aspires. Handy (1978) supports the idea that this is 'typical' and that it is the path to career success for the manager concerned. In his sample of top British executives (in mid-career) and their wives he found that the most frequent pattern (about half the 32 couples interviewed) was that of the 'thrusting male–caring female'. This he depicts as high role segregation, with the emphasis on 'separation', 'silence' and complementary activities. Historically both the company and the manager have reaped benefits from maintaining the segregation of work and home implicit in this pattern. The company thus legitimates its demand for a constant work performance from its employee, no matter what his home situation, and the manager is free to pursue his career but keeps a 'safe haven' to which he can return to relax and recuperate. The second and most frequent combination was 'involved–involved' – a dual career pattern, with the emphasis on complete sharing. This, while potentially extremely fulfilling for both parties, requires energy inputs which might well prove so excessive that none of the roles involved is fulfilled successfully.

It is unlikely that the patterns described above will be negotiated explicitly or that they will in the long term be 'in balance'. Major factors in their continuing evolution will be the work and family demands of particular life stages. A BIM report (Beattie *et al.*, 1974), for example, highlights the difficult situation of the young executive who, in order to build up his career, must devote a great deal of time and energy to his job just when his young housebound wife, with small children, is also making pressing demands. The report suggests that the executive fights to maintain the distance between his wife and the organization, so that she will not be in a position to evaluate the choices he has to make; paradoxically he does so at a time when he is most in need of sympathy and understanding. Guest and Williams (1973) examined the complete career cycle in similar terms, pointing out how the demands of the different systems change over time. The addition of role-disposition and personality-disposition variables to their 'equations' would, however, make them even more valuable.

Mobility

Home conflicts become particularly critical in relation to managerial relocation and mobility. Much of the literature on this topic comes from the USA, where mobility is much more a part of the national character than in the United Kingdom (Pierson, 1972). But there is reason to believe that mobility is an increasingly common phenomenon in Britain, too.

At an individual level the effects of mobility on the manager's wife and family have been studied (Cooper and Marshall, 1978). Researchers agree that, whether she is willing to move or not, the wife bears the brunt of relocations, and they conclude that most husbands do not appreciate what this involves. American writers point to signs that wives are suffering and becoming less co-operative. Immundo (1974) hypothesizes that increasing divorce rates are seen as the upwardly aspiring manager races ahead of his socially un-skilled, 'stay-at-home' wife. Seidenberg (1973) comments on the rise in the ratio of female to male alcoholics in the USA from 1:5 in 1962 to 1:2 in 1972 and asks the question, 'Do corporate wives have souls?' Descriptive accounts of the frustrations and loneliness of being a 'corporate wife' in the USA and the United Kingdom proliferate. Increasing teenage delinquency and violence is also laid at the door of the mobile manager and the society which he has created.

Constant mobility can have profound effects on the lifestyle of the people concerned – particularly on their relationships with others. Staying only two years or so in one place, mobile families do not have time to develop close ties with the local community. Immundo (1974) talks of the 'mobility syndro-me', a way of behaving geared to developing only temporary relationships. Packhard (1975) describes ways in which indi-viduals react to the type of fragmenting society this creates, for example treating everything as if it is temporary, being indifferent to local community amenities and organizations, living for the 'present' and becoming adept at 'instant grega-riousness'. He goes on to point out the likely consequences for local communities, the nation, and the rootless people involved.

Pahl and Pahl (1971) suggest that the British reaction is, characteristically, more reserved and that many mobiles retreat into their nuclear family. Managers, particularly, do not become involved in local affairs, due both to lack of time and to an appreciation that they are only 'short-stay' inhabi-tants. Their wives find participation easier (especially in areas where mobility is common), and a recent survey (Middle Class Housing Estate Study, 1975) suggested that, for some, 'involvement' is necessary to compensate for their husband's ambitions and career involvement which keep him away from home. From the company's point of view, the way in which a wife adjusts to her new environment can affect her husband's work performance. Guest and Williams (1973) illustrate with an example of a major international company which, on surveying 1,800 of their executives in 70 countries, concluded that the two most important influences on over-all satisfaction with the overseas assignment were the job itself and, more importantly, the adjustment of executives' wives to the foreign environment.

The Type A Manager

Sources of pressure at work evoke different reactions from different managers. Some are better able to cope with these stressors than others; they adapt their behaviour in a way that meets the environmental challenge. On the other hand, some managers are psychologically predisposed to stress, that is, they are unable to cope or adapt to the stress-provoking situations. Many factors may contribute to these differences – personality, motivation, being able or ill-equipped to deal with problems in a particular area of expertise, fluctuations in abilities (particularly with age), insight into one's own motivations and weaknesses. However, much of the research in this area has focused on personality and behavioural differences between high- and low-stressed individuals.

The major research approach to individual stress difference began with the work of Friedman and Rosenman (Friedman, 1969; Rosenman *et al.*, 1964, 1966) in the early 1960s which showed a relationship between behavioural patterns and the prevalence of CHD. They found that individuals manifesting certain behavioural traits were significantly more at risk. These individuals were later referred to as the 'coronary-prone behaviour pattern type A' as distinct from type B (low risk of CHD). Type A was characterized by extremes of competitiveness, striving for achievement, aggressiveness, haste, impatience, restlessness, hyperactiveness, explosiveness of speech, tenseness of facial musculature and feelings of being under pressure of time and under the challenge of responsibility. It was suggested that 'people having this particular behavioural pattern were often so deeply involved and committed to their work that other aspects of their lives were relatively neglected' (Jenkins, 1971). In the early studies persons were designated a type A or type B on the basis of clinical judgements of doctors and psychologists or peer ratings. These studies formed higher incidence of CHD among type A than type B. Many of the inherent methodological weaknessses of this approach were overcome by the classic Western Collaborative Group Study (Rosenman *et al.*, 1964, 1966, 1967). It was a prospective (as opposed to the earlier retrospective studies) national sample of over 3,400 men free of CHD. All these men were rated type A or B by psychiatrists after intensive interviews, without knowledge of any biological data about them and without the individuals being seen by a heart specialist. Diagnosis was made by an electrocardiographer and an independent medical practitioner, both of whom were not informed about the subjects' behavioural patterns. They found the following result: after two and half years from the start of the study, type A men between the ages 39–49 and 50–59 had 6.5 and 1.9 times respectively the incidence of CHD than type B men. They also had a large number of stress risk factors (such as high serum cholestorol levels, elevated beta-lipoproteins). After four and a half years the *same* relationship of behavioural pattern and incidence of CHD, individuals exhibiting type A behavioural patterns had significantly more incidence of acute myocardial infarction and angina pectoris. Rosenman *et al.* (1967) also found that the risk of recurrent and fatal myocardial infarction was significantly related to type A characteristics. Quinlan *et al.* (1969) found the same results among Trappist and Benedictine monks. Monks judged to be type A coronary-prone cases had 2.3 times the prevalence of angina and 4.3 times the prevalence of infarction as compared with monks judged to be type B.

An increasingly large number of studies have been carried out which support the relationship between type A behaviour and ill-health (Caplan, Cobb and French, 1975). From a management perspective, the most significant work has been carried out by Howard *et al.* (1976): 236 managers from 12 different companies were examined for type A behaviour and for a number of the known risk factors in CHD (blood pressure, cholesterol, triglycerides, uric acid, smoking and fitness). Those managers exhibiting extreme type A behaviour showed significantly higher blood pressure (systolic and diastolic) and higher cholesterol and triglyceride levels. A higher percentage of these managers were cigarette smokers, and in each age group studied type A managers were less interested in exercise (although differences in cardio-respiratory fitness were found only in the oldest age group). The authors conclude that type A managers were found to be higher on a number of risk factors known to be associated with CHD than were type B managers.

The Management of Stress

Cooper (1981a) has argued that understanding the sources of managerial pressure, as we have tried to do here, is only the first step in stress reduction. We must next begin to explore 'when' and 'how' to intervene. There are a number of changes that can be introduced in organizational life to begin to manage stress at work, for example:

1. To recreate the social, psychological and organizational environment in the workplace to encourage greater auto-nomy and participation by managers in *their* jobs.
2. To begin to build the bridges between the workplace and the home: providing opportunities for the manager's wife to understand better her husband's job, to express her views about the consequences of his work on family life, and to be involved in the decision-making processes of work that affects all members of the family unit.
3. To utilize the well-developed catalogue of social interact-ive skill training programmes to help clarify role and interpersonal relationship difficulties within organiza-tions.
4. More fundamentally, to create an organizational climate to encourage rather than discourage communication, open-ness and trust – so that individual managers are able to express their mobility to cope, their work-related fears, and are able to ask for help if needed.

There are many other methods and approaches of coping and managing stress, depending on the sources activated and the interface between these sources and the individual make-up of the manager concerned, but the important point that we are trying to raise here is that the *cure* (intervention or training technique) depends on the *diagnosis*. It is important to encourage organizations to be sensitive to the needs of its managers and begin to audit managerial stress. As Wright (1975) so aptly suggests, 'the responsibility for maintaining health should be a reflection of the basic relationship between the individual and the organization for which he works; it is in the best interests of both parties that reasonable steps are taken to live and work sensibly and not too demandingly.'

Conclusion

As this chapter has suggested throughout, the sources of job stress cannot be understood by positing single causative agents like 'long hours' or 'a lousy boss' or 'an unpleasant work environment'. It is usually more complex, involving a number of factors interacting at the same time. To get at the root of occupational health and wellbeing, we must examine all the factors discussed above and many others if we are to heed the advice of an early American president, John Adams, who wrote to his wife Abigail in July 1782 'I assure you it is much wholesomer to be a complaisant, good humored, contented Courtier, than a Grumbletonian Patriot, always whining and snarling'.

References for Chapter 7

Alban-Metcalf, B. and Nicholson, N. (1984) *The Career Development of British Male and Female Managers*, British Institute of Management: London.

Barber, R. (1976) 'Who would Marry a Director?', *Director*, March, 60–2.

Beattie, R. T., Darlington, T. G. and Cripps, D. M. (1974) *The Management Threshold*, British Institute of Management, London.

Breslow, L. and Buell, P. (1960) 'Mortality from Coronary Heart Disease and Physical Activity of Work in California', *Journal of Chronic Diseases*, 11, 615–26.

Brook, A. (1973) 'Mental Stress at Work', *The Practitioner*, 210, 500–6.

Brummett, R. L., Pyle, W. C. and Framholtz, E. G. (1968) 'Accounting for Human Resources', *Michigan Business Review*, 20(2), 20–5.

Buck, V. (1972) *Working under Pressure*, Staples Press, London.

Caplan, R. D., Cobb, S. and French, J. R. P. (1975) 'Relationships of Cessation of Smoking with Job Stress, Personality and Social Support', *Journal of Applied Psychology*, 211–19.

Constandse, W. J. (1972) 'A Neglected Personnel Problem', *Personnel Journal*, 51(2), 129–33.

Cooper, C. L. (1976) *Developing Social Skills In Managers*, Macmillan, London.

Cooper, C. L. (1981a) *The Stress Check*, Prentice-Hall, Englewood Cliffs, N.J.

Cooper, C. L. (1981b) *Executive Families under Pressure*, Prentice-Hall, Englewood Cliffs, N.J.

Cooper, C. L. (1983) *Stress Research: Issues for the 80s*, Wiley, New York.

Cooper, C. L., Davidson, M. and Robinson, P. (1982) 'Stress in the Police Service', *Journal of Occupational Medicine*, 24, 30–36.

Cooper, C. L., Cooper, R. and Eaker, L. (1988) *Living with Stress*, Penguin, London.

Cooper, C. L., Mallinger, M. and Kahn, R. (1978) 'Identifying Sources of Occupational Stress Among Dentists', *Journal of Occupational Psychology*, 51, 227–34.

Cooper, C. L. and Marshall, J. (1978) *Understanding Executive Stress*, Macmillan, London.

Cooper, C. L. and Melhuish, A. (1980) 'Occupational Stress and the Manager', *Journal of Occupational Medicine*, 22, 588–92.

Cooper, C. L. and Payne, R. (1988) 'Causes, Coping and Consequences of Stress at Work', Wiley, Chichester and New York.

Cooper, C. L. and Sloan, S. (1985) 'Occupational and Psychosocial Stress among Commercial Airline Pilots', *Journal of Occupational Medicine*, 27, 570–76.

Cooper, C. L. and Smith, M. (1985) 'Job Stress and Blue Collar Work', Wiley, Chichester and New York.

Crump, J., Cooper, C. L. and Maxwell, V. (1981) 'Stress in Air Traffic Controllers', Journal of Occupational Behaviour, 2, 293–303.

Dohrenwend, B. S. and Dohrenwend, B. P. (1974) *Stressful Life Events*, Wiley, New York.

Donaldson, J. and Gowler, D. (1975) 'Prerogatives, Participation and Managerial Stress', in Gowler, D. and Legge, K. (eds.), *Managerial Stress*, Gower, Epping.

French, J. R. P. *et al.* (1982) *The Mechanisms of Job Stress and Strain*, Wiley, Chichester.

French, J. R. P. and Caplan, R. D. (1970) 'Psychosocial Factors in Coronary Heart Disease', *Industrial Medicine*, 39, 383–97.

French, J. R. P. and Caplan, R. D. (1973) 'Organizational Stress and

Individual Strain', in Marrow, A. J. (ed), *The Failure of Success*, American Management Academy, New York, 30–66.

French, J. R. P., Tupper, C. J. and Mueller, E. I. (1965) 'Workload of University Professors', unpublished research report, University of Michigan.

Friedman, M. (1969) *Pathogenesis of Coronary Artery Disease*, McGraw-Hill, New York.

Friedman, M., Rosenman, R. H. and Carrol, V. (1958) 'Changes in Serum Cholesterol and Blood Clotting Time in Men Subject to Cyclic Variations of Occupational Stress', *Circulation*, 852–61.

Glowinkowski, S. and Nicholson, N. (1984) 'The Promotion Pathology: A Study of British Police Inspectors', SAPU, Sheffield, memo 659.

Goffman, E. (1952) 'On Cooling the Mark Out', *Psychiatry*, 15(4), 451–63.

Gowler, D. and Legge, K. (1975) 'Stress and External relationships: the "hidden contract"', in D. Gowler and K. Legge (eds.), *Managerial Stress*, Gower, Aldershot.

Guest, D. and Williams, R. (1973) 'How Home Affects Work', *New Society*, January.

Hall, D. T. (1976) *Careers in organisations*, Goodyear: New York.

Hall, D. T. and Nougain, K. (1964) 'An examination of Maslow's need hierarchy in an organisational setting', *Organisational Behaviour and Human Performance*, 3, 12–35.

Handy, C. (1978) 'The Family: Help or Hindrance?' in Cooper, C. L. and Payne, R. (eds.), *Stress at Work*, Wiley, New York.

Howard, J. H., Cunningham, D. A. and Rechnitzer, P. A. (1976) 'Health Patterns Associated with Type A Behaviour: A Managerial Population', *Journal of Human Stress*, March, 24–31.

Immundo, L. V. (1974) 'Problems Associated with Managerial Mobility', *Personnel Journal*, 53 (12), 910.

Jenkins, C. L. (1971) 'Psychologic and Social Precursors of Coronary Disease', *New England Journal of Medicine*, 284(6), 307–17.

Kahn, R. L., Wolfe, D. M., Quinn, R. P., Snoek, J. D. and Rosenthal, R. A. (1964) *Organisational Stress*, Wiley, New York.

Kasl, S. V. (1973) 'Mental Health and the Work Environment', *Journal of Occupational Medicine*, 15(6), 509–18.

Kay, E. (1974) 'Middle Management', in O'Toole, J. (ed), *Work and the Quality of Life*, MIT Press, Cambridge, Mass.

Kearns, J. L. (1973) *Stress in Industry*, Priory Press, London.

Keenan, A. and Newton, T. J. (1984) 'Frustration in organisations: Relationships to role stress, climate and psychological strain', *Journal of Occupational Psychology*, 57, 57–65.

Lazarus, R. S. (1906) *Psychological Stress and the Coping Process*, McGraw-Hill, New York.

Levinson, H. (1973) 'Problems that Worry our Executives', in Marrow,

A. J. (ed), *The Failure of Success*, American Management Academy, New York.

McMurray, R. N. (1973) 'The Executive Neurosis', in Noland, R. L. (ed), Industrial Mental Health and Employee Counselling, Behavioural Publications, New York.

Margolis, B. L. and Kroes, W. H. (1974) 'Work and the Health of Man', in O'Toole, J. (ed), *Work and the Quality of Life*, MIT Press, Cambridge, Mass.

Margolis, B. L., Kroes, W. H. and Quinn, R. P. (1974) 'Job Stress: An Unlisted Occupational Hazard', *Journal of Occupational Medicine*, 16(10), 654–61.

Marshall, J. and Cooper, C. L. (1978) *Executives Under Pressure*, Macmillan, London.

Marshall, J. and Cooper, C. L. (1979) 'Work Experiences of Middle and Senior Managers: The Pressures and Satisfactions', *Management International Review*, 19 (1) 81–96.

Martin, T. N. (1984) 'Role stress and inability to leave as predictors of mental health', *Human Relations*, 37, 969–83.

Mettlin, C. and Woelfel, J. (1974) 'Interpersonal Influence and Symptoms of Stress', *Journal of Health and Social Behaviour*, 15(4), 311–19.

Middle Class Housing Estate Study (1975), unpublished paper, Civil Service College, United Kingdom.

Miller, J. G. (1960) 'Information Input Overload and Psychopathology', *American Journal of Psychiatry*, 8, 116.

Mintzberg, H. (1973) *The Nature of Managerial Work*, Harper and Row, New York.

Morris, J. (1975) 'Managerial Stress and "The Cross of Relationships"', in Gowler, D. and Legge, K. (eds.), *Managerial Stress*, Gower, Aldershot.

Neff, W. S. (1968) *Work and Human Behavior*, Atherton Press, New York.

Packard, V. (1975) *A Nation of Strangers*, McKay, New York.

Pahl, J. M. and Pahl, R. E. (1971) *Managers and Their Wives*, Allen Lane, London.

Payne, R. 'Social Support at Work', in C. L. Cooper and Payne, R. (1980), *Current Concerns in Occupational Stress*, Wiley, Chichester.

Pierson, G. W. (1972) *The Moving Americans*, Knopf, New York.

Pincherle, G. (1972) 'Fitness for Work', *Proceedings of the Royal Society of Medicine*, 65(4), 321–4.

Quinlan, C. B., Burrow, J. G. and Hayes, C. G. (1969) 'The Association of Risk Factors and CHD in Trappist and Benedictine Monks', paper presented to the American Heart Association, New Orleans, Louisiana.

Quinn, R. P., Seashore, S. and Mangione, I. (1971) Survey of Working Conditions, US Government Printing Office, Washington, D.C.

Rosenman, R. H., Friedman, M. and Jenkins, C. D. (1967) 'Clinically

Unrecognized Myocardial Infarction in the Western Collaborative Group Study', *American Journal of Cardiology*, 19, 776–82.

Rosenman, R. H., Friedman, M. and Strauss, R. (1964) 'A Predictive Study of CHD', *Journal of the American Medical Association*, 189, 15–22.

Rosenman, R. H., Friedman, M. and Strauss, R. (1966) 'CHD in the Western Collaborative Group Study', *Journal of the American Medical Association*, 195, 86–92.

Russek, H. I. and Zohman, B. L. (1969) 'Relative Significance of Hereditary, Diet and Occupational Stress in CHD of Young Adults', *American Journal of Medical Science*, 235, 266–75.

Seidenberg, R. (1973) *Corporate Wives – Corporate Casualties*, American Management Association, New York.

Selye, H. (1946) 'The General Adaptation Syndrome and Diseases of Adaptation', *Journal of Clinical Endocrinology*, 6, 117.

Shirom, A., Eden, D., Silberwasser, S. and Kellerman, J. J. (1973) 'Job Stress and Risk Factors in Coronary Heart Disease Among Occupational Categories in Kibbutzim', *Social Science and Medicine*, 7, 875–92.

Sleeper, R. D. (1975) 'Labour Mobility Over the Life Cycle', *British Journal of Industrial Relations*, 13(2).

Sofer, C. (1970) *Men in Mid-Career*, Cambridge University Press, Cambridge.

Stewart, R. (1976) *Contrasts in Management*, McGraw-Hill, New York.

Uris, A. (1972) 'How Managers Ease Job Pressures', *International Management*, June, 45–6.

Van Maanen, J. and Schein, E. H. (1979) 'Toward a theory of organizational socialisation', in B. M. Staw (ed), *Research into Organisational Behaviour*, 1, 209–64.

Wall, T. D. and Clegg, C. W. (1981) 'A longitudinal field study of group work design', *Journal of Occupational Behaviour*, 2, 31–49.

Wardwell, W. L., Hyman, M. and Bahnson, C. B. (1964) 'Stress and Coronary Disease in Three Field Studies', *Journal of Chronic Diseases*, 17, 73–84.

Wood, C. (1984) *Living in Overdrive*, Fontana, London.

Wright, H. B. (1975) *Executive Ease and Dis-ease*, Gower, Aldershot.

Much of the material used in this chapter was first published in the Journal of Occupational Psychology, 1976, 49(1), 11–28.

8

Working in Groups

ROBIN MARTIN
Department of Psychology, University College,
Swansea

'One of the central features of work is that it is usually done in groups, groups of individuals co-operating under the direction of a leader or leaders.' Argyle (1972, p. 104).

One of the main characteristics of an organization is that people work in groups. This can be clearly seen by examining an organizational diagram. Groups, such as Personnel, Production Control, Marketing, Sales, Accounts are typical for most organizations and are instances where several individuals contribute towards a common goal. Within each group (or department) several subgroups might exist, for example in a Sales Department there may be separate groups of salespeople for each region of the country.

Typically these groups are formed to fulfil a particular organizational objective where either an individual alone could not achieve the objective or a range of skills are required. Below are some examples of groups at work which highlights the range of activities which are involved:

1. managers conducting a production meeting;
2. technicians designing a new product;
3. teams of operators assembling a product;
4. a shopfloor quality circle;
5. union officials discussing a proposal.

Working in groups is such a central part of organizational life that it is easy to forget how much of our time is actually spent in such situations. The most common form of working in groups is meetings and for some managers these take up a large proportion of their working day.

Such is the importance attached to working in groups, that many organizations involve their employees in team development programmes designed to improve their group functioning skills. The implicit belief is that better team working leads to better performance.

Given the importance of working in groups, it is appropriate that this has been the focus of a great deal of research. A comprehensive review of this literature is beyond the scope of this chapter and I have therefore been selective in the topics chosen. However, I have tried to include material which will be particularly relevant to groups in an occupational context.

The chapter is divided into five sections. The first section is concerned with the *nature of work groups* and describes what a group is and the different types of groups that can be found in organizations. The second section is concerned with *group processes* and considers how groups develop and group dynamics. The third section deals with *group structure* which supports the group processes while the fourth section examines ways of *improving group effectiveness*. The final section contains a brief *summary* of the main points of the chapter.

The Nature of Work Groups

What is a Group?

Before we can proceed further it is essential that we are clear what constitutes a *group*. Whilst there is a plethora of definitions of a group they tend to focus on a number of similar issues. The one offered by Baron (1986) summarizes the main themes. He defines a group as 'a collection of two or more interacting individuals with a stable pattern of relationships between them who share common goals and who perceive themselves as being a group' (p. 240).

It is worthwhile breaking down this definition into its four sub-units which can generally be considered to be the characteristics of a group:

1. *Groups are composed of two or more individuals engaged in social interaction.* It seems fairly obvious to consider a group as composed of more than one person but we should note, however, that not all collections of people are necessarily a group. An important defining characteristic, therefore, is that group members interact with each other on a regular basis.

2. *Groups have a structure.* As well as interaction, a group has more stable relations between group members. These relations serve to maintain the group relations and help the group adapt to meet external demands. For example, the group may have a leader who co-ordinates the group's activities and is able to foster cohesion between group members.

3. *Group members share a common goal.* Groups at work are set up to achieve a specific goal (such as, assembling a product) which cannot be achieved by a single person alone. In these cases individual group members may have their own personal goals which contribute towards a common group goal. For example, individual accountants may be in charge of different accounts but have to work together in order to present a complete company account.

4. *Group members perceive themselves as a group.* An important characteristic of groups is that group members perceive themselves as being in a group and that they share the same group identity. Group members often feel a sense of pride from being associated with a particular group.

Types of Groups

The examples given at the beginning of the chapter of different types of groups at work can be considered to be *formal* groups in the sense that they have been set up to fulfil a particular organizational objective. They tend to have a rigid structure with each group member having a particular role. In contrast to this type of group, one often observes *informal* groups, such as friends meeting each other at lunchtime, which are less structured than formal groups. In reality, most people are members of a number of formal and informal groups.

Another useful distinction concerns primary and secondary groups. *Primary groups* tend to consist of a small number of people and are concerned with a specific task or function, such as a Personnel Department or a design team. On the other hand, *secondary groups* tend to be large in numbers and contain many different functions (or primary groups), such as a company.

Group Activities

In general, the aims of a work group are to either produce a product (for example, the assembly of an automobile) or provide a service (for example, production control). In going about their objective, the group has to maintain two types of activities. In the first instance, they have to conduct the operations necessary to achieve the objective (for example, fit together a number of components or collect relevant information). These may be considered to be the *tasks* of the group. The second type of activity the group has to undertake is to co-ordinate their activities (for example, to organize who fits what component). This can be referred to as the *process* of the group. In this chapter we are primarily concerned with the group's processes and we turn to this, in more depth, in the next section.

Group Processes

Group Development

The forming of a new group can often be a traumatic experience for group members. Initially, group members are unsure about how they should behave towards other group members. Gradually, over time, the group members learn what to expect from each other and establish a way of working together. This period is termed *group development* and characterizes the process of changing from a collection of individuals into a highly cohesive unit.

The process of group development requires continual negotiation between the groups' members in order to establish appropriate behaviours. To this extent considerable social skills are required by individuals in order to avoid conflict. Some group members may be more effective in this process and cause greater influence than others. Such individuals may become 'informal' group leaders and act as a reference point for suitable group behaviours. The result of the negotiation process between group members is a set of agreed standards of behaviour. This is referred to as *group norms*.

Theories of group development conceptualize this process as occurring in stages with each stage associated with certain activities and behaviours. In reality it is often difficult to determine which stage a group is at, as stages tend to overlap. Furthermore, not all groups pass through each stage but may become 'stuck' at a particular stage due to problems either inside or outside the group. In such circumstances action may be taken to improve group functioning or, failing this, the group may be disbanded and a new group formed.

Although theories of group development vary in the number of stages proposed (usually, between three and five) they tend to focus upon a set of similar issues. Tuckman's (1965) model of group development is widely cited and nicely illustrates these main themes. This model is outlined below in Figure 8.1.

An important point to note about group development is that the process is *continuous*. Even in situations where groups have been established for a long time, new circumstances, such as a change in group membership or working practices, can re-initiate the group development process. Thus we can think of

1.	*Forming*	Establish interpersonal relationships, conform to organizational standards, testing out acceptable behaviours.
2.	*Storming*	Conflict arises between group members concerning the tasks and roles of the group, resistance to group influences.
3.	*Norming*	Group norms are established which are generally accepted, leadership roles emerge, group cohesion develops.
4.	*Performing*	Members are concerned to complete tasks, interpersonal conflict is reduced and group roles become clarified.

Figure 8.1   *Tuckman's stages of group development (1965)*

groups as being dynamic where they continually negotiate appropriate group norms. We shall now explore the nature of group norms and consider how they emerge and are changed.

Norms

As indicated earlier, norms are a set of expectations of how group members should behave. They are the rules and standards which guide individuals as to what is appropriate behaviour in terms of the tasks and processes which are performed. In many situations norms are implicit and only become realized when they are broken. When someone breaks the group norm there is usually some form of group sanction to 'bring the person back into line'. If this is not possible the person may be expelled from the group.

As well as indicating what behaviours are appropriate for group members, norms also indicate what behaviours are *in*appropriate. Thus norms can be either *prescriptive* in that they indicate what behaviours should be performed (for example, punctuality, quality control) or *proscriptive* by indicating behaviours which should be avoided (for example, wasting time, being unco-operative).

Norms serve several purposes: prominent amongst these is to reduce uncertainty between group members. Knowing how other group members will react in certain situations allows others to predict and anticipate future behaviours.

The emergence of group norms is dependent upon the aims of the group. Norms will be adopted if they increase the ability of the group to perform their duties. Thus a work group on an assembly line may decide to stagger its breaks in order to promote continuous production to meet their targets. In other situations, where a close working relationship may be required, norms which maintain positive social relationships are enhanced – for example, providing social support, going to lunch together.

Feldman (1984) has outlined four ways in which group norms are developed and these are outlined below;

1. *Explicit statements by others*. Norms are quite often set by leaders of the group or by powerful group members. For

example, a manager may set rules concerning lateness or length of coffee breaks. On the other hand, a manager may set requirements concerning how a piece of work is conducted or how it is presented.

2. *Critical events in the group's history.* There are occasions when a certain event establishes a precedent in the group. For example, a sales person may inadvertently forget to put down the delivery date on a sales order resulting in that order being delivered too late. This may lead to a norm in the sales division that only orders with a delivery date will be accepted.

3. *Primacy.* The first behaviours in a group have a powerful influence on subsequent expectations. Norms concerning seating position and behaviour during meetings quickly develop. Part of the reason why primacy effects are so strong is because group members look for regularities in group behaviours to establish group norms.

4. *Carry-over behaviours from the past.* Many norms emerge because group members bring expectations with them from previous groups. The general principle is 'we did this before so why don't we do it again?'. An example of this is leadership style. A particular manager may develop what he or she believes is a successful way to manage his or her subordinates and imposes that norm of leadership on all subsequent groups.

Group Dynamics

In order for a group to work effectively group members have to interact with each other in order to communicate information concerning both the task and process aspects of their work. The relationships and interactions between group members are referred to as *group dynamics*. Without effective group dynamics, the group is unable to co-ordinate their activities and performance is consequently poor.

Group Interaction

The frequency with which group members interact varies according to the nature of the group's work. In highly uncertain situations, where the group's goals are constantly changing and there is interdependence between group members, group interactions will be very frequent. Thus, a research and development team which is designing a new product needs to interact often and have a close working relationship. On the other hand, a group of operators on an established production line, need not interact so often.

Group interactions can be analysed on different levels. For example, Argyle (1972) analyses group interactions at the *individual level*. In doing this he uses two dimensions. First, whether the interaction is verbal (for example, spoken language) or non-verbal (for example, gestures) and, second whether the content of the interaction concerns work-oriented or social issues. Another level of analysis is the *interpersonal level* as used by Kakabadse, Ludlow and Vinnicombe (1987). They distinguish between three types of interactions; task-oriented, maintenance-oriented and self-oriented and these are described below in Figure 8.2.

Separating group interactions into both the individual and interpersonal levels highlights the fact that group members have two aims to satisfy within the group. The first concerns their own needs through interacting with others (such as, the need for achievement and the need for affiliation) and the second is to satisfy the groups' needs in terms of achieving group goals.

In balancing these two sets of needs, group members are in a state of conflict which Schulz (1966) refers to as the *interpersonal underworld*. He suggests that there is a continual struggle between group members to find an acceptable level of

Task-oriented	Maintenance-oriented	Self-oriented
Proposing	Gate-keeping	Attacking/defending
Building	(Opening/	Blocking
Clarifying	closing)	Diverting
Seeking information	Encouraging	Seeking sympathy/recognition
Supporting	Reducing tension	Withdrawing
Disagreeing	Giving feedback	Point scoring
Testing		Over-contributing
Summarizing		Trivializing

Figure 8.2 *Three types of group interaction*

interaction in terms of three important dimensions: inclusion (feeling 'in' or 'out' of the group), control (feeling high or low power in the group) and affection (feeling 'near' or 'far' from other group members). The importance of each of these dimensions varies according to the group's context. For example, in situations where the group is under external threat (such as, competition from a rival group) the inclusion dimension may be the most salient.

Social Influence in Groups

The establishment of group norms involves members of the group reaching consensus over a number of issues. This involves a two-way process where group members both influence each other and are influenced themselves. This is referred to as *social influence* which describes the process of changing judgements, opinions and attitudes of an individual as a result of being exposed to the judgements, opinions and attitudes of others.

Two forms of social influence can be identified within groups which serve the function of either maintaining group norms (social control) or changing group norms (social change). Effective group performance depends on the ability to alternate between these two sets of processes in order to meet the group's goals.

Processes of *social control* act to maintain group norms. The most dominant form of social control is *conformity*, that is, the process by which an individual accepts (or complies with) the group's view. This can often be observed when someone joins a group, whereby they conform to the group's established forms of behaviour.

The process of conformity has been vividly demonstrated in a famous set of experiments by Asch (1951). These studies showed that, even in situations where the group norm is obviously incorrect (in this case, erroneous judgement of line lengths), an individual will change their opinion to agree with the group view. Even though the subjects knew that the group view was wrong they still conformed to it in order to remain part of the group. This finding has been replicated on numerous occasions across a diversity of situations.

We may ask why individuals conform to the group norm? Deutsch and Gerrard (1955) offer two reasons. First, we tend to assume that several people are more likely to be correct than just ourselves ('several pairs of eyes are better than one') and therefore intuitively believe that the group is correct. Second, we desire to be part of a group and often conform to maintain our group membership. If we do not conform then the group might break up. Thus the more a person thinks that the group view is correct and the greater his or her desire to belong to the group, the more likely that person is to conform.

Another process of social control is *obedience to authority*. This process was observed in an (in)famous series of experiments by Milgram (1974). He showed that, under instructions from the experimenter, subjects gave what they believed to be fatal electric shocks to another subject (in fact, the 'victim' was a paid accomplice of the experimenter and no electric shocks were delivered). These provocative experiments reveal that, under certain situations, a person may blindly obey someone else and behave in a way they would not normally do. Thus group members may relinquish responsibility and obey an authoritative person.

The final process of social control which we shall consider is *power*. Power is linked to the ability of an individual to punish or reward other individuals. Leaders are in an obvious position of power, especially when they can determine working conditions such as pay. Power need not be a formal aspect of a job but may be informally held by certain members of a group. For example, senior members of a work group may exercise power over junior members due to their greater experience.

French and Raven (1959) have identified five different forms of individual power and these are briefly described below;

1. *Reward power* – refers to the ability to satisfy a need within a person. In the example above having power over someone's pay would be a form of reward power.
2. *Coercive power* – is the opposite of reward power and refers to the ability to deny a person their needs, for example, being able to stop someone being promoted.

3. *Legitimate power* – is related to the belief that the person is correct. Leadership is a good example of such power, for example, operators may assume that their supervisor has a right to influence them over their work.
4. *Referent power* – occurs when the person is attracted to the person in power and wants to be like them. Managers may copy the behaviours and mannerisms of senior managers they admire.
5. *Expert power* – occurs when the person in power is believed to have specialised skills and therefore knows more than the person being influenced. For example, an engineer may have expert power over operators due to their greater (engineering) knowledge.

If groups only exert social control over their group members then group norms would never change and thus the group would remain static. We know in real life, however, that this is not true – groups frequently adapt to meet new circumstances which require a change in group behaviours. This can be observed in, for example, a production team which is changing from a traditional form of working to a new one, such as 'just-in-time' which requires a different approach to production. The production team needs to renegotiate its group norms to fit the new circumstances: in this situation, new norms concerning stock control and work-in-progress. In order to bring about this change, mechanisms for *social change* are necessary.

The main mechanism of social change is *innovation* which we may consider to be the opposite of conformity and describes the process of replacing existing group norms with new ones. This is not an easy task, especially when group norms have been established for a long time. Indeed, Schachter (1951) shows that when someone challenges the group norm (with the view of changing it), they tend to be viewed as a deviant and consequently a lot of communication by other group members is directed towards them in an attempt to make them conform.

Against such hostility from other group members, the deviant must fulfil two objectives if he or she is to cause innovation. First, he/she must produce *convincing arguments* in favour of his/her position. He/she has to convince the group that the existing norm is incorrect and that a new one is needed. The second objective the deviant must meet is to present his or her arguments in such a way that the group believes that the new norm is a valid alternative to the existing group norm. Moscovici and Nemeth (1974) term this as the deviant's *behavioural style* and outline three important styles which the deviant needs to adopt in order to cause influence; consistency, commitment and confidence. By arguing in a consistent, committed and confident way, group members will believe that the deviant is sure of his or her position and that the alternative norm should be considered.

External conditions can either help or hinder the process of innovation. If, in the above example, the change to just-in-time had been made at a higher level in the organization, the ability to change group norms would be easier than if there were no external pressure to change.

The area of innovation at work is currently receiving a lot of attention (see West and Farr, 1990). Part of the reason for this has been the recognition of the need for organizations to adapt successfully to change. In the face of continuing competition, technological developments and dwindling resources, processes of change are becoming increasingly essential to preserve organizational functioning.

The aim of research into innovation is to identify factors which can improve group innovation. West (1989) for example, has proposed four factors which can affect both the quantity and quality of group innovations and these are described below.

1. *Vision*. This refers to the shared ideas and valued outcomes of the group. Groups are more likely to be innovative if they share the same set of values concerning the group's goals.
2. *Participative safety*. It has long been known that participation reduces resistance to change. Therefore, environments which allow individuals to freely express their ideas (without recriminations) are those which are likely to foster successful innovations.
3. *Commitment to excellence in task performance*. Commitment to excellence creates an environment in which individuals continually appraise and challenge working procedures.

Through this 'constructive controversy' new ideas will emerge. If such an environment is lacking, the group does not examine its working methods and consequently innovation is unlikely.

4. *Support for innovation.* For innovation to occur there must be support for the process of change. This support can either be from fellow group members (for example, verbal support, co-operation) or from the organization (for example, provision of time and resources).

Group Structure

In the preceding section we have been concerned with group processes which occur over time. Whilst it is true that group relations are always in a state of flux, there are aspects of groups which are more stable. In this section we shall be considering one of these aspects, namely group structure, that is, the framework within which the group processes take place. Three aspects of group structure are considered; cohesion, roles, and communication networks.

Group Cohesion

Group cohesion refers to the forces between group members to remain part of the group. Highly cohesive groups are those where group members are attracted towards each other, where they accept group norms and help the group to attain group goals. According to Piper *et al.* (1983) three separate aspects of cohesion can be identified. First, there are the forces of attraction to the group, second, forces to resist leaving the group and finally, motivation to remain a member of the group.

Many factors contribute towards group cohesion, such as, homogeneous composition (that is, group members being similar to each other), a relatively small size of group, frequent interaction between group members, clear group goals and successful group performance.

The consequences of high levels of cohesion are generally viewed as being positive both for the group members and the organization. From the group members' perspective, highly cohesive groups offer environments where group members feel secure and enjoy working together. Particularly important is the emergence of a group identity which serves the function of linking individual group members together. From the organization's point of view, in addition to the personal benefits, highly cohesive groups are able to 'pull together' and effectively co-ordinate their tasks to a greater extent than is observed in less cohesive groups.

It is often thought that high levels of group cohesion lead to greater productivity. Several studies (for example, Schriescheim, 1980; Tziner and Vardi, 1982) have shown that the relationship between group cohesion and productivity depends on the level of managerial support for the group. These studies show that high group cohesion leads to better performance when management supports the group but to *less* productivity when management does not support the group. Thus the greatest productivity results occur when the goals and support of management correspond with those of the work group.

In certain circumstances extremely high levels of cohesion can be detrimental to group performance. Janis (1972) has outlined a number of situations where highly cohesive groups enter a situation termed *groupthink*. In these situations members of a group are so cohesive that they assume that the group is always correct and consequently do not question the group's behaviours. The group then often loses touch with reality and does not take into consideration all the information that may be available to it. Consequently the group acts in an irrational way. Incidents such as the invasion of the Bay of Pigs and the Watergate break-in have been attributed to the processes of groupthink.

Group Role

A *role* is a set of expected behaviours which is associated with a particular person in a group. The most obvious role in a group is that of the leader. The leadership role involves guiding the group's behaviour and making critical decisions concerning group activities. The role of leadership (as indeed any group role) can either be *formal* (as is the case with a supervisor or departmental manager) or *informal* (such as, when an experienced worker 'leads' the group).

Unlike group norms, which indicate expected behaviours of *all* group members, roles indicate expected behaviours of *specified* individuals. Thus group members may have quite different group roles each associated with different behaviours. This is referred to as *role differentiation*.

Brown (1988) identifies three important functions which roles may serve. First, they allow a division of labour where the group can divide the tasks and processes which are necessary in order to achieve the group's goals. Hence in situations where many individuals are interdependent in achieving a particular objective, there is a need for clearly defined roles. Second, like norms, roles bring order to the group's activities and thereby reduce the level of uncertainty in the group. This is particularly noticeable when a person first joins an established group. He or she will soon learn the role of other members of the group and is therefore able to anticipate their behaviour. Third, group roles are a way in which individuals are able to identify themselves within a group. Although we may wish to belong to a group, at the same time we wish to preserve our own identity. Thus, within a construction team, work roles such as carpenter or plumber have much significance to group members.

One of the first categorizations of group roles was based upon Bales's (1951) distinction between *task-specialist* and *socio-emotional* roles. The former refers to persons who try to organize the group's activities to reach group goals. This may involve co-ordinating group members and making critical decisions. In contrast to this, people who adopt the later role are more concerned with the social wellbeing of group members and play a more supportive role.

Much attention has been placed upon the relationship between group roles and effective group functioning. Research by Belbin (1981) has been very influential. Over a number of years he observed groups participating in management games. Contrary to expectations, groups composed of very clever people consistently exhibited poor performance. This was due to the fact that these group members often didn't co-ordinate their activities and spent a long time arguing for their own position. Belbin noticed that successful teams were those which were collectively able to work in eight different roles which are outlined in more detail in Chapter 2.

Belbin's research, amongst others, clearly shows that for groups to work effectively there is a need for agreement concerning group roles. If such agreement is lacking, certain problems may arise, such as role ambiguity and role conflict.

Role ambiguity occurs when it is unclear what behaviours are expected of group members. Not unsurprisingly this can lead to a lack of co-ordination between group members and hence poor performance. Moreover, role ambiguity can cause considerable psychological strain amongst group members, particularly when the expected behaviours of a person conflicts with their normal duties or those of others.

In some situations individuals may have a role which requires certain behaviours which are inconsistent with enacting another role. This is referred to as *role conflict* and, like role ambiguity, may result in quite considerable psychological strain. Two types of role conflict can be identified. *Inter-role conflict* refers to the incompatible demands of two or more different roles by the same person. For example, a supervisor's role consists of maintaining productivity and ensuring the wellbeing of his or her subordinates. Behaviours associated with each role may sometimes be in conflict as when there is a need to discipline someone who is performing badly. The second type of role conflict is termed *intra-role conflict* and refers to situations where there are incompatible demands from within a single role. An example of this may be a sales person whose role may require him or her to be concerned for the client's needs as well as their own organization's needs.

Communication Networks

An important structural aspect of a group is how individual group members communicate with each other. These are referred to as *communication networks* which are often, in part, determined by the organizational structure. Communication networks vary in two important aspects.

1. *Vertical vs horizontal networks.* In a formal organization, communication tends to be directed up the hierarchy (vertical communication), while in less formal organizations communication often occurs across the hierarchy (lateral communications).
2. *Centralized vs decentralized networks.* Communication can either be directed through a single or small group of people with no communication by peripheral group members (centralized) or it can flow between all the members of a group (decentralized).

In analyzing group communication, Bavelas (1969) has used the concept of *information linkages* to demonstrate communication networks. These refer to the flow of information between group members. Figure 8.3 below demonstrates five typical communication networks.

How these information linkages are arranged is important in determining group performance. Leavitt (1951), for example, found that when the group task was relatively simple (that is, involving simply the collection of information) then the wheel network was more efficient than the circle. In contrast to this, Shaw (1964) found an opposite effect when the group task was more complicated (that is, requiring mathematical reasoning) with the circle being the most effective. Thus in situations where the group goal needs the integration of several people, the most effective communication network is one which allows communication between the group members.

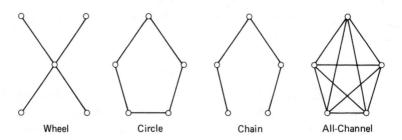

Figure 8.3　*Different types of communication networks*

Developing Effective Work Groups

In recognition of the importance of groups to organizational functioning, considerable resources are invested to improve group functioning. The aim of these activities is to increase group members' ability to work together which, in turn, should lead to better performance. Such activities are sometimes referred to as *team building*.

In order to develop team building activities it is important first to have a metric by which to evaluate group work. There are two main ways to determine group effectiveness. First we can look at *group performance*. We may assume that effective groups perform better than ineffective groups. This is generally true but should not be taken as a universal truism. Performance can be affected by many things which are beyond the groups' control, such as, unobtainable or faulty materials, lost time due to strikes, changes in currency rates. Thus a group may be functioning effectively but unable to meet its goals due to constraints beyond its control. The second way to evaluate group functioning is to examine whether it is using effective *group processes*. Woodcock (1979), for example, has outlined nine factors which lead to effective group functioning. He terms these 'building blocks' and the importance of each one varies according to the groups' activities. These building blocks are: clear objectives and agreed goals, open-ness and confrontation, support and trust, co-operation and conflict, sound procedures, appropriate leadership, regular review, individual development and sound intergroup relations.

We now turn to consider three different approaches to team building which aim to improve group functioning.

Team Development Models

Earlier in the chapter we discussed the process of group development as taking place through a number of distinct stages. In particular we considered Tuckman's (1965) model which specifies four stages: forming, storming, norming and performing (see Figure 8.1). In order for a group to function effectively it has to successfully negotiate these stages. Problems which hinder the group's progress through these stages can lead to group conflict which results in detrimental group performance. Therefore, once potential problems in the group's development have been identified, appropriate team building activities can be designed.

For example, many groups experience problems during the first stage of development (that is, forming) which involves group members testing out different ideas. It is during this stage that group norms develop. Once this problem is identified, team building activities which encourage the testing process can be developed, such as, interpersonal skills training, listening skills. If such activities are successful then the work group should proceed to the second stage of group development.

This approach to team building is particularly useful when a new work group is developed but may have limited value in long-established groups. In such situations, alternative techniques, (such as the T-group or group blockages) may be more effective and these are described below.

T-groups

An important development in team building has been the emergence of T-group or sensitivity training. T-groups are composed of groups of individuals and one or more trainers. The aim of a T-group is to encourage group members, through informal and unstructured discussion, to explore their own behaviours and attitudes and those of the other members of the group. T-groups have three main goals which are to increase the following: *sensitivity*, to be able to perceive how others react to one's own behaviour; *diagnostic ability*, the ability to perceive the state of relationships between others; and *action skill*, to be able to conduct the correct behaviour for a given situation.

The role of the trainer in T-groups is critical if the group is to benefit from the exercise. Group members receive a lot of feedback about themselves and this may be perceived as threatening and potentially upsetting. Therefore, it is important that the trainer sets an appropriately 'open' climate for the group which can overcome potential conflict. It is important to recognize that the trainer is not the leader of the group in the conventional sense. He or she may (initially) make infrequent contributions and resist attempts to structure the discussion. The aim here is to allow the group to form their own structure. This may take time and result in uncomfortably long silences.

A T-group may meet on several occasions and is likely to lead to supplementary activities which are designed to enhance the results of the group discussions. Thus we should think of T-groups as being part of a team building package.

Group Functioning Blockages

Another approach to team building is to examine factors which are blocking effective group functioning. Like the group development approach, the aim is to identify factors hindering effective group working and then design activities to overcome them. Woodcock and Francis (1982), for example, identify 10 group blockages which hinder effective group performance. These are outlined below in Figure 8.4.

The group development and group functioning approaches, however, focus on different aspects of group functioning. Whilst the team development approach focuses on the development process (and is therefore more suitable to new groups), the group functioning approach is more concerned with group processes which makes it more suitable for well-established groups.

1. Inappropriate leadership
2. Unbalanced membership/composition
3. Unconstructive climate
4. Unclear objectives
5. Poor achievement goals
6. Ineffective work methods
7. Insufficient open-ness
8. Undeveloped individuals
9. Low creative capacity
10. Unconstructive interteam relations

Figure 8.4   *Ten blockages to effective team work*

Summary

The main points arising from the four sections of this chapter are summarized below:

1. Four features were identified as being characteristic of *groups at work*. They are: two or more individuals interacting on a regular basis, having a group structure, sharing group goals and having a common group identity. Groups at work can be categorized according to formal/informal groups as well as into primary/secondary groups.

2. Several different group processes were outlined.
    Group development refers to the process of changing from a collection of individuals into a cohesive group. This process occurs through a number of stages each with specific behaviours and activities.
    Group norms are the standards of appropriate behaviours within the group. They emerge through a process of negotiation between group members. Norms serve several purposes; prominent amongst which are to reduce the level of uncertainty amongst group members and to help the group achieve its goals.
    Group dynamics refers to the different types of interaction which occur between group members. Interactions can be categorized in two dimensions, individual and interpersonal. The two aims of satisfying one's own goals with those of the group causes conflict for group members.
    Social influence is the process by which group members influence each other. These processes either act to preserve the group norms (through conformity, obedience to authority and power) or to change group norms (through innovation). The ability of the group to alternate between these processes (particularly to adapt to change) is crucial to effective group working.

3. Groups have a structure within which group processes take place. Four structural aspects of groups were considered; *cohesion* concerns the forces which keep group members to gether. Group cohesion can lead to better performance when management supports the group's activities. Extreme levels of cohesion can lead to the undesirable situation of groupthink where irrational group decisions are taken.

Roles are expected behaviours of specific group members. Successful group working depends on an appropriate mix of group roles. Role ambiguity and role conflict can arise when there is a mismatch between group roles and this can lead to conflict.

Communiction networks refers to the systems by which group members communicate with each other. These are often organizationally determined. Different types of communication networks were considered (for example, the wheel and circle) which vary in their level of decentralization. Communication networks affect group performance with the nature of the task determining which communication network is most suitable.

4. Many organizations invest enormous resources in improving group functioning through team building activities. The implicit belief is that such techniques will lead to improved performance. Three techniques were outlined:

Team development models assume that effective group working occurs when the group has successfully completed the group development process. Problems frequently arise if a group is 'stuck' at a particular stage. Team building activities can be designed to help the group overcome this problem and proceed to the next stage.

T-groups consist of groups of individuals with one or more trainers. The aim is to allow group members to exchange opinions concerning their own and other group members' attitudes and behaviours. The trainer is not the leader of the group and does not structure the discussion. It is important for the group to find their own structure.

Group functioning blockages assume that ineffective group functioning occurs under certain conditions, such as unclear objectives. By identifying conditions which hinder group functioning, it is possible to design team building activities to remedy the problem.

References for Chapter 8

Argyle, M. (1972) *The Social Psychology of Work*, Penguin, London.
Asch, S. E. (1951) 'Effects of group pressure upon the modification and distortion of judgements', in Geutzkow, H. (ed), *Groups, Leadership and Men*, Carnegie, Pittsburgh.

Bales, R. F. (1951) *Interaction Process Analysis: A Method for the Study of Small Groups*, Addison-Wesley, Reading, Mass.

Barron, R. A. (1 986) *Behaviour in Organizations*, 2nd edn, Allyn and Bacon, Newton, Mass.

Bavelas, A. (1969) 'Communications patterns in task-oriented groups', in Cartwright, D. and Zander, A. (eds.) *Group Dynamics: Research and Theory*, 3rd edn, Harper and Row, New York.

Belbin, R. M. (1981) *Management Teams: Why they Succeed or Fail*, Heinemann, Oxford.

Brown, R. (1988) *Group Processes: Dynamics Within and Between Groups*, Basil Blackwell, Oxford.

Deutsch, M. and Garrard, H. (1955) 'A study of normative and informational influence upon individual judgements', *Journal of Abnormal and Social Psychology*, *51*, 629–36.

Feldman, D. C. (1984) 'The development and enforcement of group norms', *Academy of Management Review*, *9*, 47–53.

French, J. R. P. and Raven, B. (1959) 'The bases of social power', in Cartwright, D. and Zander, A. (eds.) (1968), *Group Dynamics*, 3rd edn, Tavistock, London.

Janis, I. J. (1972) *Victims of Groupthink*, Houghton Mifflin, Boston.

Kakabadse, A., Ludlow, R. and Vinnicombe, S. (1987) *Working Organizations*, Penguin, Harmondsworth.

Leavitt, H. J. (1951) 'Some effects of certain communication patterns on group performance', *Journal of Abnormal and Social Psychology*, *46*, 38–50.

Milgram, S. (1974) *Obedience to Authority: An Experimental View*, Tavistock, London.

Moscovici, S. and Nemeth, C. (1974) 'Social Influence II: Minority influence', in Nemeth, C. (ed) *Social Psychology: Classic and Contemporary Integrations*, Rand McNally, Chicago.

Piper, W. E., Marrache, M., Lacroix, R., Richardson, A. M., and Jones, B. D. (1983) 'Cohesion as a basic bond in groups', *Human Relations*, 93–108.

Schachter, S. (1951) 'Deviation, rejection and communication', *Journal of Abnormal and Social Psychology*, *46*, 190–207.

Schriescheim, J. F. (1980) 'The social context of leader subordinate relations: An investigation of the effects of group cohesiveness', *Journal of Applied Psychology*, *65*, 183–194.

Schultz, W. C. (1966) *The Interpersonal Underworld*, Science and Behaviour Books, New York.

Shaw, M. E. (1964) 'Communiction networks', in Berkowitz, L. (ed) *Advances in Experimental Social Psychology*, Academic Press, New York.

Tuckman, B. W. (1965) 'Development sequences in small groups', *Psychological Bulletin*, *63*, 384–99.

Tziner, A. and Vardi, Y. (1982) 'Effects of command style and group cohesiveness on the performance effectiveness of self-selected tank crews', *Journal of Applied Psychology*, 67, 769–75.

West, M. A. (1989) ' and team innovation', *Changes*,

West, M. A. and Farr, J. L. (1990) *Innovation and Creativity at Work*, Wiley, Chichester.

Woodcock, M. (1979) *Team Development Manual*, Gower, Aldershot.

Woodcock, M. and Francis, D. (1982) *The Unblocked Manager: A practical Guide to Self-development*, Gower, Aldershot.

9

Organizational Structures and Processes

DIAN-MARIE HOSKING
Aston Business School

Only recently have writers attempted explicit definitions of the term 'organization'. The more usual practice has been simply to assume that there is sufficient shared agreement about its meaning. In this chapter we shall review various ways of thinking about organization, and how organization is achieved. No attempt is made to provide a comprehensive account, nor to provide a historical record of fashions. Rather, we wish gradually to lay out some basic assumptions, beliefs, and arguments about people, organizations, and their interrelations. Our intention is to show that a certain sort of perspective is needed: one which emphasizes political, cognitive, and social processes.

Our reviews pay particular attention to the relationships implied between 'Person' and 'Organization'. We take a very particular viewpoint which is that each must be theorized in commensurate terms. Our theoretical stance is that organization should be theorized in ways which reflect an adequate model of Person. We argue that this requires attention to themes which are often ignored; three themes will be emphasized. First, we will emphasize the interpretive and constructive qualities of perception – what we will broadly refer to as 'cognitive' processes. Second, we stress that 'organization' is found in meaningful activities and interactions, that is, in 'social' processes. Third, actors are seen to differ in what they value, and differ in the power they can mobilize in their support; these we refer to as 'political' processes. These themes are brought together in the argument that 'organizing' should be seen as an exercise in political decision-making: an 'exercise' performed through interrelated cognitive, social and political processes.

Early Approaches to the Design and Management of Organizations

These include the writings of 'management theorists' such as Henri Fayol, and F. W. Taylor. Each, respectively, is a well known representative of the so-called 'classical' and 'scientific' management 'schools' (see Rose, 1982; Morgan, 1986). In this section we also will outline the early 'structural' work of Max Weber (see Pugh, 1971).

Weber on Bureaucracy

In his now famous work on 'bureaucratic' organizations, Weber set out to identify the particular defining character- istics of this organizational form. He defined the pure, or 'ideal type' as characterized by: hierarchical structures of authority; specialization of tasks and functions; and an imper- sonal formalized (written) and explicit system of rules which specifies obligations. These structures are argued to be grounded in, and to reflect, the 'rational–legal' authority of managers. Management's task is to administer rules in the 'rational' pursuit of organizational goals.

It was not Weber's intention to examine the concept of Persons and social relationships implied by this view of organization; he did not do so. Instead, he focused on 'the organization' as a unit of analysis. He argued that bureaucra- cies are effective because of the importance of 'technical knowledge', and therefore, the need to exercise control through specialist techniques, knowledge, and skills. Weber reasoned that this was just as true in capitalist as well as socialist contexts and in large and small organiza- tions – whatever their products or outputs.

Social systems theorists came increasingly to question Weber's arguments. Some paid particular attention to the 'internal' dynamics of the organization, drawing attention to numerous dysfunctional consequences both of specialization/ division of labour and of the emphasis on formalized, impersonal rules. These critics included, for example, Merton, Selznick, and Gouldner (see Pugh, 1971). Researchers drew attention to the ways in which specialization and hierarchy create a lack of commitment to 'organizational goals', and create disparity between 'organizational goals' and work group activities. Specialization of functions was argued to lead to personal and sectional interests, and to conflicts of interest, as actors sought to extend their power and control. The emphasis on impersonal control, and on predictable actions, was argued to lead to lost flexibility of action and therefore to be likely to prejudice efficiency. These are arguments about the impact of certain forms of organization on people and groups, the interests to which they are committed, and the processes through which they build and mobilize commitment. Later we will take up these arguments and examine them in relation to what we shall call a political perspective of organizing.

Other social systems theorists – those whom we later shall call 'contingency theorists' – argued that there was no 'one-best-way' to organize, and therefore that bureaucracy was not necessarily the most effective form. For example, Woodward's research in manufacturing firms indicated that different patterns of structural characteristics are associated with different production technologies, and that the relationship between these two is critical to the effectiveness of 'the organization' (see Pugh, 1971). Others investigated the relationship between organization structures and characteristics of the organisation's context. The work of Burns and Stalker, and the Aston Studies, are examples of such work. We shall return to discuss these studies when we review systems approaches to organization.

Fayol and Classical Management Thought

Fayol described at length 14 'principles' of good practice. They included arguments about desirable structural characteristics of organization. For example, the principle of 'unity of command' asserted that all employees should receive orders from only one superior. A further two structural principles concerned the division of work, and the centralization of decisions concerning work standards, practices, and organization. Division of work, and centralization were said to characterize organization in the animal world. These were believed to reflect the 'natural' principles of specialization of function, and hierarchies of authority. Fayol implied that his principles were necessarily valid because this was nature's 'solution'. This line of argument led him to suggest that in order efficiently to manage social organizations it was necessary: to specialize functions, to separate 'doing' from authority, to have unity of command, and to subordinate individual interests to the general interest.

Fayol's arguments are seldom credited with the sophistication they deserve. This said, he did imply a sharp and 'natural' distinction between managers and non-managers. The former were assumed to have a right to manage through a hierarchy of authority – a natural form of organizing. Managers were seen as those who should make the decisions, for example, about organizational goals, means of payment, and discipline. Managers should see that human passions of 'employees' do not prevail over the interests of the firm and the state.

In these ways, Fayol's perspective reflects the common managerialist assumption that the goals of management rightly are beyond question and should provide the values (as standards) by which all organizing decisions and activities are judged. The goals of 'management' were taken to be a matter of 'technical' judgement, so to speak, to be value-free, and to be identical with the goals of the state. All managers were assumed to share the same goals, and the goals of non-managers to be compatible with those of management.

The assumption that all individuals and groups share the same, or at least compatible, goals and interests sometimes is described as unitary. The unitary assumption contrasts with the view that individuals and groups have multiple values and interests, and these will often conflict. This is argued to be the case, not just between management and workers, but also within the ranks of each. So, for example, within the ranks of management there will often be major differences between the interests of corporate and plant-level managers (see, for example, Parker *et al.* 1977), between production and sales, and between other managerial groups who perform different tasks. Similarly, non-managers will differ in what they value, depending on their own skills, tasks, and trade union.

We first met arguments about differences in interest and commitment in critiques of Weber's thesis about the effectiveness of bureaucracy. We will later develop the argument further to suggest that the particular values and interests of senior management may be no more legitimate than those of any other group. Rather, senior management's values may appear more legitimate for reasons to do with their greater power and influence. This implies that organizing is, to some degree, performed in relation to a diversity of values and interests. Further, the legitimacy of any (value-based) organizing activities and procedures is always potentially open to question; whether or not the question put is, to some extent, a function of the differing degrees of influence that particular individuals and groups, past and present, were and are able to achieve (see for example Pfeffer, 1981).

Such 'pluralist' arguments can be developed into a political perspective of organization. A political perspective is required in order to reflect an adequate concept of Person: political processes must be seen to be endemic to organization. To recognize this is to abandon the managerialist view of effective organization – a view which begs the question of 'effective for whom'.

Taylor and Scientific Management

Scientific management theory was emerging at around the same time as classical management theory. Taylor, an engineer, tried to build practical knowledge bases and practical techniques for organizing. The first of his 'principles' concerned the traditional practical knowledge of workers. He suggested that their rule of thumb methodology should be replaced with one which was 'scientific'. By this he meant that their knowledge should be organized: should be brought together, written down, and systematized. For him, management would be scientific when managers practised (1) the scientific measurement and organization of work through work study and (2) the scientific selection and development of employees through measurement of their personal characteristics and their work performance. Managers and workers were argued to be best organized (3) through organization structures scientifically designed to separate thinking, particularly planning, from doing. This could best be done through a centralized and hierarchical decision-making structure, and through the grouping of tasks by function.

As with Fayol, Taylor's work has been much misrepresented and it is worth consulting original texts. Three general points can be made. First, Taylor's lack of attention to organization as a political process, and second, his concept of Person which was, by todays standards, narrow and individualistic. The third, related to the other two, is that he had little regard for social processes as a vehicle for the construction and performance of organization.

Taylor's approach to work measurement and work organization provides a useful and well-known example with which to illustrate all three points. Taylor argued that one of the duties of management was deliberately to gather the 'great mass of traditional knowledge, which in the past has been in the heads of the workmen' (Taylor, in Pugh, 1971 p. 125); this could be achieved through work study – through the detailed observation and recording of the production process. He argued that this knowledge could then be reduced to laws, and applied to increase financial surpluses for the good of all. 'The principles of scientific management when properly applied. . . must in all cases produce far larger and better results, both for the employer and the employees . . .' (Taylor Pugh, p. 124).

First then, to the political issues. As with Fayol, in Taylor we find an oversimplified distinction between two groups, management and worker. Each was treated as internally homogeneous in values and interests. Each was seen to have a common, financial interest which could rationally be pursued. This being so, the interests of workers could be handed over to management for their protection and promotion. This becomes clear when it is recognized that to elicit and to codify the knowledge of workers was seen simply as a technical, value-free, device – as a scientific method. There was no thought of the implications such an intervention might have for the influence different groups could achieve in relation to their own values and interests.

Such interventions are not simply 'technical' because they are not value-free. Rather, they are interested. They are grounded in the more or less partisan interests of particular persons and groups; they are therefore political. We need not assume that Taylor, or others like him, set out with strategic intent to disenfranchise workers – conspiracy theories are not required. Instead, we need only recognize that actions, including attempts at technical change, are gounded in values, and that certain values and interests differ between individuals and groups depending on, amongst other things, the particular tasks they are performing (see earlier). Further, people and groups differ in the degree to which they may achieve influence; this is due, in part, to differences in scarce and essential resources such as task-relevant knowledge (see for example Pfeffer, 1981). As noted above, differences of this kind imply that organizing is, in part, a political process: a process which is performed both within and between groups.

Our second area of comment focuses on Taylor's assumptions about cognitive processes. Taylor treated the actions of managers and workers as though they were individual choices arrived at out of a certain sort of systematic and exhaustive process – a rational process of decision-making. Decision-making processes were believed to be of the form we now would call analytic or vigilant. They were assumed to be performed by individuals, acting in individual pursuit of their own objectives. All action was understood as a reflection of cognitive processes, oriented towards financial goals or objectives. Cognitive processes were presumed to be characterized by individual search for all relevant information to identify and evaluate alternative courses of action. Individuals were assumed to select that course of action which maximized their financial values. In other words, decision-making processes were assumed necessarily to take a certain form – to be rational processes of choice. The process was understood as a relatively solitary, analytical activity. Financial values were believed to play an exclusive and decisive role in information search, interpretation and choice.

This 'individualistic' concept of Person comes from classical economic theory. It is tied to a very particular concept of Context. The Context of values and interests, of cognitive processes and social actions, was understood to be 'out there'. The Context was viewed as a set of 'objective facts' which existed independently of the actor. This being so, cognitive processes were assumed to be characterized by search, interpretation, and choice from what was out there in the external context.

In these ways, and judged by what we understand today, Taylor greatly oversimplified and distorted what it is to be human. We now know that people seek to protect and promote many values, and not just financial ones. Further, Taylor's beliefs about the processes of cognition are also deficient. We now know that people rarely follow rational procedures. Exhaustive and systematic search, weighting preferences, evaluating and re-evaluating identified alternatives is rarely performed. Such procedures make enormous demands on the information handling skills of the actor. Further, cognitive processes typically are informed by, and performed in, a social context. The strains of data collection and evaluation are added to by the fact that different actors, be they individuals or groups, act and interact in relation to different values and interests. This introduces competition and conflict, for example, to define some values as more acceptable than others, and to achieve influence in the support and promotion of those values. As a result, cognitive processes in and about organization are best understood as both a cognitive and social process of political decision-making (see, for example, Morley and Hosking, 1984).

That cognitive processes are importantly social and political becomes perhaps more clear when it is recognized that values permeate cognitive processes. Values are not simply discreet goals against which the actor judges value-free data. Rather, cognitive processes are intrinsically *evalu*ative. When we are speaking of social, rather than 'natural' systems, fact can seldom be distinguished, simply and usefully, from value. This means that it is a mistake to sharply distinguish between Persons and their Contexts as neither can be described adequately when described independently of each other. Their interdependence is such that, for example, actors to some degree make their contexts, as well as being made by them. Individually and collectively, actors construct their contexts in relation to their own values and interests. Through their actions and interactions actors 'put into' their contexts their more or less collective constructions.

Our points so far may be brought together as a critique on the concept of Person which flowed through early theories of managers, workers, and organization. The concept of Person, particularly as it was elaborated in relation to 'workers' was an individualistic concept of Person as a machine (see for example, Morgan, 1986). These days, the machine concept looks very dated; Taylor's machine is old, simple, and lonely. The machine is simple in the sense that it has very limited cognitive capacities. The worker was a machine unable to understand its performance, and therefore unable to direct and control its performance except in relation to financial incentives. The machine is 'old' in the sense that the machines of the computer age can do much more than this. In addition, the machine is 'lonely' in the sense that it was treated as a closed system, open to its context, only through 'imports' of money and 'exports' of effort, regulated by management control. For Taylor, Person (worker), as a machine, was an un-social entitity, networked so to speak, by other agents (people and procedures) to other machines which, equally, were un-social, and which it could not understand.

We will conclude by emphasizing the relationships between concepts of Person and Organization. When workers are viewed as persons who have limited understanding and intelligence, as isolated, un-social beings, it follows that management – viewed as a different kind of person – must provide the missing organization and control. Given these assumptions, it follows that managers must: specialize and fragment tasks; remove discretion from the point of production; routinize where possible; and structure activities and decisions through a stable hierarchy of authority. There are good reasons to reject these assumptions, not least because they imply two separate and fixed types of Person: manager and worker. There are good reasons to view all persons as more or less intelligent social actors – as decision-makers organizing to protect their own values. We shall argue that actors organize in relation to projects which are more or less widely shared, and through social relationships in which they are more or less able to mobilize influence.

The Human Relations Approach

The label of human relations is typically applied to the themes which emerged from the Hawthorne Studies, conducted in America, in the Hawthorne Works of Western Electric. The names of persons directly associated with these studies are Roethlisberger, Dickson and Mayo. In his early review of different approaches to organization, Pugh (1971) referred to these as 'group theorists'. The Hawthorne Studies were conducted from the mid-1920s through to the early 1940s. Their beginnings reflected the traditions of thought and practice already described, combined with the approach and interests of British Human Factors Psychology. As far as the investigators were concerned, the studies consisted of the intentional variation of factors such as (1) physical aspects of the immediate work context (lighting levels), (2) timing and length of rest pauses, and (3) use of group bonus schemes. 'Dependent variables' such as output levels were monitored and interviews conducted.

The conduct, reporting, and interpretation of the Hawthorne Studies have been subject to considerable criticism. What is important for us here are the themes which emerged. First, the findings were taken to imply that prevailing concept of Person had to be revised to accommodate what otherwise could not be explained. A particularly important observation was the emergence, amongst production workers, of a social organization which was not planned, formalized, or legitimated by management, but rather, created and controlled by the workers themselves. These processes have come to be referred to as 'informal organization', occurring 'within' formal organization.

The study of the Bank Wiring Room, for example, is hailed as having demonstrated the emergence of informal but powerful norms specifying acceptable (that is positively valued) and unacceptable standards of behaviour. More specifically, these norms defined expected, acceptable, levels of production. 'Overproducers' and 'underproducers' were subjected to their co-workers' attempts to make the norms stick. This was attempted through social influence processes in which social acceptance, satisfying social relationships, and a sense of belonging were manipulated by co-workers. Given these new understandings about Persons, the concept of organization had to be revised to recognize that workers will, to some extent, organize themselves. They will, to some extent, create their own social relationships and social processes. Further, the concept of organization had to be revised to recognize that individuals may act as members of groups, and therefore, organizing is done by and to groups as well as individuals.

The second theme to emerge from the studies concerns the inferred existence of a 'social need'. This, like money, was understood to constitute a value which, through their actions 'in' organizations, individuals sought to protect and promote. Why else, for example, would workers conform to informal norms which resulted in restriction of output and therefore in reduced earnings? The assumed existence of such a need was seen to provide management with new strategies for organizing workers. The efforts of workers could now be harnessed through the manipulation of social processes and relationships. So for example, group-based incentive schemes could be employed with groups of workers, harnessing social influence processes and social needs. Similarly relations between workers and supervisors could be manipulated through leadership styles and through group working. New organizing strategies included employee-centred leadership styles on the part of supervisors, various forms of group working, and legitimizing a greater degree of worker participation in decision-making (for example, Coch and French; Lewin, White, and Lippitt: see, for example, Pugh, 1971; Rose, 1982).

Once again, this work has been much discussed, and much misrepresented. Some of the orginal writings can be found in Pugh (1971). A thorough and extended treatment is given by Rose (1982). As before, our review is intended to identify certain key assumptions and arguments about people, processes, and organization. As before, we wish to do so in order to create the building blocks for a very particular way of thinking about organization.

First, it should be said that the prevailing concept of Person was not revised radically. The implicit dualist distinction between managers and non-managers was little questioned. The concept of 'the worker' remained narrow and individualistic. Their values and interests were extended to include social needs. These were discussed as a means to provide managers with a larger set of needs which they could manipulate for the technical purposes of regulation and control. Needs were taken to be what explained the direction and intensity of workers' behaviour. Needs were still theorized as the properties of atomized individuals. Cognitive processes were still abstracted from social and political processes. Further, they were still theorized in relation to a very narrow set of needs. This is true, despite the emphasis on a person's need to experience a sense of belonging, despite the stress on social relationships, both with management and with co-workers, and despite the weight attached to group working.

Another way of making these points is that the dualist distinction between managers and non-managers remained, as did the machine concept of the latter. First, the cognitive competencies of Persons (as machines) were not re-evaluated in any major way. No fundamental questions were asked about the organizing strategies of specialization, centralization of decision-making, or a hierarchy of authority. There were changes in work organization, a harnessing of social relations through group incentives, supportive supervisory styles, and so on. However, these changes were introduced and understood in the context of hierarchy. No fundamental challenge was felt to assumptions about effective organization structures, and therefore, to the sources of regulation and control. The values by which effectiveness should be judged were not shaken.

The machine was still lonely (see earlier). Social processes, to the extent that they were considered at all, were theorized primarily as the expression of dynamics 'inside' the individual – as spontaneous phenomena serving intrapersonal needs. This individualistic interpretation may account for the relative lack of attention to what we would now recognize as the complexities of social interaction processes. The logic of organizing could remain unchallenged. Managers should continue technically and scientifically to structure organiza-

tion in the pursuit of what were assumed to be common goals
(values). The main difference was that managers now had to
integrate the workers' social needs with the organizations
needs for financial surpluses. Note that the managerialist
qualities of assumptions about Person and Organization
remained largely unrecognized. This way of thinking about
values as intrapersonal needs was of considerable significance.
It meant that conflicts were not considered as possible
evidence of differences, within and between groups, of values
and interests. Recognition of the political quality of organizing
would have to await rejection of the individualistic (see above)
concept of Person.

It is crucial to recognize the significance of an individualistic approach for the ways managers and researchers explained the actions of others – usually workers. Persons were
abstracted and sharply distinguished from their Contexts.
Like Russian dolls, Persons and Contexts were set apart from
one another: Persons were fitted into, or taken out of Contexts,
with each staying the same. The behaviours of workers were
believed to reflect their personal characteristics. Since Contexts were seen as independent of Persons, Contexts could be
manipulated. Managers were seen to have the technical task
of manipulating structures and controls so as best to harness
the personal characteristics of workers; a model of simple
cause and effect.

Eventually there came another shift in published works on
Organization. Researchers further consolidated their sup-
planting of managers as writers on organization. They did so
perhaps because of the methods they came increasingly to
employ, and the perceived legitimacy of those methods as the
methods of science. Increasingly sophisticated measures and
statistical methods achieved prominence. Research went
beyond the typical case study methodology to investigate
quantified relationships between large sets of variables. Researchers became able to handle large samples of Persons,
Organizations, and their possible interrelations. Attention
came largely to focus on relationships between structures and
technologies as Contexts of action, independent of and affecting individual characteristics such as attitudes towards tasks,
work performance (output measures), social interactions,

values and conflict relations. Much of this work follows
naturally from Weber's arguments about bureaucracy. It
includes the analysis of 'bureaucratic dysfunctions' described
earlier, along with the well-known studies of Woodward,
Burns and Stalker, and the Aston Studies.

Organizations came to be viewed explicitly as systems,
more or less open to their environments. Organic systems
models, including 'contingency theories', became especially
popular. Empirical studies examined relationships between
organizational characteristics such as structures, technology,
and size. These also were examined for their relations with
extraorganizational characteristics – especially environmental
turbulence and change. The relations between organizational
and environmental characteristics were then examined in
relation to organizational performance. In other words, researchers investigated a greater range and complexity of
relations between Person and Context, and the range of
contextual characteristics was extended to include more organizational, and environmental characteristics. However, little attention was directed to a better understanding of Person,
and Person and Context each continued to be theorized
independently of the other. As a result, the roles and significance of cognitive, social, and political processes were not
seriously considered.

Organic Systems Approaches

The 1960s and '70s witnessed a blossoming of approaches
which were explicitly described as open systems perspectives
of social organization. Like the term organization, the term
system may be used to mean many things. Often the term is
used in a very general way to refer to a bounded set, or entity,
made up of interrelated parts. A key argument is that a
change in any one of the parts is likely to effect a change in one
or more of the others, depending on the structure of the
system.

There are many kinds of systems approach, and we shall
not attempt to describe them all. They differ in whether they
are are open or closed, and in the underlying model: tradi-

tional mechanistic or machine; organic or biological; and cybernetic. Few systems models of organizations make explicit their underlying model of Person. The mechanistic and organic models in particular, typically embrace a physicalist view of realities as objective facts, existing independently of the person who describes them.

We found the concept of Person as a machine implicit in the classical and scientific management approaches reviewed earlier. 'The organization', viewed as a machine, was seen as analogous to a closed, mechanical system – the sort that necessarily tends to a state of equilibrium. Person and Organization were set apart, the view being taken that each could satisfactorily be theorized independently of the other. An organization was theorized, like Person, as an entity. Like Person, the organization was thought to be capable of being theorized as independent of 'its' context, the speed of technical change, competition, and so on.

The mechanical analogy came to be increasingly criticized. Critics drew on research findings and on argument to suggest that social organizations cannot rightly be viewed as closed systems, viable, regardless of the nature of their context. Critics argued that just as Person and Context cannot sharply be distinguished, organizations are in varying ways, and to varying degrees, open to their contexts. However, different writers had quite different reasons for arguing against closed systems assumptions. Probably only a few wanted to seriously question the validity of treating the organization as an actor in its own right. Such reification was thought acceptable, given the need to study units of analysis more macro than the social group. The debates seldom were focused on the status of 'an organization' as a reality which exists independently of the person. Instead, researchers discussed what, from theory, made organizations open, and investigated empirical relationships between 'organizational characteristics', the organization's Context, and organizational effectiveness.

As certain weaknesses of the mechanical analogy became evident, models variously described as organic or biological received more attention. Researchers focused on structures and functions, just as many had done before. In an organic model of social organization, the theory of system functioning draws from the biological system model. The equivalent of the biological 'need' is the social system 'need' to achieve survival or homeostasis. The system parts, or subsystems, are understood to function in ways which service the needs of the system whole or entity. In sum the perspective depends upon the assumption of functional unity – an assumption usually left unstated.

The approaches to which we are referring here comprise a major portion of the fields of organization studies and organizational behaviour. We will describe a few particularly well-known examples, focusing on empirical studies of organization structures and other organizational characteristics.

Structure of Organization

'The structure of an organization is often taken to comprise all the tangible and regularly occurring features which help to shape its member's behaviour' (Child, 1977, p. 9) So what are these features? We have previously described Weber's descriptions of the bureaucratic form. Such a form is now often termed 'mechanistic' (Burns and Stalker, 1966) or called a 'machine bureaucracy' (Mintzberg, 1983). It is worth repeating the structural characteristics of bureaucracy. First, there is emphasis on a high degree of specialization such that different people perform different tasks. Great care is also devoted to formalization, that is, to the precise definition and standardization of those tasks. Duties, methods, and the discretion attached to the position/job are often specified through written descriptions. Tasks are grouped in different specialist departments, usually according to the functions they are understood to perform for the organization (system) as a whole. A managerial hierarchy of authority and command is created, with each level having delegated authority to control the level below. Authority is delegated 'down the hierarchy' and information is regulated to flow 'upward'. The hierarchy acts as a simple control system with the emphasis on vertical relations, and with horizontal relations relatively under-emphasized.

'Structural theorists' (Pugh, 1971) took the view that any organization may be described in terms of varying degrees of these characteristics – centralization and so on. This made it possible, for example, to speak of the overall shape of the organizational whole. Particularly popular was the debate about 'tall' versus 'flat': the more levels in the hierarchy, the more narrow the associated spans of control, and the more tall the organization.

It has become usual to summarize structural characteristics in terms of three principle components: complexity, formalization, and centralization. (a) *Complexity* embraces: the degree of horizontal differentiation between units such as tasks, teams, and departments; vertical differentiation, that is, the height of the hierarchy; and spatial differentiation of personnel and locations. (b) *Formalization* refers to the degree to which jobs are programmed and routinized to specify and limit the discretion of the job holder. (c) *Centralization* refers to the degree to which formal authority is focused in the positions of senior management (see for example, Child, 1983).

These structural characteristic of organizations have been examined for their relations with other organizational and environmental characteristics. The former include, for example, the size, and technologies of the organization. The size of the organization – usually measured by the number of employees – frequently has been found to show systematic relations with structures. So, for example, complexity increases with size, and centralization decreases as numbers increase (see Child, 1983). The technology of the organization also has been related to structural characteristics.

The technology of an organization was defined in terms of the way 'the organization' transformed inputs into outputs. Woodward's research provides a well-known illustration of the application of this approach to manufacturing enterprises. Woodward (see Child, 1983) distinguished between 'small batch and unit', 'mass', and 'process' production systems. These she described as representing a scale of technical complexity, with process technologies being seen as most complex, and unit the least. She investigated these in 100 firms in the south-east of England. Her findings led her to conclude that each production system was associated with a different pattern of structural characteristics. There are now many studies which show systematic but complex relations between technologies and structures (Child, 1983). Debate has tended to focus on the extent to which technologies have simple causal effects on structural characteristics, and on the extent to which management can exercise choice over these arrangements.

Others have investigated relations between organization structures and environmental characteristics. This work includes the socio-technical systems studies of Rice, Emery and Trist, and others at the Tavistock Institute in London; the work of Burns and Stalker (1961), and that of Lawrence and Lorsch (1970). The environment, viewed as the Context of the organization, tends to be defined in terms of other organizations and forces which affect the organization but over which it has little control. So, for example, Burns and Stalker focused on 'mechanistic' (see earlier) and 'organismic' structural forms in the electronics industry. These firms had markets for their products which were rapidly changing; large-scale research and development activities were increasingly seen as sources of environmental turbulence and environmental complexity. Their research seemed to suggest that 'more successful firms' were structured in ways which were appropriate for their environments. Put very crudely, mechanistic structures appeared more appropriate in stable, simple, that is, 'certain' environments, and organismic in turbulent, complex, 'uncertain' environments.

Taken together, these studies of structure, technology and environmental characteristics, represent examples of the 'contingency' approach to organization. They illustrate many of the concepts and arguments which are implicit in large areas of organization theory and organizational behaviour. They have provided the empirical basis for arguments about how best to match organizations to their environments. They reflect an implicit, managerialist perspective in that they leave unquestioned the assumption of functional unity, and therefore, leave unquestioned the values by which organization is identified and organizational effectiveness judged. For example, socio-technical systems theory argues that social, technical, and economic values must jointly be optimized. Joint optimization often means sub-optimizing in the particular areas. Yet, as we have seen, individuals and groups are likely to differ over which values they seek to protect and promote. In sum, it seems a political perspective is preferable to a managerialist one.

Organizing: Political, Cognitive, and Social Processes

Critical Themes

The organic analogy, like many analogies, has certain strengths. However, analogies tend to get overstretched to the point where similarities are over-emphasized and important differences ignored. There are important differences between social and organic systems; excellent and extended critiques can be found elsewhere (for example, Buckley, 1967; Morgan, 1986). Here we wish only to continue the argument already begun. We will do so by developing three themes. The first theme concerns the unitary assumption which underlies biological, structural–functionalist approaches, an assumption which underplays the political qualities of organization. The second theme concerns the emphasis on relatively unchanging structures at the expense of a more dynamic, processual perspective. The third theme concerns the oversharp distinction between Person and Context, a distinction which ignores the extent to which Persons make their Contexts whilst also being made by them.

1. *The political qualities of organization.* Our first point concerns the failure to consider sufficiently political processes as a characteristic of organization. We have already shown why unitary and managerialist assumptions should be rejected. We indicated that values, and therefore goals, are not necessarily shared by all workers or all managers. We suggested that no particular group, including senior management, has values which are necessarily more legitimate than the values of any other group, be they shareholders, production management, craft workers, or whoever. We observed that groups differ in the extent to which they are able to protect and/or promote their own values and interests. From this we see that, for example,

senior management may only have the power to make their values and interests appear more legitimate than those of others. This political perspective offers a fundamental challenge to the assumption that social systems, like biological systems, have functional unity characterized by shared needs.

2. *A processual perspective.* Our second concern is with the treatment of social structures and functions as relatively unchanging. As we have seen, social structures have been taken to be comparable to biological structures. It seems that biological species evolve slowly in relation to their environments, making a relatively static, structural emphasis appropriate and efficient. Radical, disjunctive changes are rare in biological systems. Where social systems are concerned, such an emphasis is less obviously appropriate, particularly where individual organizations, members of the species so to speak, are concerned. The emphasis on structures understates the essentially processual and dynamic qualities of social organizations as systems of activity.

In the literatures of organizational characteristics described above, organizational structures are theorized as the relatively static characteristics of a relatively unchanging organizational whole. The whole is treated as though it can be adequately theorized independently of Persons and Contexts. The language of structures hinders attention to a more dynamic, processual perspective. It carries away attention to the making and performing of structures, and away from the different contributions that different actors make to those processes. The biological metaphor obscures the issue of functions by glossing the question of whose values and interests should set the standards by which functionality should be judged.

We take the view that social organization is better understood in processual terms. This requires attention to 'organizing' as an activity which is achieved in and through cognitive, political, and social processes. Translated into systems terms: structures emerge through functioning. They do so, not in relation to system needs, but in relation to the values, interests, and power of participants.

In systems terms, the 'parts' are interrelated, not by shared needs, but by the influential actions of persons past and present. These are reflected, for example, in operating procedures, workplace layouts, and in what is valued more generally. System parts are related by people who seek the resources that others may provide in order to help them add value to their lives (Hosking and Morley, forthcoming).

3. *Relations between Person and Organization.* The research and theory we have here reviewed draws oversharp and oversimple distinctions between Person and Organization, and between Organizations and their Contexts. The systems perspectives we have reviewed, both open and closed, treat organizations as though they have an objective, physical status, existing as entities, independent of peoples activities, interactions, and value-based cognitions. Persons are set apart from their Contexts and treated as basically passive, compelled into action by the physical realities of payment systems, work organization, and organization structures.

We suggested earlier that Persons, through their activities and social interactions, to some degree construct their own social realities. They create more or less widely shared constructions of their Contexts, how these relate to their values and interests, and what they must do to protect and promote the latter. These are what we have broadly referred to as 'cognitive processes', processes which are intertwined with the social and political. The significance of socially constructed realities cannot be overstated. Once they are recognized it becomes possible to theorize Person and Organization in commensurate terms.

Cognitive Processes

The reference to cognitive is here intended to be just about as broad as it could be. It is intended to refer to 'all processes involved in knowing' (see Hosking, 1988). Cognition is not simply a process in which given external realities are, as it were, registered; understandings are not defined as knowledge only when their truth value can be verified against an appropriate physicalist criterion. Rather, actors construct understandings (knowledge) in their heads, so to speak. Further, these processes are not 'lonely' (see earlier). Rather, they are more or less collective: actors construct views of their Contexts in interaction with others who also are constructing their realities. This means that cognitive processes are intertwined with social processes such as social exchange, social competition, negotiation, and social influence. By these means, actors produce descriptions of their Contexts which are to some degree shared. Terms such as schemas, scripts and ideologies have been invented to describe such descriptions or knowledge representations. Shared descriptions make possible co-ordinated action. Such agreements to describe and act exist in the context of disagreements, actual and potential. The making, supporting, and breaking of such agreements are processes of organizing (see Hosking and Morley, forthcoming).

Surprisingly few have attempted to theorize cognitive processes as the link between Person and Organization (see Pfeffer, 1981 for a discussion of these literatures). Of those who have, most have taken organizational procedures, strategies, and structures to be selected out of a more or less rational process of conscious choice. Given our present interest in cognitive processes, what we lack in particular is attention to the ways in which they are interwoven with social and political processes in the performance of organization. The theorists considered so far set Person and Organization apart and employed a physicalist view in which external 'structural' realities constrained the understandings and activities of workers. So far we have seen little attention paid to the ways actors more or less collectively construct what is taken to be real, that is, might make their Contexts meaningful. This general approach is often referred to as 'interpretive'.

The interpretive approach embraces wide differences of emphasis. The approach sometimes focuses, for example, on *social interaction* processes such as role-making. Sometimes the emphasis is on the *symbolic* qualities of interaction in which words, acts, roles and so on are recognized as signifiers of something which physically is not present. Sometimes the focus is on the *negotiated* qualities of interactions, and in particular, on the negotiation of meaning that is how something should be described and understood. Generally, concepts such as norms, values, and roles are argued to be the more or less shared creations of actors, who are seeking to make sense of activities and relationships. Organization structures are understood as actors' creations: created through the social interactions and relationships of actors, past and present. Actors are seen actively to create their Contexts in thought and deed. Organizations are seen, not as entities characterized by shared goals, but as created through the activities of individuals and groups. Actors negotiate some values, some meanings and some activities with others; they do so in a variety of groups and more or less temporary coalitions of interest. In so doing, they organize their worlds in relation to value (see, for example, Sims *et al.*, 1986).

Karl Weick is perhaps one of the best known interpretive theorists. He argues that cognitive processes characterize organizing in a very particular way: actors are said to 'put out there' their constructions of their Contexts, and to act in relation to their social realities: news organizations may create the realities which they report as news, hospitals may create the illnesses that they treat, governments may create the evidence which justifies their hostile acts.

Arguments in favour of social realities do not require that the existence of external realities either be denied or accepted. The point, and it is an important one, is that if we want to understand the organizing activities of actors, we need to know their constructions, how these are formed and reformed, and how these reflect their values and interests. Further, we need to recognize that such processes are necessarily political. Most ignore the parochial quality of values and interests, and fail to consider influence processes as they support *particular* values and interests.

Social Processes

To bring to life the social qualities of organization, theorists focus on for example: interpersonal relations, lateral (non-authority) and vertical (authority) relations; within and between group relations; cliques; coalitions; and networks. Theorists also may emphasize that individuals are members of many groupings and bring out the significance of this. The concepts developed for discussing relations include the concepts of role, norms, values, ideology, social status and influence, patterns of exchange, and negotiation. Of course these may be discussed as features of organization which are largely or minimally constrained by realities external to the individual – formal organization structures, technologies and the like. Equally, 'formal' organization may be considered only from the actors' point of view, or be ignored altogether. Our particular interest is in processual accounts which bring out the ways in which actors *create* these social relations. More particularly, we are especially interested in accounts which also emphasize the cognitive and political aspects of these processes.

Processual accounts of large collectivities are hard to find, for reasons which are perhaps obvious: to track the emergence of social relations, the emergence of systems of value and influence, is hard to do. Particularly rare are interpretive accounts, emphasising the sense-making aspects of activities and interactions and how these change.

Silverman's (1970) reinterpretation of the 'Wildcat Strike' (Gouldner, 1965) illustrates the way in which interdependent actors (individuals and groups) may have very different values and interests which are reflected in very different descriptions of their situations. His analysis illustrates the conflict relations that arise between their (different) definitions, and the asymmetric influence relations which mean that some actors are better able than others to make their definitions prevail. Gouldner described the development of an 'indulgency pattern': unwritten rules, tacitly agreed by management and workers, in which the latter were allowed to exercise considerable discretion in their work and in the use of company materials. These tacit agreements were breached when a new manager, not party to the agreement, promptly broke it. Silverman points to the processes of organization as revealed in the more or less temporary agreements of interdependent actors, seeking to protect and promote their own, different values.

Strauss also discussed Gouldner's work (Strauss 1978). He did so in order to make the point that the relationships described were characterized by a great deal of negotiation. He argued that Gouldner missed this because he failed to consider negotiation as a process – a process in which actors effectively decide what's acceptable, and what constitutes a violation of tolerance. Gouldner was interested primarily in the dysfunctions of formal bureaucracies – in the constraining effects of formal organization. Strauss suggested that had Gouldner attended to the processes of negotiation, to the opportunities for mobilizing a range of resources wider than thos provided by formal organization, he would have reached a very different conclusion: the newly appointed manager did not know how to negotiate successfully. We would like to see more work of this kind, work in which such arguments are develped to make central the political qualities of organizing processes.

Organization as Political Decision-Making

In 1981, Pfeffer observed that empirical studies of power and politics were rare in the literature on organizatians. There are a number of reasons why this is so. First, as we have seen, writings on organization have often been characterized by a managerialist bias in which the values and interests of (senior) management were taken as legitimate, and as shared by all participants. Associated biases are found, for example, in descriptions of managerial initiatives as 'industrial democracy', whilst worker initiatives are described as sabotage; in references to 'organizational' objectives, suggesting by implication that they are not therefore the partisan values of a particular group; in the concept of 'informal' organization, invented to describe the exercise of discretion which is not consistent with legitimate 'organizational' goals and procedures; by wording away, so to speak, the political quality of power through the language of authority and leadership, and as a result, defining political activity as illegitimate, as something which is marginal to organization.

Power and politics have been also obscured through focusing on organizational characteristics as realities independent of actors value-based cognitions and actions. Such a divorce forces attention away from the value-based qualities of organization. As a result, relatively few have described organization as expressed in the meaningful actions of identified individuals and groups. Power and politics have been hidden by the focus on relatively static structures; they are revealed when organizing processes are examined. Attention to processes, in their own right so to speak, can reveal the making, performance, and breaking of agreements to define situations in certain ways, through action, and therefore, to support and promote particular values. Such a focus puts politics centre stage, so to speak, as actors seek to protect and promote their own values whilst others attempt to do likewise.

Andrew Pettigrew's account of *The Politics of Organizational Decision-Making* (1973) provides a vivid illustration of many of our arguments. Pettigrew set out to explore the implications of assuming that organizations consist of diverse, interdependent interest groups who have to engage in joint decision-making to manage their relationships. He focused on a group of computer programmers who formed a coalition to protect their status (valued) which seemed to them to be threatened by changes in the status quo – the new elite of systems analysts. One of their most favoured influence strategies was in various ways to manipulate 'information'. So, for example, the programmers tried to manage meanings – to achieve acceptance of their definition of the situation – their descriptions of reality. They tried to gain acceptance for their view that theirs was extremely difficult work, work which could not be proceduralised, work which was both indispensable and uniquely provided by them.

The programmers acted to ensure that their expertise, their specialist information and skills, were kept on a rule-of-thumb basis – so as not to give it away so to speak.[1] They exercised close control over socialization into group norms (values) by insisting on a traditional apprenticeship training, rather than formal schemes run by others. Pettigrew also described the events involved in the purchase of a new computer system.

[1] See the earlier discussion of Taylor's arguments about 'scientific management'.

Three persons, Kenny, Reilly, and Turner, valued conflicting choices. Kenny was successfully able to promote his own values at the expense of others. He did so by using his relationships strategically. For example, he was able to act as a gatekeeper between his technical subordinates and the Board, and between the Board and the competing computer manufacturers. In this way, he was able to select and interpret 'information' which supported the particular view of reality which he wished to gain commitment, and filter out data which were inconsistent with that view.

Summary and Conclusion

We have focused our review on approaches to organization which set person and organization apart. We have directed attention to the ways in which such approaches fail adequately to theorise the processes through which persons more or less collectively make organization. We have argued that Person and Organization must be theorized in terms which are commensurate. When 'organization' is theorized as a Context independent of Persons' meaningful social actions, this is incommensurate with an adequate theory of Person. A theory of organizing is required. Such a theory should attend to the interrelated cognitive, social and political processes of organizing. This will require attention to social relations of collaboration and conflict, negotiation, exchange. These processes are grounded in, and contribute to, differences in power and influence. Such processes are grounded in value, and serve to protect and promote some values better than others. We have selected from the literature illustrations of aspects of these arguments. Elsewhere, we have attempted a systematic and detailed elaboration in relation to particular 'topics' (Hosking, 1988; Hosking and Morley, forthcoming). Work of this kind has much to recommend it.

References for Chapter 9

Buckley, W. (1967) *Sociology and Modern Systems Theory*, Prentice-Hall, Englewood Cliffs, N.J.

Burns, T. and Stalker, G. M. (1961, 1966) *The Management of Innovation*, Tavistock, London.

Child, J. (1977, 1983) *Organization: A Guide to Problems and Practice*, Harper and Row, London.

Gouldner, A. W. (1965) *Wildcat Strike*, Harper and Row, New York.

Hosking, D. M. (1988) 'Organizing, leadership and skilful process', *Journal of Management Studies*, 25(2), 147–66.

Hosking, D. M. and Morley, I. E. (forthcoming) *A Social Psychology of Organizing*, Harvester Wheatsheaf, London.

Lawrence, P. P. and Lorsch, J. W. (1967) *Organization and Environment: Managing Differentiation and Integration* Harvard University Press, Boston.

Mintzberg, H. (1983) *Structure in Fives: Designing Effective Organizations*, Prentice-Hall, Englewood Cliffs, N.J.

Morgan, G. (1986) *Images of Organization* Sage, London.

Morley, I. E. and Hosking, D. M. (1984) 'Decision-making and negotiation: Leadership and social skills', in Gruneberg, M. and Wall, T. (eds.) *Social Psychology and Organizational Behaviour*, Wiley, Chichester.

Parker, S. R., Brown, R. K., Child, J. and Smith, M. A. (1977) *The Sociology of Industry*, George Allen and Unwin, London.

Pettigrew, A. M. (1973) *The Politics of Organizational Decision Making*, Tavistock, London.

Pfeffer, J. (1981) *Power in Organizations* Pitman, Marshfield, Mass.

Pugh, D. S. (ed) (1971) *Organization Theory*, Penguin, Harmondsworth.

Rose, M. (1982) *Industrial Behaviour: Theoretical Development Since Taylor*, Penguin, Harmondsworth.

Silverman, D. (1970) *The Theory of Organizations*, Heinemann, London.

Sims, H. P. Gioia, D. A. and Associates (1986) *The Thinking Organization*, Jossey Bass, London.

Strauss, A. (1978) *Negotiations: Varieties, Contexts, Processes and Social Order*, Jossey Base, London.

Woodward, J. (1958) 'Management and technology', in Pugh, D. S. (ed), (1971) *Organization Theory*, Penguin, Harmondsworth.

10

Leadership and Supervision

MIKE SMITH
School of Management, UMIST

They had something to celebrate, so it was quite a party. A small research team in the North-west had upstaged Silicon Valley and had given the company a competitive edge with their refinement of the laser zapping of silicon chips. They were also drinking to build up their Dutch courage to help them endure a congratulatory speech by an executive from Headquarters. The speech took its predictable course: perfunctory appreciation; an acknowledgement of their world lead amongst laser zappers; an acknowledgement of the lead they had shown to other research teams within the company. The executive knew little about the technicalities of laser zapping but he considered himself an expert on the subject of leadership – the country needs more strong leaders. . . leaders are born not made. . . a leader must inspire awe in others. . . a leader must ruthlessly rivet everyone's attention to the objectives and make sure that there is no faltering or slacking until the goal is reached.

The leader of the laser zappers flushed with embarrassment. He knew that the reality of leadership was quite different. He knew that leadership had to be learned the hard way; he remembered the early days when his formal position as a leader contrasted strongly with his informal position, and he recalled that in leading his team he often had to modify his leadership style according to the task and the situation. He also recalled that, as leader, a great deal of his time was spent on things that were not directly related to the task but helped to ensure that his team was cohesive and could maximize the collective experience of its members.

Definitions of Leadership

Probably the first step in the study of any area is to define the subject. In the case of leadership, this is not so easy since people have used many definitions and there is no single universally accepted definition. However, the core of leadership is influencing other people. A leader is someone who influences other people to do things they otherwise would not. In other words, a leader is someone who influences the direction of other people's behaviour. This definition presents quite a lot of problems since in any social interaction, influence is mutual. Even the most lowly member of any group has *some* influence on the other members. Consequently, the essence of leadership becomes relative influence. A leader is someone who has more influence over others than they have over him or her. Coleman (1969) listed four main ways that a leader influences the direction of the group:

1. *Structuring the situation*: making it clear where the group is going and what has to be done;
2. *controlling group behaviour*: creating and enforcing appropriate rules;
3. *personifying the group*: acting as spokesperson to other groups and expressing the feelings and decisions of the group both within and outside the group;
4. *helping the group achieve its goals and potential*: mobilizing and organizing the group's resources and decisions.

Types of Leaders

Some writers emphasize particular aspects of the influence process. Power is often important (see French and Raven, 1959) and a leader is someone who can apply more power to others in the group than they can apply to him. The position of power in a relationship may be complex and arise in many ways. A leader may have power because he or she controls *rewards*, such as promotion or pay, which are wanted by the other members of the group. A leader may also have power because he or she has knowledge or *expertise* which others need. A leader may also have power because people identify with him and want to be like him (*referent power*). Leaders may also have *legitimate power* and *coercive power*. Either directly or indirectly most sources of power come down to reward power. Applying the concept of power to specific groups is quite complex. Different people may hold different types of power. One person may hold the key to material rewards. Another person may hold key technical knowledge. Someone else may be the person who is most admired. To add even greater complexity, the importance of the different types of power may vary from day to day. If the group is facing a technical problem, the person with technical knowledge will be the true leader. If there are material rewards to distribute the leader may be someone else.

Formal and Informal Leaders

In many situations, it is not sufficient to use a global definition of leadership. Two separate types need to be distinguished. First there are *formal leaders* who are usually imposed on a group and who occupy a well-defined position in an organization hierarchy. Often, but not always, formal leaders have reward and coercive power. Second, there are *informal leaders* who emerge from the group itself. Informal leaders usually have expert power or referent power. Another distinction is between *leader emergence* and *leader effectiveness*. Some people are good at getting themselves into leadership positions but are quite hopeless once they are there. Distinctions between formal and informal leaders or emergent and effective leaders need to be borne clearly in mind when reading the literature on leadership. Authors are not always clear about which type of leader they are investigating. Many of the apparent contra-dictions in research results would evaporate if they clearly defined the type of leadership under investigation. Usually, we are most concerned with the effectiveness of informal leaders. Usually, we investigate some aspect of emergent leaders.

Traits of Leadership

Most organizations are totally convinced that leadership is a good thing and they want more. One way of providing more leadership is to identify the type of person who becomes a leader. People who fit the description can then be hired and put into formal leadership positions. During the 1940s and 1950s a great deal of effort was put into identifying the traits of leaders. In a typical investigation, the characteristics of a large sample of students would be measured either by a fairly crude questionnaire or on the basis of interview ratings. The characteristics measured included such things as intelligence, emotional adjustment, extroversion, dominance, empathy and masculinity. The students would be split into small groups and asked, as a group, to complete some ambiguous tasks. On the basis of behaviour in these artificial situations observers would note who emerged as leaders. An attempt would then be made to identify those traits which these leaders held in common.

This genre of leadership research was summarized in two influential reviews (Stodgill, 1948; and Mann, 1959). These reviews were interpreted as saying that there were few, if any, worthwhile and stable relationships between leadership and personal traits. Indeed, one very influential textbook in the 1980s commented, 'Stodgill (1948) and Mann (1959) have demonstrated no relationship between personality factors and leadership effectiveness' (Landy, 1985). As a result of these conclusions, interest in identifying the traits of leaders waned and psychologists turned elsewhere in their attempt to provide organizations with the leadership they so earnestly desired. As we shall see later, the conclusion was wrong!

One-Dimensional Leadership Styles: Autocracy-Democracy

If traits did not hold the key to improving leadership then perhaps the style that leaders adopted would be a better area for research. If the right leadership style could be identified it might then be possible to train leaders to adopt the right style. Three major investigators focused upon one aspect of leadership style.

Lewin, Lippit and White

In the mid-1930s Lewin, Lippit and White (1939) conducted what is probably *the* classic experiment on leadership style. The study involved 10-year-olds in a boys' club. The boys were organized into small groups engaged in hobbies and led by an adult. Lewin, Lippit and White arranged for the leaders to adopt one of three styles on an autocratic–democratic continuum.

1. *authoritarian leaders* made all the decisions and told the boys what to do;
2. *laissez-faire leaders* left everthing up to the group;
3. *democratic leaders* encouraged and helped the group to make decisions.

The leaders took it in turns to adopt the three styles so their traits could not influence the results. The groups were then observed as they went about doing their hobbies. The results were interesting. The groups with authoritarian leaders worked well enough when the leader was present but slacked off noticeably when he was absent. The group atmosphere was characterized either by tension and hostility or by passivity. The groups led by the *laissez-faire* leaders did little work and achieved little. The group lead by the democratic leader did as much, if not more work than the authoritarian group *and* they continued to work at the same rate when the leader left the room. The group atmosphere was positive, cohesive and involved.

Tannenbaum and Schmidt

Tannenbaum and Schmidt (1959) refined the ideas of Lewin, Lippitt and White and applied them to the work of managers. They also saw authority as a key aspect of leadership styles. But, instead of isolating three types, they saw authority as a continuum. Figure 10.1 shows that, at the authoritarian end, a manager uses a great deal of power to coerce followers into action. Because of the high level of power he or she simply *tells* followers what to do. As the manager's power decreases a slightly different style is needed. The manager still makes the decision and tightly controls subordinates' behaviour but he or she will make some attempt to make this palatable and will try to *sell* the decision to subordinates. As the manager's authority weakens further the manager will retain the key strategic functions and will define the situation and possible courses of action. He or she will then *test* which course is best by asking subordinates for comment and opinions. The framework is set by the manager and he or she reserves the right to accept or reject the comments of subordinates as he or she thinks fit. As the authority retained by the manager decreases still further to the point where significant authority lies with the subordinate, a *consulting style* is adopted. In participative leadership the manager retains very little authority to him or herself. A totally participative style is adopted in

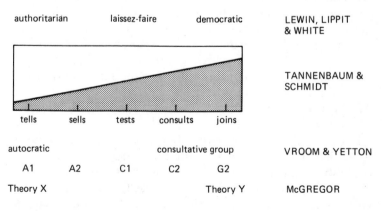

Figure 10.1 *Comparison of one-dimensional models of leadership style*

which the manager and the subordinate jointly review the situation and reach a joint decision on the appropriate action. The manager is said to have a *joining* management style.

According to Tannenbaum and Schmidt, an effective manager is one who can move along the continuum selecting the style which is most appropriate to the situation. Appropriateness will be the result of three major forces. First there are forces in the *manager*. Each manager will have their own blend of characteristics such as self-confidence, ability to tolerate ambiguous situations or, perhaps, sociability. These characteristics will predispose a manager to adopt one style rather than another. For example, an insecure, unsociable and intolerant manager might be more likely to adopt a 'tells' style of management. Forces in the *subordinate* also influence the style of management. Inexperienced, immature and uncommitted subordinates may force even the most participative manager to adopt an autocratic, telling, style. Finally, the nature of the *situation* helps to determine the management style. If there is little time to make simple decisions that are vital, again a 'telling' style is probably most appropriate.

Vroom and Yetton

A theory by Vroom and Yetton (1973) focused on the way that leaders make decisions. They produced a spectrum of decision-making styles which was similar to the spectrum proposed by Tannenbaum and Schmidt. When making decisions a manager can be autocratic (A1 or A2), consultative (C1 or C2) or delegate the decision to the group (G2). He can:

A1. make the decision himself using the information available to him at the time;

A2. get the necessary information from subordinates and then make the decision;

C1. share the problem with subordinates as individuals, get their ideas and then decide himself;

C2. share the problem with subordinates as a group, get their ideas and then decide himself;

G2. share the problem with subordinates as a group, get their ideas and accept decision which has group support.

Like Tannenbaum and Schmidt, Vroom and Yetton thought that a successful manager would be someone who was able to move about the continuum to select the range which was most appropriate to the situation. They produced a decision tree to help managers locate the most appropriate style. Very often it boiled down to three choices:

1. If acceptance does not matter or can be taken for granted use an autocratic style;
2. if acceptance by subordinates is important, and if there is a chance it might not be accepted, use a consultative style;
3. if subordinates share organizational goals, let the group decide.

Vroom and Yetton's actual decision tree is inordinately complicated and involves seven steps and multiple nodes.

McGregor

The final major theorist who focused on a single dimension of leadership was McGregor (1960). McGregor's idea) were not based on empirical research but arose from his experience. In some ways McGregor added very little to the underlying ideas but his work does shed some light on management philosophy and behaviour of leaders occupying extreme points of the continuum. McGregor suggested that managers hold implicit assumptions about the nature of subordinates. These assumptions influence the leadership style which managers adopt. He identified two sets of assumptions, *theory X* and *theory Y*.

Managers who hold theory X believe that subordinates dislike work and will avoid it if they can. Consequently people must be made to work either by threats (dismissal or other disciplinary action) or, slightly more benignly, by inducements) (bonuses, raises). Under theory X, subordinates cannot be trusted and need close control and supervision. Managers who hold theory Y believe that people are naturally active and enjoy work. The main task for a theory Y manager is to enable people to work productively by making sure that the goals are clear and that efforts are properly co-ordinated within an efficient organization. A final aspect of McGregor's thoughts is that management styles can become a self-fulfilling prophecy. A manager who treats people as workshy and needing constant supervision is likely to produce resentment among subordinates who as a result dislike their work and avoid it whenever possible.

Clearly the works of Lewin, Lippit and White, Tannenbaum and Schmidt, Vroom and Yetton, and McGregor have much in common. They all identify one dimension of leadership. That dimension seems to be concerned with overt use of power and authoritarianism on the one hand and participation and democracy on the other. Unfortunately, as these ideas were tested, it became clear that other things were involved because, for example, some autocratic leaders were successful whereas others were failures. Considerations of this kind led on to a more sophisticated approach involving two dimensions.

Two-Dimensional Leadership Styles: Authority and Consideration

The two-dimensional leadership styles were arrived at more or less independently, at two centres in the mid-west USA. The *Ohio State Studies* were conducted by Stodgill and Hemphill and their colleagues. Researchers at Ohio State wrote out 1800 different things that managers might do. After eliminating close duplications they were left with a final list of 150 activities which they believed covered nine categories. The 150 questions were cast into a questionnaire called the Leader Behaviour Description Questionnaire (LBDQ) (Hemphill and Coons, 1957). The LBDQ was administered to a large number of people. When the results were analyzed, it was found that there were two main categories rather nthan the nine the researchers had expected (Halpin and Winer, 1957). The two factors were called *consideration* and *initiating structure*. Consideration is the extent to which a manager is concerned about the wellbeing and the feelings of his subordinates. Structure is the extent to which managers organize, define and control the work of their subordinates. A great deal of research was conducted to assess the effects of these factors. Research by Fleishman, for example, showed that considerate managers tended to achieve a lower turnover of subordinates and fewer grievances against them. Managers who scored highly on structure tended to have a high turnover of subordinates and a high rate of grievances.

Meanwhile, at *Michigan State* University, Renis Likert (1961) and co-workers were investigating the differences between low productivity units and high productivity units. A part of their work concerned managerial style. They too established two primary dimensions which they called production emphasis and employee emphasis. The similarities with the structuring and consideration dimensions identified at Ohio are obvious. They also found that there was a strong relationship between productivity and employee emphasis.

The findings from the Ohio and Michigan studies were very popular and influential. Many people adopted the findings and developed them into management training packages. One of the most successful was Blake and Mouton's (1964) Man-

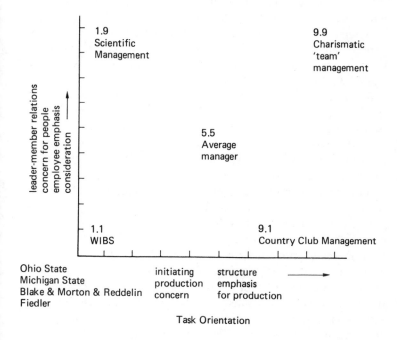

Figure 10.2 *Comparison of two-dimensional models of leadership style*

agerial Grid. They took the two factors and developed them into nine-point scales. When set at right angles, they formed a 9 × 9 grid. With the help of a questionnaire managers could be placed on a grid according to their managerial style. Blake and mouton Mouton then developed descriptions of the extreme styles.

A 9.1 manager has very high concern for people but little concern for production. This type of manager believes that if you avoid conflict and look after people, productivity will automatically follow. This type of manager is often called the 'country club' manager since his main task is simply to keep everybody happy.

A 1.9 manager has a high concern for production but a low concern for people. This type of manager emphasizes efficiency, good scheduling and a scientific approach to management. The danger with this type of management is that it alienates subordinates so that they leave the group or organization so that there is no-one left to undertake production. Managers with this style are often called scientific managers.

A 1.1 manager is neither concerned with production or with people. He or she gets little done and does not keep people happy. Sometimes 1.1 managers are called WIBs (Weak, Inefficient Bastards!)

5.5 managers are the compromisers who try, probably like most managers, to strike a balance between people and productivity. Often this type of manager is left with the worst of both worlds. They are not sufficiently people-oriented to earn the loyalty of their subordinates nor do they achieve the production required by their superiors.

The ideal type of manager is the 9.9 manager. This is the team manager where production is achieved through people. The idea of training based on the Managerial Grid is to establish the style that a manager adopts and then encourage him or her to move nearer the ideal 9.9 position.

A great deal of work was conducted on the implications of a two-dimensional view of leadership. There did, indeed, seem to be a consistent relationship between a people-oriented style and work group productivity. However, the situation is not straightforward. Some researchers agreed that there was a link but thought that it worked the opposite way round. Good productivity would allow a supervisor to be more considerate to subordinates. The two-factor theories encountered a second problem. Even with this greater sophistication, only a small proportion of managerial behaviour was explained. In a search for a more powerful explanation, researchers turned to a three-factor theory of leadership.

Three-Factor Leadership

Reddin's 3D Grid

The simplest modification of the basic people *vs* task model of leadership was made by Reddin (1970). He took the Blake and Mouton approach and said that for each of the quadrants there were effective and ineffective modes of action as follows:

1.1 Low people orientation, low task orientation:
    effective – bureaucratic approach
    ineffective – desertion of the situation
1.9 Low people orientation, high task orientation
    effective – benevolent autocracy
    ineffective – autocracy
9.1 High people orientation, low task orientation
    effective – developer
    ineffective – missionary
9.9 High people orientation, high task orientation
    effective – executive
    ineffective – compromiser

For example, a 9.9 manager could be quite ineffective if he or she only carefully balanced vested interests and the objectives to produce a compromise situation. One person may maintain that $2 + 2 = 4$. Another may say that $2 + 2 = 6$. A compromise manager would say that $2 + 2 = 5$. On the other hand, a 9.9 manager could act as an executive. He or she would work out ways of resolving the issue so that the correct answer was reached but no-one would feel a loss of face or humiliated.

Fiedler's Contingency Model

Fiedler (1967) refocused the two basic dimensions. Instead of using people orientation he focused upon leader–member relations. But he retained the idea of task orientation. Fiedler resurrected the concept of power as the third dimension of leadership. According to Fiedler, there were three aspects of leadership leading to eight possibilities called octants:

1.   good relations, high structure, strong power
2.   good relations, high structure, low power
3.   good relations, low structure, strong power
4.   good relations, low structure, low power

5.   poor relations, high structure, strong power
6.   poor relations, high structure, weak power
7.   poor relations, low structure, high power
8.   poor relations, low structure, low power.

Fiedler attempted to link this with the type of person who was the leader. The way that he attempted to measure this type of person was with the least-preferred–co-worker-scale (LPCWS). The idea behind the LPCWS was quite simple. First, the leader would nominate the person in his or her group with whom they would least like to work. Second, the leader would then rate this person on a number of character-istics such as pleasant or unpleasant, friendly or unfriendly. A total of eight aspects of this kind were used. The LPCWS was held to be a particularly sophisticated measurement. A manager who disliked someone (the least preferred co-worker) but who could still recognize the positive attributes of that person would probably be a better manager than someone who disliked a person and who let that dislike alter their judgement on all the merits and demerits of that person.

   Fiedler then linked the eight octants to the results of the LPCWS as shown in Figure 8.3. A leader who could dislike working with someone but who could also appreciate their advantages was quite different from a leader who could dislike

someone and would therefore think that they had no advantages. The former would thrive in some situations and the
latter would thrive in others. The way that Fiedler linked the
LPCWS scores with the octants of his contingency model are
given in Figure 10.3.

A leader who underrated people who he or she disliked would
be best when dealing with situations in octants 1, 2, 7 and 8. A
leader who would be able to appreciate even those who they
disliked would be best when dealing with situations in octants
3, 4, 5 and 6. To many people in the 1970s, Fiedler's theory
was magic. It represented the best research in organizational
psychology and had the allure of applicability to specific
situations.

Slowly, however, it began to dawn that Fiedler's theory left
something to be desired – just how did it square with the
facts? Peters *et al.* (1985) did a meta-analysis of 11 laboratory
studies. The laboratory studies did produce evidence to
support Fiedler's ideas. Peters also did a meta-analysis of 12
field studies. The results were quite discouraging. Fiedler's
theory was supported in three octants but it was not supported in the five remaining octants. It would thus seem that
contingency theory is something which exists in a laboratory
but does not exist in realistic situations.

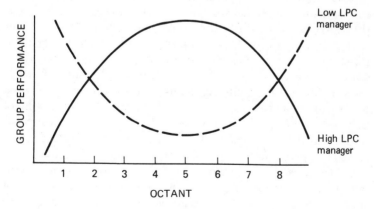

Figure 10.3   *Relationship between LPC score, performance and octant of situation
as predicted by Fiedler*

Newer Theories of Leadership

A response to the disappointing results from dimensional theories has been the development of a new set of leadership theories. The three main ones are path–goal theory, the vertical dyad linkage model and transformational leadership.

Path–Goal Theory

In a nutshell the *path–goal* theory (House and Mitchell, 1974) says that leaders will be effective if they help the followers attain their goals. It was once hailed as a sophisticated theory which integrated job satisfaction, motivation and leadership. There are two basic ideas:

1. A leader's actions are acceptable if the followers think it will bring them satisfaction either immediately or in the future;
2. subordinates will make more effort if they believe the effort will bring them the rewards they want and if they see the leader helping those efforts.

The task of the leader is therefore to use a style which leads a subordinate to believe that the leader is helping them reach their goals. The best style will depend on two things: the characteristics of the subordinates and the characteristic of the environment. For example, if subordinates who feel that they have a lot of ability themselves are usually less ready to accept guidance and direction from a leader. Another characteristic of subordinates is their locus of control. The locus of control concerns a person's beliefs about who controls their lives. People with an internal locus of control believe that they control their own lives. People with external locus of control believe other people control their lives. According to path–goal theory of leadership non-directive styles of leadership should be used with 'internals' and a directive style should be used with externals. Internals like to be asked, externals like to be told. A third important characteristic of the followers in their latent authoritarianism – the degree to which people see things in rigid, often moralistic, categories and their acceptance of formal authority. Not surprisingly, directive styles of leadership are more appropriate with authoritarian followers. The characteristics of the environment also determine appropriate leader behaviour. There are three main environmental characteristics: the task, the authority system and the primary work group. The more a task is unpleasant or dissatisfying, the more a directive style of leadership is disliked.

According to path–goal theories of leadership, leaders should strive to achieve three main things: (1) help subordinates decide on the goals that are important to them; (2) remove obstacles that lie between subordinates and their goals; (3) reward and encourage subordinates to achieve their goals.

Unfortunately, path–goal theory has been criticized on two grounds. The first is largely a matter of semantics. In path–goal theory the leader has to follow the group's aspirations. If this is so, can he or she really be said to be leading the group? The second criticism is a matter of data. Many studies have failed to obtain results that support the theory. Indeed, some studies have produced results which are the reverse of what the theory would predict (see House and Singh, 1987).

Vertical Dyad Linkage Theory

The vertical dyad linkage model (VDLM) grew out of mutual influence theory. Leadership is seen to be a series of relationships, *a dyad*, between two people – the leader and the follower. This dyadic relationship is much like any other dyadic relationship in the sense that both people influence the other. But in a leadership situation the leader has more power to influence the follower than vice versa. In a sense the dyad is a vertical one. Dansereau, Grean and Haga (1975) based a theory of leadership on these ideas. Leaders operate by forming special relationships with some subordinates and not others. Generally, they judge subordinates on two main things: their competence and the degree to which they can be trusted. Subordinates with these characteristics become members of a special in-group. They do more than is formally required of them and they are given tasks which are more vital to the group's effective performance. 'In-group' subordinates receive more support and attention from their leaders. Members in the 'out-group' do the more routine tasks and it is more likely that formal authority is used to influence them. The VDLT has important implications for other theories of leadership. If the VDLT is correct, it is useless to talk about average group characteristics in the way that Vroom and Yetton, and Fiedler do. Research results seem to support VDLT. It helps predict turnover of group members and job satisfaction.

Transformational Leadership

Path–goal theory and to a lesser extent the VDLT focus on the balance of exchange between what the leader offers and what the follower gives. Theories of these types are sometimes called transactional theories of leadership. Some workers say that real leaders do more than exchange cost-benefits with followers, they drastically alter the followers: they transform their behaviour. *Transformational Leadership* (Burns, 1978) is closely related to Charismatic Leadership. Instead of focusing on the style of the leader, they focus on the emotions and feelings that their followers have towards work, self-esteem, trust, and the motivation to perform above and beyond the call of duty. Transformational leaders are those who provide their followers with a vision of the future in which their lives will be better and more meaningful. The achievement of charismatic and transformational leaders is to turn humdrum followers into people who have higher self-esteem and who have a mission in life and work longer hours. A particularly important finding is that transformational leaders are able to overcome the effects of poor conditions and productivity. House (1985) classified US presidents into charismatic and non-charismatic leaders and he then looked at the record of the two groups. Charismatic presidents tended to be re-elected or assassinated! Only one of the non-charismatic presidents was given a second term. The charismatic leaders took stronger actions, were more prestigious and accomplished more. Research suggests that transformational leaders have three main effects on their followers. The largest factor which accounted for 66 per cent of their impact was the faith and inspiration provided by the leader. Two smaller factors involved consideration of individuals and intellectual stimulation. The degree to which transformational leadership is relevant to commercial organizations is debatable. Commercial concerns and organizational realities may mean that charismatic leaders are unlikely to emerge and they might be quite dangerous if they do: their charisma may lead others to ignore basic realities and put the organization's viability in jeopardy. However, charismatic and transformational leadership are clearly relevant to other organizations such as voluntary, reform or political organizations.

The Resurrection of Trait Theory

An astute reader will have noticed that the research on charismatic leaders indicated that they had certain traits in common. But, earlier in this chapter it was noted that many researchers had abandoned the idea that leadership is linked to specific traits. In fact, in recent years there has been a notable turn of opinion. This change has been brought about by the realization that many of the earlier studies were very crude. They used small samples Elementary statistical laws say that results based on small samples are bound to be erratic. Consequently, it is little wonder that early trait theorists could not find consistent results. The early studies also used very artificial situations using student groups that operated over relatively short periods of time.

Equally, the early studies did not measure leadership very well – often it was just a subjective rating by one person. If the criterion is measured badly it is almost impossible for other things to correlate with it – for example if a micrometer is calibrated against a hand drawn scale the micrometer seems quite inaccurate. The identification of these problems led investigators to look again at trait research and the work of Stodgill and Mann. One of the early conclusions was that much of Stodgill and Mann's work had been misrepresented. For example there had been 196 attempts to relate intelligence to leadership. Eighty-eight per cent of these attempts had yielded positive relations and in 47 per cent of these attempts the relationship was statistically significant. In 1986 Lord, De Vader and Alliger reanalysed the data using the techniques of meta-analysis (see Chapter 3). They found that there were clear correlations between leadership and intelligence (.52), masculinity (.34), conservatism (.22) and emotional adjustment (.21). In view of the fact that the technique of meta-analysis could not compensate for poor measurement of personality and the artificiality of the designs, these results are quite surprising.

Recently, Fiedler (1989) has suggested what is in essence a trait theory of leadership – the *Cognitive Resource Utilization Theory (CRUT)*. The basic idea behind CRUT is that under normal circumstances, the leader's intelligence is a crucial aspect of both his or her ability as a leader. The leader uses intelligence to identify goals, structure the situation and control the behaviour of the followers so that the goal is reached. Thus, the leader's intelligence is a key resource for the group and it normally correlates highly with group success. However, things are not always normal. Under certain circumstances, there are things which stop the leader utilizing his or her intelligence. Under these circumstances there is little or no relationship between intelligence and leader success. Fiedler maintains that there are three main factors which prevent a leader using the resources of his or her intelligence to the full. Probably the most important is stress – especially stress between the leader and his or her boss. Stress from the job such as time or production pressure is not too important. Stress from the boss, however, diverts the leader's attention to thoughts such as, 'How can I avoid another conflict?', or, 'How can I get another job' It is suggested that stress with superiors inhibits the leader from analysing a situation, making plans, communicating to the group and monitoring events. Other important factors which prevent leaders using their intelligence are poor interpersonal relationships and a non-directive style. In general, the research data gives quite strong support to cognitive resource utilization theory. But it is a very recent theory and much more work is needed.

Cynical Views of Leadership

Looking back on half a century of research into leadership is quite depressing. What it amounts to is a seemingly endless succession of theories which hold sway for a few years and then fall because of lack of empirical support. Part of the problem is caused by different authors using diffierent terms to describe what is almost the same idea. Another part of the problem arises because it is difficult to pin down the cause and effect (for example, does a considerate leader give rise to a productive group or, does a productive group give rise to a considerate leader?)

Some researchers take quite a cynical view of leadership and influence. They doubt whether leaders actually influence the direction of the behaviour of their followers. Writers such as Calder (1977) and House and Baetz (1979) say that the direction a group takes will be largely determined by outside forces and the situation the group faces. However, the group comes to believe that the direction was influenced by one person – their leader. According to this *attribution view* of leadership the leader is the person who is best able to persuade the group that he or she was responsible for things which were to happen in any event. In this analysis of leadership, the main requirements are to be in the right place at the right time and to be able to persuade others that you made it so.

Others such as Manz (1986) try to avoid the problem of leadership altogether. Are leaders at all necessary to direct the energies of a group? Maybe not. Perhaps the same ends could be achieved by devising jobs which are more motivating, promoting professionalism and formalizing plans so that they are clear to all. Particularly important leadership substitutes might be self-monitoring and self-management, either by individuals or by the group.

References for Chapter 10

Blake, R. R. and Mouton, J. S. (1964) *The Management Grid*, Gulf Publishing Co., Houston.

Burns, J. M. (1978) *Transformational Leadership*, Harper and Row, New York.

Calder, B. J. (1977) An attribution theory of leadership. In Straw, B. M. and Salanick, G. R. (eds), *New directions in organisational behaviour* St. Clair, Chicago.

Coleman, J. C. (1969) *Psychology and Effective Behaviour*, Scott Foresman, Glenview, Illinois.

Dansereau, F., Grean, G. and Haga, W. (1975) 'A vertical dyad linkage approach to leadership in formal organisations', *Organizational Behaviour and Human Performance*, 13, 46–78.

Fiedler, F. E. (1989) 'The effective utilisation of intellectual abilities and job relevant knowledge in group performance:cognitive resource theory and an agenda for the future', *Applied Psychology: An International Review*, 38, 3, 289–304.

French, J. R. P. and Raven, B. (1959) 'The bases of social power', in Cartwright, D. (ed) *Studies in Social Power*, Institute for Social Research, University of Michigan, Ann Arbor, Michigan.

Halpin, A. W. and Winer, B. J. (1957) 'A factorial study of leader behaviour description', Stodgill, R. M. and Coons, A. E. (eds.) *Leader Behaviour: its Description and Measurement*, Bureau of Business Research, Ohio State University, Columbus.

Hemphill, J. K. and Coons, A. E. (1957) 'Development of the Leader Behaviour Description Questionnaire', in Stodgill, R. M. and Coons (eds.) *Leader Behaviour: its Description and Measurement*, Bureau of Business Research, Ohio State University, Columbus.

House, R. J. (1985) *Research contrasting the behaviour and effect of reputed charismatic versus non-charismatic US Presidents*, presented at Annual General meeting of the Administrative Science Association, Montreal, Canada.

House, R. J. and Baetz, M. L. (1979) Leadership: some empirical generalizations and new research directions. In Straw, B. (ed.) Research in organisational behaviours (vol 1) J A. I Press, Greenwich, CT.

House, R. J. and Mitchell, T. (1974) Path–goal theory of leadership, *Journal of Contemporary Business*, 3, 81–98.

House, R. J. and Singh, J. V. (1987) 'Organisational behaviour: some new directions for I/O Psychology', *Annual Review of Psychology*, 38, 669–718.

Landy, F. J. (1985) *Psychology of Work Behaviour*, Dorsey Press, Homewood, Illinois.

Lewin, K., Lippitt, R. and White, R. K. (1939) 'Patterns of Aggressive Behaviour in Experimentally created Social Climates', *Journal of Social Psychology*, 10, 271–301.

Likert, R. (1961) *New Patterns of Management*, McGraw-Hill, New York.

Lord, R. G., De Vader, C. L. and Alliger, G. M. (1986) 'A meta-analysis of the relation between personality traits and leadership perceptions: an application of validity generalisation procedures', *Journal of Applied Psychology*, 71, 402–10.

Mann, R. D. (1959) 'A review of the relationships between personality in small groups', *Psychological Bulletin,* 56, 241 270.

Manz, C. (1986) 'Self leadership:towards an expanded theory of self influence processes in organisations', *Academy of Management Review.* 11, 585–600.

McGregor, D. (1960) *The Human Side of the Enterprise,* McGraw-Hill, New York.

Peters, L. H., Hartke, D. D. and Pohlmann, J. T. (1985) 'Fiedler's contingency theory of leadership: an application of the meta-analysis procedures of Schmidt and Hunter', *Psychological Bulletin.* 97, 2, 274–85.

Stodgill, R. M. (1948) 'Personal factors associated with leadership: a review of the literature', *Journal of Psychology,* 25, 35–71.

Tannenbaum, R. and Schmidt, W. H. (1958) 'How to choose a leadership Pattern', *Harvard Business Review,* 36, 95–101.

Vroom, V. H. and Yetton, P. (1973) *Leadership and Decision Making,* University of Pittsburgh Press, Pittsburgh.

11

Change in Organizations

STEPHEN FINEMAN
School of Management, University of Bath

We are told that the pace of life in the late twentieth century is speeding up, if not hurtling along. In 1970 Alvin Toffler warned of 'future shock', where the super-mobile employee had to keep running faster in order to survive. Now rapid technological change has created organizations which do not require many people at all, let alone ones who run fast. Production and services are achieved by button pushers, seated at flickering computer terminals and fax machines. Electronic and mechnical slaves do much of the work. We seem unsure as to where all this will lead. Some are apocalyptic in their predictions: we are on an inexorable route to a deskilled life, void of job satisfaction. Others see light at the end of the tunnel: ingenious information technologies will provide the opportunity for exciting new ways of collaboration.

A high-tech view of the world of work fits with what is happening in many industries and services – but it is a partial picture. The pressures for change from new technologies, and other sources, are powerfully matched by forces for non-change: stability and the preservation of the old. Inherent in the very notion of organization is the reduction of uncertainty and protection of what one already has. A peaceful, predictable life is a thing to be treasured, not cast to the whims of 'the market', the latest computerized system, or to the whims of the next managing director. Old hands in organizations tell stories about ambitious programmes for change which ultimately flounder, ending at the point where they began. Some seem to amount to no more than rearranging the deck chairs on the Titanic. A long-serving executive at Co-Operative Retail Services (a once-potent retailing force in the United Kingdom) confided in me his despair that, even after successive restructurings of their product and style operations, they were still finding it difficult to survive.

So change, its extent and its manipulation, has something to do with the very lifeblood of an organization. Not just large commercial corporations (which get most attention) but businesses and services of all sorts, from the village shop and the doctor's surgery to the social services department and government offices. There are inevitable tensions between maintaining an organizational order and reforming it. People at work are likely to feel a tug in both directons. Old habits and familiar routines die hard – and so they should. They have taken a long time to form and have often served their owners well; hence it is not surprising that people will resist change. On the other hand, a very predictable work life can be boring and lack creative sparkle. Conflicts can turn out to be more destructive than constructive. Gradually (or sometimes suddenly) the viability, or survival, of an enterprise can become threatened. The need for change in these circumstances may be overwhelming. But in what direction? How can it be achieved? This chapter will address these questions.

Assumptions and Techniques

The study of organizational change is seductive in that it holds promise of *useful* enlightenment – the discovery of a technique 'that works'. A glance at the 'management' shelves of bookshops provides a flavour of that promise. There, between very glossy covers, are the stories of those who have found the secret – which can soon be yours. From Peters and Waterman (1982) we are informed about the key characteristics of 'excellent' cultures and, more recently, about how we can learn 'to love change' (Peters, 1987). Blanchard and Johnson (1981) tell us how it is a matter of managing better by the minute, literally. Lee Iacocca (1986) shows how his American drive to achieve and his deep suspicion of accountants ('bean counters'), can move corporations as vast and complex as Chrysler. Local heroes, such as Michael Edwardes (1983) and John Harvey-Jones (1988) take us with them on their recent journeys as top executives in, respectively, British Leyland and ICI. Their techniques and skills at weaving between the interests of managers, unions and government are portrayed as testimonies to their effectiveness at managing change.

What these people show us (apart from something of the politics of publishing 'instant' management texts) is that the magic required to achieve change can come from very different spells. That is confusing. How do we judge what type of change is required? And how is such change to be achieved? The research in the area should help clear the air.

An initial impulse is to examine what we know about the strengths and weaknesses of different techniques for bringing about change. The tack has merit, but such pragmatism can be arid without a firm context for the techniques. Furthermore, the number of available methods for achieving change is becoming bewildering – over 350 are listed in a recent review of the area (Huczynski, 1987). It is more helpful to start elsewhere – with the assumptions we hold about how an organization functions. In other words, how we create or manage change in an organization depends first and foremost on how we think that organization works – and, as will be apparent, there is more than one set of principles to consider. The assumptions we take for granted may be the first thing that should be challenged, before we latch on to one or another change technique. Rarely is this a problem for successful managers who, operating at a particular time and place, use their intuition in appraising the organization, and seem to get it about right. For those of us with less of a flair for diagnosing and managing change, there are perspectives from social science to consider.

Perspective 1: Organizations are Rational/ Behaviouristic

The roots of this perspective go back to some of the earliest theorizing about organization. Rational/behaviouristic thinking starts from the premise that organizations exist to accomplish goals prescribed by 'superior' people (now known as managers and executives). The goals are achieved through the standardization of behaviour and tasks, tied together by an appropriate structure – a specific arrangement of people, a chain of command and job responsibilities. People work towards task goals because there are financial and security rewards in doing so. The rules have to be followed and superiors ensure that people cannot indulge their inclination to duck them. Amongst the doyens of this perspective we find Frederick 'Speedy' Taylor (1911) whose attempts to programme every physical movement of labourers took the principle of rational control of work methods to new heights (or unfortunate depths, as would have critics of Taylorism). Also in the early twentieth century Max Weber (1947) was showing how the rise of capitalism favoured formal, rational means of doing things, and the co-ordination of efforts through bureaucratic procedure. He argued that bureaucracy, with its sense of a place for everything and everything in its place, may not be perfect, but it suited well the rational pursuit of profit and the co-ordination of complex activities and services.

Organizations, from this perspective, look distinctly militaristic and owe much of their rationale to organized warfare. Terms such as targets, mission, commands, battlefield, enemies and troops can be found in companies with products as diverse as chocolate bars to microprocessors. A casual observer of the precision of High Street hamburger production will witness a clear, and garish, expression of up-to-date Taylorism and bureaucracy. Rational/behaviouristic principles are deeply rooted in the design of a vast proportion of organizations: characteristically symbolized by the organizational chart, job descriptions, and the rule book.

Changing a rational/behaviouristic organization means, essentially, restructuring. If the purpose or objective of the enterprise is ill-served by the present structure then a new structure can be devised to achieve a better fit. There is an industry of experts concerned with rearranging roles, relationships, technologies and the co-ordination of activities, to provide a more 'sensible' shape and style organization. The experts journey under various labels – such as personnel,

work study, organization and methods, information technology and systems engineer. Together they can recast the
organization in a form which is structurally more efficient – or
such is their claim. There is now detailed guidance available
on the type of structure which best suits a particular organization – according to its particular configuration of goals, needs,
history, tasks and markets. For example, Henry Mintzberg
(1983) describes a 'simple structure' which is appropriate for
young, small, organizations with a highly controlling top
manager, compared with more elaborate 'divisionalized form'
which applies to organizations which have a strong middle
management, diversified markets, and standardized output.
The essential point is that there is a template, a rational
document, from which an organization can be shaped.
Change is an exercise in fundamental design, impressed by
experts. The popularity of this form of thinking is revealed in a
study by Miles (1975). Miles questioned 1,000 managers to
discover that the top-down approach was their most favoured
method when it came to the reorganization of their subordinates' work methods, a finding which also reminds us the
managerial perogative often has the first, and last, say in the
change process.

The emphasis on organizational goals and objectives in the
present perspective is the key to much-cited approach to
change – *management by objectives* (MBO) (Odiorne, 1979).
MBO engineers change through precise objective-setting, and
standards against which an individual's performance can be
judged. A typical objective for a television sales manager
might read: '(1) increase sales for the year by 5 per cent; (2)
sell all remaining stock monochrome sets at 30 per cent
discount; and (3) hold advertising expenses at last year's
level.' MBO can cascade from the top of an organization with
broad objectives through to strategic, departmental and then
individual job objectives. Sometimes objectives are jointly set
by the employee and the manager, sometimes it is the
manager who lays out the objectives. An MBOd organization
looks tidy and very rational on paper, and it proceeds
according to a simple motivational principle: that people will
contribute to the overall organizational goal if they know
exactly what they are responsible for and how their success
will be recognized and rewarded.

MBO has strong connections with techniques of *behaviour modification*, which in turn takes its principles from stimulus-response psychology (such as Skinner, 1971). The heart of behaviour modification is the arrangement and structuring of rewards ('positive reinforcement'), and punishment ('negative reinforcement') to encourage certain behaviours and discourage others. The early experiments on behaviour modification took place in psychological laboratories on animals, such as pigeons and dogs. The principles by which these animals learned to behave in some ways, and not in others, are, argue proponents of behaviourism, just as relevant for human beings. It is simply a matter of becoming systematic with rewards and punishments that have long been accepted in organizations, such as pay rises for good performance, delays in promotion for under-performance, and piece-work systems. The trick is to find rewards that are valued by the people affected.

Targets of organizational change found susceptible to behaviour modification include absenteeism, lateness, safety and sales performance. In a much quoted application of behaviour modification in industry, an air freight company, Emery Air Freight, attempted to reduce the unfilled space in shipping containers – and so improve their profits. Workers believed they were loading the containers fuller than they really were, so the company encouraged supervisors to praise (positively reinforce) workers when their loading increased and give them consistent feedback on their performance. This had the effect of sharply improving the loading problem – but not for long. The company was forced to seek more creative reinforcers when the glow from feeling the subject of special attention faded in the workers' eyes. Invitations to luncheons, special letters of praise, more responsibility and time off from the job were added to the armoury of rewards (Hammer and Hammer, 1976).

As is evident, change in the rational/behaviouristic organization is matter of finding the right framework and pulling the appropriate levers. There is convincing evidence that change can be effected in this manner, and it is hard to argue that attention to the structure and rewards of an organization is unnecessary. But those wedded to this perspective are also confronted with the *unintended* consequences of their efforts.

For example, employees may resent having their jobs minutely analysed, and despite apparent agreement on goals and objectives, output may decrease rather than improve. Carefully designed communication structures may be by-passed. New technology can be resisted or sabotaged, even though it offers the prospect of better working conditions.

There is something uniquely human in these responses, and there is the rub. The quest for profit, growth, productivity and efficiency makes much managerial sense, but it cannot be assumed that everyone shares that vision. There are people at work who feel bored, stressed, trapped in the job, ideologically at odds with their employer, in conflict with their immediate colleagues, concerned about house repairs, a failing marriage, a new baby, or next month's holiday. . . and so on. The important concerns of life may be very distant from the organization's priorities. Tony Watson, an industrial socio-logist, makes a similar points:

> Every organization is thus confronted by a basic paradox: the means used by the controlling management of the organization to achieve whatever goals they choose or are required to pursue in an efficient way (i.e. at the lowest cost – short and long term) do not necessarily facilitate the effective achievement of these goals since these 'means' involve human beings who have goals of their own, which may not be congruent with those of the people managing them (1987: p. 174).

Perspective 2:   Humans Needs, Human Resources

The image of an organization as a bureaucracy and structure, a depersonalized phenomenon, was being challenged by social scientists after the Second World War. Features of bureau-cracy were recognized as often petty, obsessive and self-serving, alienating people from the organization's purpose and sometimes from themselves. Traditional organizational structures were seen to sweep over, or homogenize human needs. The powerful effects on performance of informal human groupings, 'human relations', at work were being acknowledged – effects that could far outweigh managerial efforts to manipulate the working conditions or environment (Roethlisberger and Dickson, 1939).

The human needs/human resources perspective does not turn the structuralist view on its head; rather it argues for 'humanizing' structures. It assumes individuals have needs which they seek to satisfy, regardless of the formal purpose of the organization. So, if the organization cannot accommodate individual needs then it cannot expect the energy, enthusiasm and commitment it requires from people in order to be productive and profitable.

A variety of writers have been influential in specifying what human needs we should consider. Maslow (1943), McGregor (1960), Herzberg (1966) and Argyris (1962) have suggested that people should have the opportunity to grow psychologically at work by self-actualizing ('becoming everything that one is capable of becoming'), and by exercizing self-control, responsibility and autonomy. Such prescriptions initially were regarded as a bit quirky, but today are presented as a respectable part of a broad package of considerations for 'human resource management'. This recast of human relations thinking brings individual needs and abilities to the centre of the organizational stage. In practice it has meant that people's feelings about the design of their job, workspace layout, career security, satisfaction with the organization, training and rewards are now central to the organization's planning and functioning. 'People are our most important asset' is a phrase commonly found in brochures of companies which accentuate human resource management. It is worth noting tht the human resources approach does not make any claim to value human beings simply as human beings, as the 'pure' humanistic writers would prefer (see for example Rogers, 1961). People are regarded as *resources* to serve the commercial, or other, ends of the organization, and are judged accordingly. At this point the approach deviates little from the rational behavioural perspective. Nevertheless, how the human resources are 'used' does look very different.

Changing organization by means of human resource principles meant, in early applications, participation – a cornerstone of the then new management style (Likert, 1961).

Effective change was seen to require the involvement of those affected by the change – although the desirable extent and stage of involvement has been much debated. Participation challenges the managerial prerogative, so it has been employed with various degrees of seriousness and depth. At one level it can represent little more than a kindly way for a manager to tell staff what to do. At another extreme it can be full-blooded, consensual decision-making involving a high level of trust across the hierarchical and functional boundaries. In recent years it has been recognized that Japanese organizations have been most at ease with participative approaches, and executives from Western countries have eyed their success with a mixture of concern and envy. One participative method, second nature to Japanese corporate management, is the quality circle. Quality circles are designed to give a constant impetus to organizational change. They comprise groups of employees from the same work area meeting regularly, outside the normal hierarchy, to identify problems and propose solutions on issues such as productivity, costs, quality and conditions of work. Their powers to implement solutions do not usually extend beyond recommending solutions to management. The main reward from participating in quality circles is seeing one's recommendations implemented.

Quality circles have been adopted by many organizations outside Japan. In 1986 the International Association of Quality Circles had over 7,000 members. Evidence on their success is mixed. The Japanese cultural system, which places responsibility on groups rather than on individuals, and offers long term security within an employing company, is unlike the individualistic, top-down ethos of many American and European organizations (Ouchi, 1981). Consequently quality circles have not always been welcome: lack of volunteers to participate, hostility amongst non-participants, and cynicism among participants if management dictates the terms and conditions of participation (Griffen, 1988). When actual changes in quality, costs and productivity are examined we find many reported failures to set against evidence of positive change (Barrick and Alexander, 1987). Quality circles share the verdict on other variants of participative change: participation, while solid and liberal in conception, cannot simply be grafted on to organizational systems which normally operate by bureaucratic or self-seeking principles. A much broader cultural shift is required, which may be unfeasible, or inappropriate, within the total context of an enterprise.

Organization Development

Despite difficulties in sustaining participative programmes, efforts at co-operative organizational change continue, with some vigour, under the umbrella of *Organization Development* (OD). Traditionally, OD takes humanistic behavioural science knowledge, and harnesses it for change through a variety of intervention techniques. The target of change may be the organization as a whole, a specific part of it, or even a particular individual. One of ODs important goals is to increase the level of trust and openness in organizations through the freer expression of feelings.

OD has its genesis in the work of Kurt Lewin in America in the 1940s. Lewin and his team at the National Training Laboratories pioneered training groups (abbreviated to T-groups) where small groups of strangers could learn about their own behaviour, needs and difficulties in intensive inter-personal exchanges. The learnings were then to be applied to changes back at work. The people themselves are the agenda in the T-group; there are no tasks, exercises or games. Typically, over a period of time, the ambiguous situation provokes frank and confronting exchanges between partici-pants (steered by occasional interventions from a trainer). But the intensity of contact also engenders trust, which helps participants gain insight into their own and others feelings and behaviours. T-groups can be very disturbing because of their very personal nature. However their potential for harm seems more than outweighed by the increased flexibility and more open communications they can produce. Change within an individual needs to be supported in the workplace if T-groups are to influence job behaviour and organizational processes. This is often the weak link in the chain (Nicholas, 1982). Clearly, the virtues of open expression of one's views and trust in one's colleagues are much reduced if the organization, or department, is regidly bureaucratized, hierarchical, or tends to be punitive in its management style.

T-groups continue to be used, but less so than *survey feedback*. Survey feedback presents organizational members with a candid, warts 'n' all, picture of the organization in which they work, from which they can suggest change. The information is gleaned from customized survey questionnaires where managers and their staff report, anonymously, their views about the organization, their work unit and their individual manager. The key to effective change lies in the rapid feedback of survey results to participants, and the frank discussion of the findings. Action is expected following recommendations from these discussions.

Survey feedback reflects a simple concept of change, originally articulated by Kurt Lewin in 1951. He spoke of *unfreezing* people's views from which *movement* can occur – changes to new behaviours and structures. These are then *refrozen* in a new set of norms, policies and work practices. The simplicity of this logic belies its psychological complexity. For example, it has been found that many individuals, when confronted with aspects of themselves which produce difficulties for others, will change their behaviour only if they can do so without examining the underlying causes. This has been called 'single loop learning' (Argyris and Schon, 1978). In other words, the change is in surface behaviour, remote from the roots of the problem. This may be fine for easily manageable, routine activities, but may interpersonal issues and team problems are more confused, and less amenable to 'a quick fix' to get through the day. For example, it may be that an individual's over-aggressive behaviour is based in his or her mistrust of management, inability to listen to others' points of view, or career insecurities in the organization. A 'double look' at the situation may expose the anxieties, fears and operating norms which underpin the problem, and it is here where change is required. Change of this sort is referred to as 'double loop learning' because it does more than simply realign out-of-phase behaviour.

Many organizations have institutionalized single loop learning through their bureaucratic and behaviouristic principles. Accounting systems, targets, profits and budgets are designed to keep the organization 'on course', and deviations have to be corrected – as an end in itself. Challenging the relevance of the various indicators, or indeed the course that is being charted, is not part of the culture. In this way organizational problems become over-simplified, and operating assumptions go unchallenged – as the organization is steered unwittingly onto the rocks. The snappy quips of management-speak ('We run a tight ship here', 'We're on top of the facts', 'It's a matter of being firm and fair with people') can add to the self-delusion that 'everything is under control' and, consequently, there is no need to question the principles behind the actions.

It should be apparent that the openness and reflectivity required to double loop learn cannot be assumed. Even if individuals identify what they should change in their basic thinking, many do not know how to go about it. They feel lost, deskilled in unfamiliar territory. It is fair to conclude that the OD specialist who uses surveys, or similar devices, to achieve change, is faced with considerable difficulties in bringing about double loop learning. The benefits, however, are considerable when the obstacles are surmounted, as has been demonstrated in changes ranging from employee attitudes to organizational strategy (Argyris, 1982).

Team and individual interventions

OD interventions with specific work teams or individuals may take various forms, although the goal remains consistent – to improve organizational effectiveness through increased self-awareness, trust and harmony. A 'process consultant' can be present as a team goes about its business. The consultant will give team members concrete feedback on how they make decisions, their different styles of interaction (effective and less effective) and points of stress, confusion and conflict. The consultant will also assist the group in formulating where and what it wishes to change (although the major impetus for change comes from group members themselves) (Schein, 1987). There is evidence that process consultation can often improve feelings of group effectiveness, and is one way of strengthening or 'building' a team, especially when there is poor cohesion, conflict or low morale (Kaplan, 1969). Some OD consultants will enhance process feedback with tasks or exercises so that teams can experiment with new ways of operating.

Interventions with individuals are aimed at changing self-knowledge, coping skills, attitudes or expectations which have a bearing on organizational relationships. The more psychologically healthy the individual, the more healthy the organization, runs the argument. Consequently, many interventions have a strong psycho-therapeutic flavour, such as gestalt therapy (Harman, 1974) transactional analysis (Berne, 1964), stress counselling (Fineman, 1983) and life–career planning (Lippitt, 1970). Other individualistic approaches look more towards role dynamics – how an individual performs his or her role in relation to others, and how role behaviours can be changed, or 'renegotiated' (see for example Harrison, 1972).

OD has become firmly established in management and organizational literature. It has also established its own professional identity with specialist journals and practitioner training courses. But there are tensions. While some writers wish to reaffirm the importance of collaborative values as fundamental to the purpose of OD (Harrison, 1983), others see that premise as too simplistic, especially if one is seeking changes to the organization as a whole. The inevitable mix of values and orientations within any single enterprise requires more than a single-value change strategy.

Perspective 3: Coalitions, Constructions and Performances

According to this perspective organizational goals emerge, and re-emerge, from struggles between people who wish to have their views heard, and who seek a slice of the organizational cake. Organizational life is markedly more turbulent than the previous perspectives would have us believe. There are many rationalities to consider, and many different, and competing, values and interests. Openness and trust may be the least of people's concerns – not because they are inherently suspicious, but because experience tells them that their personal interests are not always best served by being open. This perspective portrays organizations as inevitably 'political'. They are arenas where individuals and groups vie with other to promote their own desires (Pfeffer, 1981; Morgan, 1986). Organizations are, therefore, inherently conflictual. There will be conflicts because people carry with them different social backgrounds, different ambitions, a variety of tolerances and competencies, and so forth.

These human 'givens' are bound up in the texture of the organizational processes. They cannot be democratized away or harmonized within the rational purpose of the organization. So organization, management and change are constantly-to-be-worked-on, moving, processes which seek temporary bargains and agreements which fit, for a time, with where 'people are'. It is people's experienced, 'socially constructed', realities which give meaning to organized life, and it is those meanings which determine action. Change is part of the flow of everyday politics. The way such processes are construed and managed by the parties involved provides us with the material for understanding organizational change. The case below illustrates the points. It is taken from recent experiences of the author at the University of Bath.

Case Study – Change: Politics and Passion

As a director of Undergraduate Studies, my research into our students' grievances revealed that one problem had festered for years. Promise after promise had been made to the students that we would get a technician to maintain the laboratories and provide them with a reliable service for their studies – but nothing had happened. Shortage of money, unavailability of personnel, disinterest, and lack of political will conspired to reinforce the status quo.

I could fix that, I thought, and fast. I had money in my control to employ someone – at least for a six-month period to get things straight. Whatever the ambiguities of my role and limits to my influence, I could use my money as a powerful voice. I even knew someone who could do the job – Alan – who new the computer system well. He was already employed elsewhere in the university, but he could work in his spare time for us. He was delighted with this prospect.

I checked out my plans with the Head of School, and he, Alan I met together in his office to thrash out an agreeable contract. We succeeded. We shook hands and we were all delighted with the deal. Most crucial for me was that the students would get good service right away. I passed the good news to my colleagues and to the students. It was received with a mixture of relief and disbelief. I returned to my office feeling very satisfied with myself. I wrote a polite note to our Personnel Department informing them of the arrangement, and how it was to be financed. Systems can work smoothly, I thought, as long as you find the right buttons to press, and the right people press them.

My delight was short-lived – 48 hours short-lived to be precise. On arriving at work two days later I found two messages marked 'urgent'. I was to contact Simon Andrews in the Personnel Department. Simon, normally a mild-mannered soul, was barely recognizable on the phone. The conversation went something like this:

Simon: (*angrily*) Steve, you *can't* do it!

Me: (*taken aback*) Can't do what Simon?

Simon: You can't agree to employ someone just like that!

Me: Why not?

Simon: (*very firmly*) Because *I* set the rates. *I* set the contracts. *I* have to agree!

Me: (*very indignantly*) Of course I can do it. We have been negotiating our own contracts for sometime now. You should know that. And it's my own budget to manage.

Simon: (*officiously*) No-one's been negotiating separate contracts with me – maybe elsewhere in our department. And it doesn't matter whether or not you manage the budget, *I* have to make sure that payments fall in line with university rates.

Me: (*rattled*) Why are you getting all bureaucratic with me, Simon!? If I had offered Alan standard university rates he would run out laughing. He's a skilled computer technician and has a doctorate – and we need him urgently. We are still paying him *half* the commercial rate!

Simon: Well, he's not going to get paid anything at all unless
   I agree. And there's no way I can agree to what you have
   offered.

And he was right. The actual payment would not go ahead
unless Personnel approved. I paced up and down my room in
quiet fury. Apart from feeling undermined, I had now become
entangled in inter-departmental politics and territory
squabbles. I had no direct authority to unpick it all. Simon, of
course, was much offended for being bypassed. All the more
because, unbeknown to me, he had previously been in
discussions with my Head of School about a technician, so he
believed that he was part of the ongoing process.

The situation looked impossible, and very embarrassing. It
seemed that an inpenetrable screen had been thrown up – and
indeed that is what Simon wished to create. My right to take
the decision had been challenged, and my influence could not
penetrate stiffly-defined rules, further hardened by the hurt
feelings of the enactor of those rules.

Well, hurt feelings I could do a little about. After a couple of
days Simon and I buried the hatchet – this time not in each
other's heads. Shortly after, his boss called me to gently
explain their own position, and for the first time suggest the
need in his own department 'to be somewhat flexible given the
circumstances.'

An immutable situation was softening. Significant actors
were trading words and feelings, gradually shifting to a
position which, perhaps, could make the impossible possible.

The grand finale was set, once more, in the Head of
School's office. Seated in a semi-circle were myself, the Head
of School, Alan the technician – looking a little confused – and, this time, Simon from Personnel. Everyone said
something about the value of the new position and the
conditions of employment. Within 20 minutes we had run out
of things to say, and we reached an agreement. It was
virtually identical to the original one. (Extracted from Fineman, 1989)

This case illustrates the ebb and flow of organizing and
change. Different actors, with varied purposes, personal agendas, objectives and threats, worked away at influencing each
other. They used words, the main medium of exchange, and
harnessed their power and coalitions wherever possible. Out

of the 'mess' a new strand of organization was born. But that creation is temporary and require renewal and renegotiation as the people involved shift their expectations and aspirations. A consultant concerned with facilitating change would look at the way the various parties 'defined' the situations which confronted them, and how the definitions were influenced by different social settings.

When we look at the minutiae of interactions in this manner, it is evident that the ability and skill with which people conduct their political affairs has a significant bearing on the nature and progress of change in organizations. We talk of 'skilled performers' and 'sharp' negotiators. The term 'actor', prominent in the writing on this perspective connotes the language of the dramatist, with rehearsed scripts, carefully created roles, stages and directors. Indeed, authors such as Goffman (1959) and Mangham (1978) explore the notion that organizational life *is* theatre, and change requires a new performance of role based upon the 'rewritten script'. Creating convincing impressions is the key to the actor's craft. As an example, Mangham and Overington (1987) examine Sir Michael Edwardes' 'dramatics' in achieving change at British Leyland:

> As a performer Edwardes is in the grand tradition of Beerbohm Tree and Sir Donald Wolfit. He writes his own parts, selects his cast and puts the show on the road . . . 'There is no better way to achieve mobility of executive management than to change the structure sufficiently to create transparency – that is, to create a climate in which each and every job must be subjected to a spotlight. . .' Edwardes, in his tenure of the Leyland National Theatre, took great pains to select and cast each and every senior manager for his part. (p. 176)

The master performers in big corporations are attractive fodder for organizational analysts. However, argue protagonists of dramaturgy, office managers, shopkeepers, or head waiters who seek change are also subject to 'performance' rules. They must perform with skill to persuade their staff that new situations are desirable and worth the effort of change. Similar processes are evident in formal negotiations – across the table bargaining for changes in work methods, pay, or other employment conditions. They often resemble a cross between theatre and chess. Successful outcomes depend on how negotiators play their hand, and the postures they take (Stephenson and Allen, 1987).

Symbols and Change

The present perspective offers a fragile view of organizational reality – no more enduring than how we represent, and then manipulate, what hit our senses. We attribute meaning to what is around us, so objects and events have *symbolic* significance. Further symbols – our thoughts and words – provide order and sense to what we believe is 'out there'. By this analysis, organizations are fictions. They are psychological creations. But, of course, they are very real in their impact and consequences. Peters and Rothenbuhler (1989) take up this point:

> The discovery that all the world is symbolic doesn't call for a rejection of the world, but a more appropriate understanding of how it works. That journalism is a symbolic performance doesn't mean that they've been lying to us all along and should never be trusted again. It means that we can read of, and resist, Reagan's scandals with the knowledge that many of these same actors were central in the Watergate ritual dance. . . How will the drama unfold?. . . The answers depend more on the meanings of the situation than on some purported reality lurking behind them – the meanings of the situation are its reality. (p. 25)

Organizations, therefore, are to be found in people's heads and hearts. Interpretations of 'what is going on' are shared, to a greater or lesser extent, by organization members, and provide the basis for joint and individual effort. In Karl Weick's (1979) term, we *enact* our environments. We consciously and unconsciously shape them, put meaning into them, rather than blindly respond to a given set of rules or structures. We may feel stuck in predictable, unchanging circumstances, but that says as much about what we create for ourselves as what others impose upon us.

How does symbolic analysis clarify the nature of the organizational change? Change will occur when organizational members 'own' new interpretations, or meanings, of a situation. The wider these are shared, the more organizationally-established is the change. For example, the basis of a change in style of an organization may pivot around management convincing employees that a new 'open, achieving and rewarding' climate will be fostered. Initially it is a matter of leadership. A skilful leader offers new visions on purpose or progress (symbols) which capture imaginations. Events and structures are then added which further symbolize management's commitment to the new style of operating – such as seminars, open discussions of problems, access to previously restricted information, and easy-to-contact supervisors and managers. 'Glossy' symbols reinforce the new message, such as an eye-catching booklet and a neat company motto. The latter is a common device – for example, 'The Listening Bank' (Midland Bank), and 'IBM mans Service'.

A symbolic approach to change acknowledges that vitually every aspect of organizational life has symbolic significance which can contribute to an individual's image of the organization (an image which may be radically different from the one intended by its designers). The subleties are crucial. For example, a committee meeting is not just a committee meeting. Who sets the agenda, the timing, the way the chairs are arranged, where the chairperson sits, who the chairperson addresses, the permitted content and range of discussion; all are 'meaning signals' to participants. They symbolize the extent to which the organization is open, caring, listening, responsive or status-ridden. Other organizational practices will contain their own coded messages – the accessibility of senior managers, the rituals of joining and leaving the organization (a new recruit to my own academic department is rarely introduced to colleagues, symbolizing the do-it-alone, find-your-own-way culture), the forms of dress and address, how documents are written and circulated, and the stories that are told.

Given the complexity of the meaning-making process, close attention to various levels of symbolism – the explicit and the implicit – is required if organizational change is to be effective. For example, tidy brochures exhorting bank staff to 'listen to customers' or 'act fast' are likely to have little, or even reverse, impact if staff do not see such values demonstrated in a variety of managerial actions. It is difficult for an employee to be serious about caring for customers when the organization seems to care little for its own staff.

Clearly, an important major message for the symbolically-attuned manager or change agent is to be alert to the range of possible meanings which could be attached to a change-effort or intention. Decreasing that range to 'strengthen' an organization's culture has been extensively promoted as a way to improve organizational performance (see for example Deal and Kennedy 1988; Peters and Waterman, 1982). This has meant designing procedures and rituals which engender a sense of corporateness, openness, and shared mission. For example, organizations such as Marks and Spencer, McDonald's, IBM, and 3M take care to present the core values and mission of their company to new recruits, and *their* way of doing things. There is a special company language, secret processes are divulged, well-prepared stories are told about the organization's history, heroes, and future plans. The workspace is designed and coloured with the company values and image in mind. Employees can soon find their identity fusing with that of the company, and in this manner an 'IBM', 'M&S' or 'Procter & Gamble' person is produced. Individual performance and rewards are linked-in with the core values, supported by seminars, training, and company literature (often on 'designer' paper). There is little ambiguity about the means and ends of the organization, and everyone can share openly in effort and reward.

The quest to create strong cultures illustrates well the symbolic perspective to change. What is sometimes missed, however, is that strong cultures, by their very nature, are also resistant to change. Their homogeneity can stifle the innovative spark which finds nourishment in the more segmented, 'weak' culture. (I have visited bright management students on placement, in blue-chip companies, reduced to tears of frustration at being unable to express their individual ideas and talents.) The challenge for managers is to design organizations which benefit simultaneously from cultural strength and cultural diversity.

Conclusion

The three perspectives on change in this chapter suggest something of the complexity of an area which, at first glance, appears rather simple and obvious. In practice, an organization may operate according to a mix of underlying assumptions, further confusing efforts to produce or manage change. It should be clear that there are pitfalls in adopting a flavour-of-the-month change technique, and an appraisal of the organization is a crucial prerequisite to any programme of change. Yet, in the end, it is people who are going to be the focus of change, not some abstract thing called 'an organization'. It is people individually, in groups, and in mass, who comprise the organization, and it is they who will change – or stay pretty much as they are. Change, therefore, is intimately bound up with psychology and sociology of organizing. The extent, level, and purpose of change are all relevant considerations, and the perspectives in this chapter address these points. Thereafter we must decide whether it is surface behaviour, underlying values and attitudes, personal meanings, skilled performances and their attendant symbols, or maybe all of these, that are relevant for attention. Each offers something different to the manifestation and progress of change, and each requires a rather different form of intervention.

References for Chapter 11

Argyris, C. (1962) *Interpersonal Competence and Organizational Effectiveness*, Irwin, Homewood, Illinois.

Argyris, C. (1982) 'How learning and reasoning processes affect organizational change', in P. S. Goodman and Associates (eds.), *Change in Organizations*, Jossey Bass, San Francisco.

Argyris, C. and Schon, D. (1978) *Organizational Learning*, Addison-Wesley, Reading, Mass.

Barrick, M. R. and Alexander, R. A. (1987) 'A review of quality circles and the existence of positive finding bias', *Personnel Psychology*, 40, 579–92.

Berne, E. (1964) *Games People Play*, Grove Press, New York.

Blanchard, K. and Johnson, S. (1981) *The One Minute Manager*, Fontana/Collins, London.

Deal, T. and Kennedy, A. (1988) *Corporate Cultures*, Penguin, Harmondsworth.

Edwardes, M. (1983) *Back from the Brink*, Collins, London.

Fineman, S. (1983) *Social Work Stress and Intervention*, Gower, Aldershot.

Fineman, S. (1989) 'Leading to. . .what?' Paper presented at Standing Conference of Organizational Symbolism, *The Symbolics of Leadership*, INSEAD, Fontainebleau, June 28–30.

Goffman, E. (1959) *The Presentation of Self in Everyday Life*, Doubleday Anchor, New York.

Griffen, R. (1988) 'Consequences of Quality Circles in an Industrial setting: A longitudinal assessment', *Academy of Management Journal*, 31, 338–58.

Hammer, W. C. and Hammer, E. P. (1976) 'Behaviour modification on the bottom line', *Organizational Dynamics*, 4, 8–21.

Harman, R. L. (1974) 'Goals of Gestalt therapy', *Professional Psychology*, 178–84.

Harrison, R. (1972) 'Role negotiation. A tough minded approach to team development', in W. M. Burke and H. A. Hornstein (eds.), *The Social Technology of Organization Development*, NTL Learning Resources Corp, Virginia.

Harrison, R. (1983) 'Strategies for a New Age: Releasing love in the workplace', *Human Resource Management*, Fall, 209–35.

Harvey-Jones, J. (1988) *Making It Happen*, Collins, London.

Herzberg, F. (1966) *Work and the Nature of Man*, World Publishing Company, Cleveland, Ohio.

Huczynski, A. (1987) *Encyclopedia of Oreganizational Change Methods*, Gower, Aldershot.

Iacocca, L. (1986) *Iacocca. An Autobiography*, Bantam, New York.

Kaplan, R. (1979) 'The conspicuous absence of evidences that process consultation enhances task performance', *Journal of Applied Behavioural Science*, 15, 346–60.

Lewin, K. (1951), *Field Theory in Social Science*, Harper and Row, New York.

Likert, R. (1961), *New Patterns of Management*, McGraw-Hill, New York.

Lippitt, G. L. (1970) 'Developing life plans: a new concept and design for training and development', *Training and Development Journal*, May 2–7.

Mangham, I. L. (1978) *Interactions and Interventions in Organizations*, Wiley, Chichester.

Mangham, I. L. and Overington, M. A. (1987) *Organisations as Theatre: A Social Psychology of Dramatic Appearances*, Wiley, Chichester.

Maslow, A. (1943) 'A theory of human motivation', *Psychological Development*, 50, 370–96.

Miles, R. E. (1975) *Theories of Management*, McGraw-Hill, New York.

Mintzberg, H. (1983) *Structure in Fives: Designing Effective Organizations*, Prentice-Hall, Englewood Cliffs, N.J.

Morgan, G. (1986) *Images of Organization*, Sage, California.

McGregor, D. C. (1960) *The Human Side of Enterprise*, McGraw-Hill, New York.

Nicholas, J. (1982) 'The comparative impact of Organization Development interventions on hard criteria measures', *Academy of Management Review*, 7, 531–42.

Odiorne, G. S. (1979) *MBO II: A System of Managerial Leadership for the 80's*, Pitman, California.

Ouchi, W. (1981) *Theory Z*, Addison-Wesley, Reading, Mass.

Peters, T. J. (1987) *Thriving on Chaos: Handbook for a Managerial Revolution*, Knopf, New York.

Peters, T. J. and Waterman, R. H. (1982) *In Search of Excellence: Lessons from America's Best-run Companies*, Harper and Row, New York.

Peters, J. D. and Rothenbuhler, E. W. (1989) 'The reality of construction', in H. W. Simons (ed), *Rhetoric in the Human Sciences*, Sage, London.

Pfeffer, J. (1981) *Power in Organizations*, Pitman, Marshfield, Mass.

Roethlisberger, F. J. and Dickson, W. J. (1939) *Management and the Worker*, Harvard University Press, Cambridge, Mass.

Rogers, C. (1961) *On Becoming a Person*, Constable, London.

Schein, E. H. (1987) *Process Consultation Vol II*, Addison-Wesley, Reading, Mass.

Skinner, B. F. (1971) *Beyond Freedom and Dignity*, Knopf, New York.

Stephenson, G. M. and Allen, P. (1987), 'Bargaining and industrial relations', in P. B. Warr (ed), *Psychology at Work*, Penguin, Harmondsworth.

Taylor, F. W. (1911) *The Principles of Scientific Management*, Harper, New York.

Toffler, A. (1970) *Future Shock*, Random House, New York.

Watson, T. J. (1987) *Sociology, Work and Industry*, Routledge and Kegan Paul, London.

Weber, R. M. (1947) *The Theory of Social and Economic Organization*, Free Press, New York.

Weick, K. E. (1979) *The Social Psychology of Organizing*, Addison-Wesley, Reading Mass.

12

You and Your Career

MIKE SMITH
School of Management, UMIST

This chapter is fundamentally different from the others in the book. They aim to help manage others better. This chapter focuses on you and your career. Many people do not take an active part in managing their own careers. There is a substantial random element in their progress and often talent is wasted. The aim of this chapter is to give some guidelines so that the random element is reduced. It is important to emphasize that the purpose of this chapter is to put you in charge of your life so that you get closer to obtaining whatever you find fulfilling. The ideas are fairly value-free. Some, probably most, readers will want to use the techniques to advance to higher level, better-paid and more interesting jobs. Others will use the techniques to find work which avoids hassle and which is consonant with a particular set of values. The choice is yours.

The Stages of Men's Careers

Super (1983) defines an occupational career as 'a sequence of positions occupied by a person throughout his or her preoccupational, occupational and post-occupational life. It includes work-related roles such as those of student, employee and pensioner or annuitant'. This definition emphasizes two major points: a career is a *sequence* of jobs and it extends on either side of actual employment. People think of a career as a sequence of jobs each of which is related but better than the previous one. Careers are related to a sense of vocation. Super defines a vocation as an occupation to which a person has a sense of commitment; it is distinguished from an occupation by the psychological meaning it has to the individual rather than its economic meaning to society.

In fact, careers can involve all kinds of movements, upwards, sideways and downwards. Often, the jobs in the sequence have little relation to each other. The idea of an 'onward and upwards' sequence is seen by many people to be a middle-class idea. Willis (1977) studied working-class boys in their transition from work to school and identified two groups. One group accepted the need for qualifications and held something like the 'onward and upward' view. The other group, 'the lads', rejected this view and held that all jobs were basically the same.

Why people enter their careers is a major issue. There are two main explanations. The first explanation is favoured by psychologists. It can be called 'talent matching'. People differ in their skills and abilities. Jobs require different skills and abilities. There is some sort of process which matches the people to the jobs. Hence most people eventually find themselves in jobs which suit them. The second explanation is favoured by sociologists and can be called the 'sociological' explanation. It starts with two major observations: most people follow similar careers to their parents and people usually find work via family contacts. According to this explanation, people are brought up by their parents to be suitable for jobs similar to their own and the family network means that people only learn about those jobs which are similar to their parents. There is some truth in the sociological explanation but the number of people who do not follow the pattern of their parents is high and means other factors are at work.

Super and Hall (1978) put forward a model of career paths in which there are five main occupational stages.

The first stage is the *exploration stage*. It is usually assumed that people have a large degree of vocational maturity and are realistic and willing to enter the world of work. During the exploration stage young people gather information about themselves and various jobs. The way that they do this varies enormously. Some people gather the information at random. Others are highly systematic. Some are very passive and wait

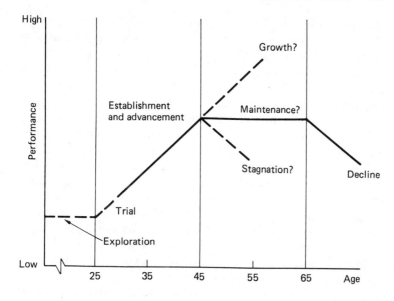

Figure 12.1 *Super and Hall's model of career paths*

for the information and others actively search it out. Research suggests that much of this activity is not systematic: rather more than half of the job changes before the age of 25 are floundering and unplanned (Super, Kowalski and Gotkin, 1967). After the age of 25 about a quarter of all changes involve floundering or drifting. Consequently, during their early 20s most people decide to try out a particular job. If this trial proves successful, they move to the second stage. A fuller description of this and other stages is given by Watts (1981).

The stage of *establishment and advancement* is characterized by acquiring seniority and competence. This is often accompanied by feelings of quick progress. Some have called this the stage of the workaholic. Long hours and great effort bring noticeable advancement which in turn generates greater effort and longer hours. Berger and Wright (1978) suggest that at this stage there is a need for counselling in alternative career patterns such as dual career marriages, part-time employment and househusbanding. the advancement and establishment stage has a good image that fits the Prostestant work ethic.

However, there is evidence (Levinson, 1978) that when the party ends there are many sad hearts. Only a minority of people come through this stage in a satisfactory way.

According to Super and Hall's model, there comes a point during the mid-40s age range when a career reaches an important choice point. It can continue to grow. It can maintain a constant level. It can decline.

The *continued growth stage* is perhaps the happiest outcome. The career continues to advance. Contrary to popular myth not every man or woman encounters a mid-life crisis. They continue to develop and break new ground. The main difference is that at this stage people 'become one's own man' and act quite independently. Their own mentors have retired and are no longer available for guidance and advice. Indeed, in this stage people become mentors for the next generation.

The *maintenance stage* is when there is a concern to hold onto the position that has been established in the place of work. This means acquiring new information in order to fend off obsolescence. Little new ground is broken but there is a continuation of the past. This stage is often referred to as the *career plateau* which is usually defined as, 'the point in a career where the likelihood of any organizational promotion is very low'. Ference, Stoner and Warren (1977) identified two major types of plateaued manager. First there are those who, according to the well-known 'Peter Principle' have risen to the limit of their incompetence. They have been promoted to the level at which they can only just cope – certainly they could not cope with a still more demanding job. The other type of plateaued manager still has reserves of talent but the organization is somehow unable to utilize it. the main sources of organizational plateaus are:

1. A narrow hierarchical structure with only a few places at the top;
2. intensive competition from others both inside and outside the organization;
3. age prejudice and an organizational 'youth culture';
4. the fact that someone is too good at their present job and thus too valuable to be moved upward.

An excellent discussion of plateauing and other aspects of career development in industry is given by Shullman and Carder (1983).

The *decline stage* occurs when physical and mental powers decline. In fact, the work of gerontologists suggests that this decline is much less than was once believed. Work on the relationship between ability and age began in the early part of the century. Researchers used cross-sectional methods and tested groups of teenagers, 20-year-olds, 30-year-olds and so on. When the results were plotted on a graph they showed that mental ability reached a peak in the late teens. there was a decline until the 50s and then a steep decline. Longitudinal data takes longer to collect. It follows up specific people over several decades. When the data from longitudinal studies is plotted it shows that ability reaches its peak in the late teens but the level is maintained much longer – often into the 70s. Another interesting effect became apparent.

People who start with high ability seem to maintain their ability better. Schaie (1967) provided an explanation for these contradictory findings. He noted that the early studies mixed

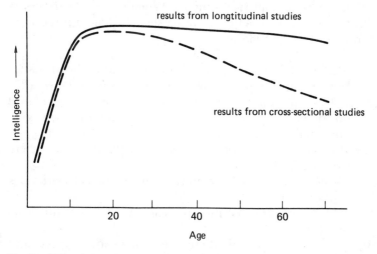

Figure 12.2 *Schematised diagram showing the relationship between age and ability from two kinds of studies*

up the influence of ageing with the influence of history. In the cross-sectional studies, the 20-, 30- and 40-year-olds had had reasonable schooling. Many of the 50- and 60-year-olds had not had any secondary schooling. The cross-sectional studies were highlighting a difference due to the past rather than an actual decline in ability. Recent meta-analyses (such as Hunter and Hunter, 1984) suggest that the link between age and performance in the working population is precisely zero. Hall and Mansfield (1975) showed that work involvement continues to increase into late career for professional and research workers. Indeed, one of the main problems of later career is to prepare people for the time when work disengages itself from them and they are formally retired.

The Stages of Women's Careers

Most research about the stages of a career applies to men. The pattern in women is usually quite different – although in recent years more women have been following career patterns similar to Super and Hall's model. When women's carrers are investigated, seven major patterns seem to emerge (see Fitzgerald and Betz, 1983):

1. *Stable homemaking pattern.* Women marry shortly after leaving education and have no real work experience. (22)
2. *Conventional women's pattern.* Women follow a career until marriage in early 20s and then devote themselves to homemaking. (27)
3. *Working pattern.* Women work through life span where work is their career. (3)
4. *Double track pattern.* Women combine home and work roles continuously. (14)
5. *Interrupted pattern.* Women return to work after childrearing. (16)
6. *Unstable career pattern.* Women who have an irregular and repeated cycle of home *vs* work involvement. (18)
7. *Multiple trial pattern.* Women have an unstable job history. (no. not known)

The approximate percentage of women in the USA in 1973 following these patterns is given in brackets.

A Survivor's Guide to Managing your Career

The previous sections in this chapter will have shown that a career is not a straightforward sequence of jobs. To most people it is a major part of their lives and probably represents the biggest financial commitment they will ever make. Careers need managing as carefully as any other major project or financial commitment. Many senior excecutives obtain the services of professional career consultants to help with the task. This involves periodic, perhaps five-yearly, assessments of their career, research of the job market, preparation of CVs and interview training plus secretarial support facilities. In this way, an individual takes full responsibility for his or her own career rather than delegating it to their employer. In many cases, employers do not accept a role in furthering the career of their employees. In addition, at certain key points the interests of an employer may be diametrically opposed to the interests of the employee.

In a chapter of this natue it is impossible to duplicate the services of a careers consultancy. It is necessary to come to terms with the fact that if another candidate is supported by professional consultants, it is likely that he gets the job and you do not! However, a chapter like this can provide general advice particularly for those at the start of their career who are unlikely to be able to afford professional advice.

Getting a Job

The chance element in getting any job is very high. For example, you will have no control over who else applies. If the six other candidates are paragons, your chances are slim. But for a similar job advertised a few weeks later your chances could be high. The paragons will be out of town attending interviews for the first job and they may have missed the advert. Similarly, you will have little control over your interviewer. Few interviewers are properly trained. It is largely a matter of luck whether you are interviewed by someone whose style suits you. Because so much chance is involved, you should apply for a lot of jobs so that the chance factors have the opportunity of cancelling each other out. You should also adopt a systematic approach so that you do not add any extra chance to what is already a chancy business. A systematic approach to getting a job will involve five main stages: personal stocktaking, finding a vacancy, making an application, attending selection, and accepting or rejecting the offer. Each of these stages needs to be handled with care. A mistake at one stage can ruin the careful preparatians of another. The job finding chain is no longer than its weakest link.

Personal Stocktaking

The first stage in getting a job consists of a cool, deliberate assessment of your strengths and weaknesses. Many applications go wrong because this stage is skimped or ignored. Personal stocktaking is important. It ensures that you do not waste time applying for unsuitable jobs. It is also important because unless you have a very clear idea of what you can offer, you will have difficulty in convincing others of your merits.

A simple method of taking stock of yourself is to set aside a weekend when your social life is less hectic than usual. On Friday, start three list: (1) a list of everything your have achieved in your life; (2) a list of things you have failed or missed; (3) a list of influential people you have met. Spread the lists out somewhere that is convenient, private and where they will not be disturbed. Keep adding to the list as you think of items during the weekend. Include every little achievement – everything you have organized and everthing you have passed. People are often surprised that their achievements list requires several continuation pages.

On the Sunday afternoon find a quiet place to organize the lists. Many interviewers use a plan. The most frequent is probably Rogers' Seven-Point Plan (see Chapter 3). Write three sentences about yourself under each of the headings in the plan. When you have finished your stocktaking show it to two trusted friends or parents. Ask if your stocktaking is reasonable and whether you have omitted anything.

If you have difficulty in arriving at a stocktaking of your talents it may be useful to obtain outside advice from University or Polytechnic Appointments Boards, local authority careers service or private agencies. Be careful in your choice of private agency. Establish the fees in advance. Check the qualifications of the counsellor – they should be chartered psychologists and preferably a member of the Division of Occupational Psychology of the British Psychological Society (0533 549568), the American Psychological Association (202 955 7600) or the Australian Psychological Society (3 347 2622). Tactfully ask them how long they have been giving careers advice and how many people they have advised: make excuses if they have practised for a short period of, say, less than two years or less than, say, 100 cases.

The final part of stocktaking is to use this information to choose a job which is most suited to your characteristics. Ask other people. Visit the local library and consult careers books. Ask if there are any computer based systems you can use. Be careful not to overlook any possibilities simply because your home background has narrowed your field of view. When you have identified a job, it is wise to take extra steps. First check that you are not joining a profession such as university teaching where the prospect is one of continuing decline. Second, find someone who is already doing the job you have selected. Obtain an introduction and ask to meet them for 30 minutes to talk about their work. As they are talking, pay particular attention to two things: is this a job which would suit your competences and what are the problems which people who do this job need to solve?

Finding a Vacancy

Use all available sources to locate vacancies. *Printed sources* include national papers, local papers and trade and professional publications. When planning your sweeps of relevant adverts remember to look at every issue: jobs are rarely advertised twice. Read the adverts carefully and do not be put off by titles. An assistant in one organization can have a more interesting job at a higher salary than the chief in another. Except perhaps in a civil service job, do not be put off if you fail to meet all the essential requirements – employers usually ask for more than they need. They will be realistic when replies are received.

Many people overlook the importance of *personal contacts*. Once they were *the* method of finding jobs. The 'old boy' or the 'old girl' network is still very strong. Your contacts cannot help if they do not know that you are looking for a job. There is nothing reprehensible about seeking work, so do not keep quiet. In most cases it might be a good idea to let them have details of your experience, qualifications and the type of work you want. This saves them wasting their efforts on unsuitable jobs. Do not mislead your contacts because it may put their reputation at risk. To keep your contacts sweet, always follow up openings they make even if it is only a short courteous letter thanking a firm for their interest and explaining that you have now found a job. Remember to offer to pay any postage or phone costs they incur on your behalf. As a final courtesy, always let them know the results arising from their efforts – you never know when you may need their help again.

Few people exploit the full potential of *speculative applications* yet they are amazingly successful. You hope that your letter arrives on the day a vacancy arises and that the employer jumps at the chance of short circuiting a long and expensive recruitment campaign. You have shown initiative and you are on the inside track with no competitors. There are two elements to a good speculative application: a carefully targeted mailshot and a good application package.

You should use telephone directories and business directories such as 'Kompass' to locate firms which are likely to have vacancies. Keep an eye on the press for news of firms that are expanding. Write to them even if the publicized expansion is in another department – expansion will produce momentum in other areas. If you use directories remember that they are certainly out of date. Never use a name on your letters unless you have first verified it by phone: some people are upset by receiving a personalized letter addressed to their predecessor. Your application should consist of two items: a copy of your CV and a short letter. The letter should not begin with the word 'I'. It should not say what they can do for you. It should say how you can help them and what the next step will be. A good closing line is, 'may I phone you on Thursday to discuss any possibilities?' Students should ignore all advice from careers services or central personnel establishments which seek to dissuade the use of speculative applications. Despite the fact that they may be frowned upon, the evidence is that speculative applications can be very successful and that the managers who make the final employment decisions like receiving them.

Making an Application: the Stage when the Odds Against you are Highest

This is the most vital of all the stages yet it is one that candidates often rush and bodge. An employer may have hundreds of replies and will need to whittle them down to four or five to be invited to an interview. The odds against you will, perhaps be 50:1. Once you get an interview the odds will be about 5:1. The employer will whittle the applications down to a reasonable number using all sorts of criteria, neatness, legibility and, above all else, ease of comprehension. Pay minute attention to detail. Ensure that your application is neat, legible and easy to understand.

If a firm asks you to complete an application form, read the form carefully. Reread the advert. Reread your personal stocktaking. Next, draft your replies on spare paper. Only then should you complete the form. *Never* fill out an application form while eating, drinking or making love. Crumples and stains of any kind will count against you and all sorts of things become enclosed in application forms by mistake!

Unless there are specific instructions to the contrary, have your answers typed on a modern typewriter that uses a carbon ribbon. If you write your replies use *black* ink: never use light blue ink which does not photocopy well. Do not draw attention to your weak points. Unless there are specific instructions to the contrary, leave a section blank rather than pepper the form with 'none' or 'no experience'. Try to answer in a positive way. 'I am looking for a job' is a more positive response than 'I am out of work'. 'I am seeking a new opportunity' gives a more positive image than 'I am bored with my present job'.

Many application forms have a section headed 'any other information'. This gives you an opportunity to underline your strong points by repeating them in different words. Most of the suggestions for application forms also apply to your Curriculum Vitae (CV). Remember, the sole purpose of a CV is to create a favourable impression so that you will be invited to an interview. Make your CV appear distinctive but tasteful. Avoid using strongly coloured paper. Be very generous with spacing. A CV which looks cramped will count against you. Organize the material in a CV under a few headings. The most frequently used headings are:

1. *Previous experience* – start with your most recent job and work backwards. Make sure that your achievements in the job stand out. Give dates and numbers whenever possible.

2. *Qualifications* – include educational qualifications but don't forget licences and membership of professional bodies.

3. *Interests* – give three: not more, not less. Make sure they are active interests and preferably they should have some relation to the job involved. Preferably they should be interests you have held for some time (give dates) and where you have reached some level of proficiency (e.g. black belt, handicap of 10). Do not give 'watching TV' as one of your interests.

4. *Biographical information* – age, marital status etc.

At the application form stage you will often be asked to give the names of referees. If possible, select people who are good at writing and who sound prestigious. Secondary considerations are how well they know the job and how well they know you (in fact the priorities *should* be the other way around!). Before you give anyone's name ask their permission and take the opportunity to check their initials, job title and qualification. To avoid pestering your referees, explain that you might be making several applications. Send the referee a copy of your CV and a short note saying why you want that type of job. Hopefully, the referee will transmit this information to the employer concerned.

In most circumstances, your CV or application form should have a covering letter which is very similar to the covering letters sent out with speculative applications.

The Selection Stage

Preparing for the selection stage involves three main activities: finding out about the organization, anticipating questions and sorting out personal appearance.

It is vital that you obtain background information about the organization especially:

1. its size;
2. its origins and age;
3. its three main products and services;
4. its three main customers or customer groups;
5. its location and location of major branches.

You can get this information from existing employees or recruitment literature. Never hesitate to phone your interviewer's secretary and explain that you have a meeting with Mr X next Thursday and that you want to be fully briefed – could you please be sent copies of the annual report and other up-to-date literature? With luck, your foresight and efficiency will be reported to your interviewer and you will be on the inside track.

Anticipating questions is much more difficult. Remember, the interviewer does not want to hear what he can do for you. He wants to hear how you can help him meet his targets and goals. Always anticipate this underlying question. Also work out answers to the following question:

1. Why do you want this job?
2. What do you think you will be doing in two (five) year's time?
3. Why did you leave your last job?
4. What are your strong points?

5. What are your weak points – be truthful but do not hestitate to turn the question into a positive statement.
6. What salary are you asking – at this stage quote a wide range rather than an exact figure.
7. Have you made any other applications – tell them about two others but be ready to say why this one has greatest opportunities.

Sorting out your personal appearance should not be left to the last minute. Always have a clean blouse or shirt ready so that you can respond to a surprise invitation to an interview. The style of dress is not particularly important so long as it is reasonably formal. Pay particular attention to your grooming: have your hair trimmed a week before any likely interview. On campus interviewers are used to scruffy students but for interviews at a firm, especially with line managers, you should be smart and formal in your dress.

Arrive five to ten minutes before your appointment. Be pleasant but guarded in your relations with any secretaries. Some interviewers may be so indecisive that they may ask their secretary's opinion. The first few minutes of an interview are crucial. Research shows that many interviewers make up their mind in the first four minutes. Respond to the interviewer in an open and friendly way. Establish lots of eye contact but don't stare the interviewer in the eyes – look at the end of his nose! Avoid using one word or very long answers – three of four sentences per answer is about right. Don't take offensive remarks personally. The interviewer is probably trying to see how your react to stress. In most situations, stress interviews are a wast of time. As Chapter 2 has shown, interviews are not very good ways of selecting people so the interviewee's job is largely a matter of humouring the interviewer.

The main value of an interview is that it allows you to find out more about the firm. Your are likely to be given the change to ask questions. Avoid asking trivial questions such as 'Do I get free Hershey Bars?' An early question should be, 'Do you have any reservations about my ability to do this job?' It gives you a change to bring their doubts to the surface and hopefully you can then remove these doubts. Your other questions should point to the future:

1. What new skills will I be able to learn?
2. What is the training scheme?
3. What are the prospects for further careers?
4. What are the last year's intake doing now?

Do not ask too many questions.

Organizations may ask you to complete *psychological tests.* Always approach tests in a positive frame of mind. They give you an opportunity to show your real strengths without being handicapped by an interviewer's prejudices against certain types of background. If a firm is using psychological tests, at least it is trying to be up to date and fair. If you wear glasses take them to any interview so that if you are asked to do any tests you will not be handicapped.

The most frequently used tests are tests of mental ability. Usually firms will be testing your general mental alertness but sometimes they may focus on more specific aspects such as verbal, numerical, spatial or mechnical ability. It is no use trying to get hold of these tests in advance. They are only made available to qualified testers and no qualified tester will lend you a copy or coach you in how to answer. Almost all tests of mental ability have instructions that will give you all the information you need. Almost all have practice items so that you can tune your mind to what is required. When you come to answer the test itself, there will be no surprises. Listen carefully to the instructions.

Listen especially for any time limits. If a time limit is not stated, take any opportunity to ask what the time limit is. If the time limit is less than 30 minutes, speed is of the essence. It will be worth making one or two mistakes in order to attempt a greater number of questions. Do not expect to finish all the questions or get them all right – people very, very rarely do. Do not let this discourage you in any way. If the time limit is greater than 40 minutes you will know that you are in for a rough ride and you can expect to find even the examples difficult. Again, do not be discouraged. Every one else will find the questions hard. In a sense, the organization is paying you a compliment – it thinks that you are clever and wants to see exactly how clever you are.

The use of *personality tests* is increasing very rapidly. Again look upon them as an opportunityto show your true strengths (everybody has some strengths and yours may be just the ones the organziation needs!). You are unlikely to encounter the more zany methods of testing personality. Inkblot tests went out with the ark. Most modern tests ask you to read a statement and then mark a box which indicates your view. Personality tests are not strictly timed but most last about 40 minutes and contain about 200 questions. It is almost certain that before you are asked to answer any questions, you will be given full instructions and several practice questions.

Your approach to answering the questions is vital. None of the major personality tests (16PF, OPQ, CPI, EPQ) have trick questions or questions with hidden meanings. So *do not spend a lot of time pondering or trying to fathom some inner significance.* Take each question at its face value and answer fairly briskly – about four or five questions a minute. Give your first natural reaction as it comes to you. There will rarely be any right or wrong answers. You are entitled to put your best foot forward but do not tell any blatant untruths. Most tests contain lie scales. Make absolutely sure that you answer all questions. Do not miss any out. Even though a question does not apply to you very well, give your best guess. Don't worry about contradicting yourself (lie scales do not work on that principle). None of the questions will be exactly the same as another and, up to a point, it is human nature to be contradictory. So, do not spend ages trying to cross check your answers. Do not try to play safe by sticking to the middle answer. You will emerge without a personality at all! Use the middle answer only when the answers at either side clearly do not apply to you – about once every four or five questions.

More and more firms are using *assessment centres*. Assessment centres are very costly so you should feel flattered that an organization considers that you might justify the cost. Indeed, at the School of Management, UMIST, the best students seem to take it as a personal insult if they are *not* selected by this method. Assessment centres are described in more detail in Chapter 3. If you are invited to an assessment centre the most vital thing is to find out the dimensions on which you are being assessed. Make sure you then demonstrate the qualities relevant to these dimensions. There is little you can do to prepare for an assessment centre except, perhaps, organize your thoughts for a presentation.

Presentations are a common feature of assessment centres. Often, you will be asked to give a presentation on a specific topic, but you may also be allowed to choose your own topic. Think out this choice in advance. Avoid wine-making, pets, do-it-yourself and my holiday in Yugoslavia. The assessors will have heard these so many times before that they will have difficulty keeping awake. A good choice is someone you admire and why you admire them. Provided you have thought out the facts ahead of time you should be able to adjust the presentation in a way that underlines at least some of the dimensions being measured by the assessment centre. Avoid making your presentation boring. Involve the audience and use visual aids.

Assessment centres often involve *group discussions*. About four assessors will watch you and your fellow candidates discuss a topic. Usually the topic does not have a right or wrong answer. You will almost certainly be given a written briefing. Make sure you know how long the discussion will last. Quietly check with your neighbours that you all have the same briefings. A favourite trick of assessors is to give everyone a slightly incomplete brief and watch how the group puts the whole picture together. A key and obvious point is that you must say *something*. Do not leave it to the last few minutes to blurt out a panic contribution. Be able to break into a discussion without seeming too argumentative – prepare half a dozen phrases that will allow you to get a word in. For example:

1. I can't entirely agree with that because. . .
2. I think that's right but shouldn't we also consider. . .
3. I'm glad that you mentioned that because. . .
4. That's interesting. I'd like to hear exactly how that worked because I'm, not sure it would apply in a case where. . .

Group discussions are usually used to measure how logically you can argue, marshall your facts, phrase your arguments and how you relate to other people. Do not overlook the social side. Be sensitive to the needs of others. Get your points across but don't talk too much. Listen, and be seen to be listening. Try to involve others. For example:

1. Mavis hasn't spoken yet; let's hear what she thinks. . .
2. John, do you think that is reasonable?

Do not openly despise the naïve and stupid comments of the more gormless members of the group. At the start of the group discussion, it will probably be appropriate to clarify the goals and the expertise of the group members. After about five minutes, it might be appropriate to generate ideas and to build upon the ideas of others. Shortly after halfway through, start to emphasize the need to complete the task you were given. Be on the look out for errors and omissions. Five minutes before the end, it might be appropriate to sum up the achievements and feelings of the group by articulating group verdicts. Be prepared to praise and acknowledge the contributions of others. Start smoothing over any animosities that have arisen. Now would be the time for quips or even jokes.

The Offer or the Rejection

Hopefully, you will be offered the job and you will have to decide whether to accept. If this is your first job, the most important factors are whether it will give you challenge, experience and visibility. Think back over your contacts with the organization. Were they efficient, fair and businesslike? How did they treat each other? How did the bosses treat their staff? Is the industry expanding or declining? Will you be happy in the job? A survey by the Consumer's Association suggests that you will be happy in your job if you:

1. Work long hours and have lots of work to do;
2. earn 50 per cent more than the national average wage;
3. have some choice in what you do;
4. have a job that is relevant to your qualifications;
5. work for a small organization or a small unit in a larger one.

People also tend to be happy if they are somewhere near the top of their organization. Check for blocks to your promotion. It may be exciting and yuppie to be working for someone who is only five years older than yourself but it may also mean that you need to wait many years before you are promoted.

Don't be dejected if you are rejected. Retain your self-confidence. Remember that there is a great deal of chance involved in getting a job and because chance works against you at one time does not mean that it will always work against you. Furthermore you may not know the real reason why you were rejected. The organization may have been looking for someone who would be stupid enough to work alongside Sid who has eccentric and revolting habits. They are likely to have concealed this fact from all applicants. The fact that you have been rejected from this job is to your credit.

However, you should also avoid being complacent. When you are rejected, think back to see if you could have handled any stage better. Make a note of any of these points and resolve to improve them for your next job application.

The Tactics of Promotion

Once you have obtained proficiency in your job, your thoughts will probably turn to promotion. Many people think that simply by being proficient or even excellent at their job will bring promotion. Nothing could be further from the truth. Because you are good at your job, things rarely go wrong. Superiors tend to devote their time to dealing with crises and consequently your efforts are taken for granted. Promotion needs to be managed as actively as your own job. Some aspects of the tactics of promotion are described by Wood (1984).

The first stage is to decide whether or not you want to be promoted. There is no commandment which says that everyone must strive for promotion. It is a personal choice you must make. Take account of the work activities and lifestyle of the job you may be promoted into. Also take account of the effort you will have to make and the things that you will have to forego in order to get promoted. If you still wish to be promoted, your chances will be noticeably improved if you follow some of the following tactics.

Tactic one: be in the right place, especially at the start. Being in the right place at the right time is a key ingredient of success. Research by Berlew and Hall (1964) indicates that success is closely correlated with the degree of challenge given to an executive in the first job and to success in meeting these challenges. You should also look at the career structure. Does it lead to the top or are there only one of two rungs on that career ladder? – which means that you might stagnate. If you find yourself stuck in a job without much promise, consider a sideways or even backward move to get yourself onto a career ladder with many rungs. Situations change. Be mobile. In the early stages of your career, be prepared to change employer every two or three years. However, there is the danger of being seen to be too mobile. Avoid a series of jobs held less than a year each.

Tactic two: be a high performer. Low performers are not promoted. Find the indices which are used to judge success in your organization. There are usually only three or four indices. Work hard and skilfully to out perform your rivals on these indices. Waste no time on side issues.

Tactic three: be visible. Modern organizations are very complex. It is very difficult for senior people to see who has achieved what. Quiet, efficient people tend to be overlooked. The first part of being visible is to know your own successes. Keep a 'hero' or 'heroine' file and a 'brag' sheet. The file should contain cuttings from newsletters or letter and memos of congratulation. The brag sheet is a record of your achievements which is updated every six months. Once you are clear about your own success, you can start communicating it to others. This needs care and tact. Avoid bragging overtly. Be visible. Attend meetings and make your presence felt by talking to people informally before and after the meeting. Make intelligent comments and ask intelligent questions during the meeting. Write occasional articles or letters to your organization's magazine or newsletter.

Tactic four: support your boss. Rightly or wrongly, your boss can make or break your career. He will be the first to be consulted if there is promotion in the air. Pointing out your boss's drawbacks to others might seem clever but others will conclude you are disloyal. Rumours will get back to your boss. You will not be trusted with anything important again. Supporting your boss means more than taking his or her side in times of departmental warfare. Adopt a complementary role. Volunteer to fill out reports or draft memos if your boss is not good at these tasks. If you can be relied on, you will be asked to substitute at meetings and functions. You will then meet people of a higher rank who will notice you and may have a positive impact on your career.

Suporting your boss does not involve being a 'yes person'. Arrive at an explicit or implicit contract that in return for public loyalty, you should be allowed to express freely your own opinions within the department. In these situations, be frank, direct and polite.

Tactic five: Find a sponsor. A sponsor or mentor can be a great help. They are individuals of a higher rank who will supplement and support the views of your boss. At every promotion meeting practically every boss speaks up for their own candidate. Promotion often goes to those who have another, supposedly neutral, person speak up for them. First you should identify who is likely to be involved in the decision-making process. Make yourself visible to these people. Find ways of letting them know you are a high performer. Avoid being pushy but take opportunities for small talk when you meet informally in lifts or corridors. It is dangerous to play your boss off against your sponsor but having a sponsor brings an additional advantage. A spiteful boss thinks twice about being unfair at promotion meetings if someone else who takes an interest in you is present.

Tactic six: develop your network. Having a network can give you access to a much wider range of information but networks do not happen on their own: they need to be created and maintained. Plug into the organization's grapevine. Be friendly and approachable. Cultivate and maintain contacts. Once you have developed your network, maintain it regularly. Keep in touch by sending cards and brief messages of congratulations or sympathy.

Tactic seven: play the part and make your ambitions known. If you want promotion, act and dress like someone with potential.

The way you dress will be taken to indicate the type of person you are. If you want promotion let people know. A frequent comment at promotion meetings is, 'Yes, she is competent but she is not really interested in promotion'. The comment is usually made about women but it is also often wrong. The individual would often like promotion but is too embarrassed to say so. The lesson is that if you are ambitious let other people know. This needs to be done tactfully. The annual appraisal meetings is probably a good time to broach the subject by asking your boss for advice and support.

Tactic eight: be human and learn to influence people. Dale Carnegie's book *How to Win Friends and Influence People* contains good advice. An important general strategy is to avoid habitually criticizing, condemning and complaining. Do not become labelled as the departmental moan or the organization's whinge. Be genuinely interested in people. Talk in terms of *their* interests. Respect their opinions. Some fairly universal ways of influencing people are:

1. Begin in a friendly way;
2. start at points of agreement and work towards contention;
3. let them do the talking and if possible think that the idea is theirs;
4. appeal to nobler motives such as justice or excellence;
5. dramatize your ideas to make them memorable;
6. use short words and short sentences. Do not talk too much yourself.

Keeping Track of your Career

If you seriously embark on a high flying managerial career, you need to monitor your progress every few years against the following benchmarks:

Age 22 establish yourself as an independent person who has gained a good education and is working in a responsible job;

22–25 gain experience as an individual worker. After perhaps two or three jobs, choose one for major commitment. Develop competence in this job;

26–30   work as a line manager, responsible for the work of
          a small team;
31–35   hold second level management positions such as
          'production manager' or 'area sales manager';
36–45   head a broad corporate function such as Sales
          Director or Director of Research;
46–55   be Managing Director or Chief Executive.

Of course this idealized profile applies only to a managerial career. The benchmarks for professions will be different and involve competent discharge of professional duties (22–25); acknowledgement as local expert in some field (26–30); holding office at a national level in an appropriate professional body (31–35); and acknowledgement as a national or international expert.

When you are undertaking the reviews of the progress of your career it is always important to start with the question, 'Do I want further promotion?' The fact that you wanted promotion at the age of 20 does not necessarily mean that you will want promotion 15 years later. Your values can change. The tactics of promotion are only relevant if they help *you* to to what *you* want with *your* life. Good luck.

References for Chapter 12

Berger, M. and Wright, L. (1978) 'Divided allegiance: men, work and family life', *The Counselling Psychologist*, 7, 50–2.

Berlew, D. E., and Hall, D. T. (1964) *Some Determinants of Early Managerial Success*, Working paper 81–64, Massachusetts Institute of Technology: Sloan School of Management.

Ference, T. P., Stoner, J. A. and Warren, E. K. (1977) 'Managing the career plateau', *Academy of Management Review*, 602–12.

Fitzgerald, L. F., and Betz, N. E. (1983) in Walsh, W. B. and Osipow, S. H. (eds.) *Handbook of Vocational Psychology, Vol 1, Foundations*, Erlbaum, London.

Hall, D. T. Y. and Mansfield, R. (1975) 'Relationships of age and seniority with career variables of engineers and scientists', *Journal of Applied Psychology*, 60, 201–10.

Hunter, J. E. and Hunter, R. (1984) 'Validity and utility of alternate predictors of job performance', *Psychological Bulletin*, 96, 72–92.

Levinson, D. J. (1978) *The Seasons of a Man's Life*, Knopf, New York.

Lunneborg, P. W. (1983) 'Career Counselling Techniques', in Walsh, W. B. and Osipow, S. H. (eds.) *Handbook of Vocational Psychology, Vol 2, Applications*, Erlbaum, London.

Schaie, K. W. (1967) 'Age changes and age differences', *Gerontologist*, 7, 2, 128–32.

Shullman, S. L. and Carder, C. E. (1983) in Walsh, W. B. and Osipow, S. H. (eds.) *Handbook of Vocational Psychology, Vol 2, Applications*, Erlbaum, London.

Super, D. E., Kowalski, R. and Gotkin, E. (1967) *Floundering and Trial After High School*, Teachers' College, Columbia University, New York.

Super, D. E. (1983) 'The history and development of vocational psychology: a personal perspective', in Walsh, W. B. and Osipow, S. H. (eds.) *Handbook of Vocational Psychology, Vol 1, Foundations*. Erlbaum, London.

Super, D. E. and Hall, D. T. (1978) 'Career development: exploration and planning', *Annual Review of Psychology*, 29, 33–72.

Watts, A. G. (1981) 'Career Patterns', in Watts, A. G., Super, D. E. and Kidd, J. M. *Career Development in Britain*, Hobsons Press, Cambridge.

Willis, P. (1977) *Learning to Labour: how working class kids get working class jobs*, Saxon House, Farnborough.

Wood, J. E. (1984) 'The Tactics of Promotion', in Smith, J. M., *A Development Program for Women in Management*, Gower, Aldershot.

Author Index

Subject Index